Operative Optimism

Prologue and initial concept **Manuel Gausa** General coordination and editing **Susanna Cros**

1 tActar Arquitectura
2 njiric + njiric
3 Neutelings & Riedijk
4 NL ARCHITECTS
5 Périphériques
6 IaN+
7 WMA Willy Müller
8 Ábalos & Herreros
9 Lacaton & Vassal
10 Duncan Lewis
11 R&Sie... François Roche
12 Federico Soriano (S&Aa)
13 NO.MAD
14 Vicente Guallart
15 MVRDV
16 UN STUDIO
17 NOX
18 FOA

A WORLD OF POSSIBILITIES

Reality is subjective because it involves the interpretation we make of it in our minds. As the different individuals that we are, we all therefore have our own views of the world and our own ways of intervening in it. The will to act, change or expect something of reality according to a way of understanding the world depends on individual character and the education that each receives. It is this point in the process, the moment of intervening in exterior reality, that we aim to highlight with this publication. And architecture is one of the disciplines that has the most direct physical repercussion on reality.

Hence the title: Operative Optimism. Optimism, because we have chosen an optimistic, open, cheerful, playful way of addressing reality in a positive fashion, understanding that ours is a world of possibilities, that problems are challenges and that chaos leads to progress. And operative because we can turn this chaos, these problems and these circumstances to good account and achieve results that multiply the pre-existences and the context.

The approach chosen is very direct and forceful; it is based on contemporary visual culture, advertising strategies, capitalist consumerism, frenetic mobility and constant change; but also on social awareness and attention to the individual.

It is also based on globalization and regionalization: it is when we take our place in a global world that we realise we form part of a local culture; it is when we possess a regional identity that we find our place in a global world.

It represents a step beyond the academic rigour which is in some cases an inhibitor and prioritizes a spontaneity that leaves prejudice behind and concentrates on offering society what it really needs rather than what is, theoretically, advisable. It is an energetic attitude of action and one that attracts attention.

All this represents a consistent decision to adopt a transdisciplinary approach, with two objectives: firstly, to produce a greater wealth of knowledge by creating a two-way channel of information between different ways of seeing the world; and secondly, to make high culture accessible to the masses, to disseminate apparently elitist architecture to people who have not necessarily received an architectural culture.

The result is the fusion of sport, consumerism, culture, housing and recycling.

Worthy of mention is the dissemination work carried out by the teams whose work we present. Some of them have edited architecture magazines and others have issued minor publications, all with the constant desire to publicise their ideas.

It is this theoretical desire to publicise that marks the texts that present the teams. They might be regarded as small-scale manifestos that call for or advocate a way of producing architecture, of understanding the world and of acting consequently.

There are no hermetic compartments because there are no closed minds or single-minded objectives; because the world is complex; change is constant; and people are sensitive. (Susanna Cros)

OPERATIVE OPTIMISM
TOWARD A NEW PRAGMATIC IDEALISM IN EUROPE

(FOREWORD FOR AN UNWRITTEN TEXT)

'Nous ne nous moquâmes pas de lui, bien au contraire; car un homme qui sait se rendre heureux avec une simple illusion est infiniment plus malin que celui qui désespère avec la réalité.'

Alphonse Allais, 'La forêt enchantée', from *Oeuvres Posthumes*, 1877 à 1905, Robert Laffont, Paris, 1990.

'Everything has a beginning. The longest book begins with a single word. The longest journey begins with a single step.'

Patrick Redmond, *The Wishing Game*, Hodder & Stoughton, London, 1999.

1. INTRODUCTION

The beginning of certain projects is always slippery. They often come about as a reaction to a diffuse set of impulses and demands that thus become the catalysts, more or less concealed or more or less explicit, more or less ambiguous or more or less accurate, according to the circumstances.

In the case of the present essay, this had its origin as the culmination of the series of issues of the magazine *Quaderns*, which I edited from 1990 until 2000. Its intrinsic logic was that of a final message –or rather that of an intermediate conclusion– intended to transmit a certain conviction: that of confidence in a new kind of propositive action that I had been championing in the magazine. For reasons of an administrative nature this summing-up was never finished, although it immediately assumed the format of a possible publishing project. The thesis I wanted to defend at that time was that of the appearance of a new international framework of architectural research with a marked commitment to the reactivation not only of the discipline itself but of the social, cultural, economic and productive reality that at once convokes it and defines it, and that would imply, more than the acritical and/or cynical acceptance of an environment in which to fluctuate, a desire for pragmatic –and at the same time activist– involvement from which to reorient processes positively.

A new kind of 'operative optimism', less arrogant than the strictly doctrinal modern (more willing to accept the logics of the surrounding reality and its implicit capacity for qualitative reorientation), apparent in multiple facets of contemporary creation that could be interpreted as autonomous traces of a hypothetical shared action.
This change of approach (more dynamically disposed toward reality) should be understood, then, as a complementary derivation from a change of logic –formal, organizational, ordering, in short– that had been studied by extension in the essay 'open logic', which appeared not long after.[1]

The lengthy preparation of this study, as well as the decisive concentration on a professional practice particularly demanding in time and commitment and the change of circumstances that every delayed project entails combined to set back –without postponing *sine die*– a project that was always going to be especially complex both in theoretical analysis and in projectual situations. The team at the Actar publishing house have now assembled the testimony of that deferred project in the form of the more selective

and synthetic work that these lines aim to preface, rather than to analyse in depth. This present text should thus be seen as the foreword to a hypothetical study still waiting to be written than as a genuine closely-argued essay.
There is room for discussion, then, in the light of this 'change of approach', as to whether its focus –on the eighteen referential trajectories, confined to the European context, that are presented here– is sufficiently rigorous or complete.
All the more so because I have been affirming for quite some time that the greatest contribution made by the change of logic generated from various fronts is, precisely, its possible conception as a shared scenario of investigation more than as a 'hit parade' of brands or 'heroicised' figures (prompted by iconographic fascination, by spectacular limelight-stealing or simply by good old-fashioned cronyism). That change would be fundamental to understanding, for example, the differences between the 90s generation and its immediate predecessor: although the 80s generation pioneered innovative modes and manners, continued to trust not only in the apparent formality implicit in their concepts and designs but, above all, in a decisive –and professionally more profitable– desire to regard themselves more as an 'intellectual elite' (vocational and culturally officialized) than as a genuine collective field of research that would conceive of closeness to power only from the closeness to ideas.

The propositive slowing-down and/or the intellectual fatigue of some of the chief 'legends' of this 'limelight-stealing' scenario illustrate the difficulty of continuing to posit an architecture conceived solely as a specular/spectacular object (trusting in the greater or lesser competitiveness –whether this means attractiveness or rivalry– of an increasingly singularized 'one-off' creative action, deriving from the current trends of a market economy subject to consumption and expectation) and the need to understand that new will to change simply in terms of a new will to ideological account and plural exchange, associated with a new kind of projectual logic. The monumentalising of a handful of privileged careers would thus seem to contradict the very convictions they championed: that that change of logic could be discerned not only in certain iconic experiences but in a whole host of creative attempts, proposals and explorations –whether productive or merely speculative, developed or barely intuited, anonymous or widely recognized, tried and tested or

still experimental, formed or in formation– that would share a given degree of commitment and intensity in their orientation.
It is also true that the most high-profile and (why not?) most mediatic defence of this conceptual transformation can be traced in many of the different theoretical or practical facets characteristic of most of the careers presented here. These are careers that have manifested themselves on more than one occasion as 'standard bearers' of that possible propositive option (at once critical and compliant) by being remarkable not only for the more or less evident quality of their works but for a constant promotional, propagandistic or banner-waving action, based on the conviction entailed in upholding a certain alternative creative ambition, both individual and collective.

In the last few years, in effect, some of the most interesting experiences on the current European international scene have sought –perhaps as a response to the increasing inclination of official criticism toward the description of panoramas rather than the advancing of genuine theoretical positions– to conjugate a two-sided approach, theorizing and active, publicising and projective, laying the bases of a new critical and productive action understood more as operative instrument than as mere neutral position. Dual proposals for action and reflection such as *Quaderns* (Gausa/Prat), *Fisuras* (Ballesteros/Soriano-Palacios) and *New Media* (Guallart/Díaz) thus intersected and overlapped in their approaches, in different means and formats, connecting with the lines of argument presented in other, more or less episodic projects of diffusion such as *Exit* (Ábalos-Herreros), *Rizoma* (Solà-Morales) and *Circo* (Tuñón-Mansilla) in Spain, or *In-Ex* by the Périphériques group (Paillard-Jumeau, Marin-Trottin and, initially, Jakob-MacFarlane) in France, and GAM (Riewe) in Austria, or the numbers of *Forum* edited by Winy Maas in Holland, as well as the important critical work done by Alejandro Zaera during his involvement with *El Croquis*; UN Studio (Van Berkel & Bos) and their writings on the new transdisciplinary phenomena; François Roche (Roche, DSV & Sie) and his network mobilizations; the early explorations by Willem Jan Neutelings in the realm of mobility (*The Ring Cultuur, The Patchwork City*), by MVRDV in that of data processes and urban growth (*Farmax*, *Digital Cities*, *Costa Ibérica*, etc.) or the most militant manifestations of Luca Galofaro (IaN+), Njiric+Njiric, NOX, NL, Lacaton & Vassal or Eduardo Arroyo, etc., signified as explicit actions in specific field.

These are also the dynamics within we should situate the action carried out in the last few years by Actar Arquitectura and the Actar publishing house and their foundational link to the Metápolis group, whose motors are Vicente Guallart, Willy Müller, Ramon Prat and Manuel Gausa, the author of these lines: this is a somewhat unusual project (only explicable in terms of the coincidence of different trajectories in synergy with the concerns that engage us here, and revealing the fundamental contribution made in recent years and at the international level by certain ventures in this country, involved with that new will to action diffusion and oriented, from such premises, at interlinking R & D & T & D —that is, Research + Development + Teaching + Diffusion— in a multiple approach as ambitious as it is rigorous in its objectives.

The position common to most of these proposals was that of attempting to understand those links or relationships that seemed to emerge forcefully in the end-of-century international debate and were to end up taking concrete shape in various forums for exchange, such as the first Europan competitions, the Metápolis encounters, the Archi-lab laboratory and so on, all of which seemed to have a stimulating innovative energy supplied by theoretical concerns and of evident search experiences, although often lacking an authentic global interpretation. These forums did, in any case, provide the first physical materialization of that other, more virtual kind of encounter made up of networks of conceptual interest, which at the same time served to identify, in possible scenarios for common discussion, some of the most advanced lines of research at the international level. The great strength of all of these initiatives was their recognition of a common territory (previously registered in other platforms such as *Quaderns*, *Arch+*, *Archis*, etc.) defined by careers that although physically distant were connected by a similar will to innovation. Far from the old familiar academic congresses and politically correct get-togethers, the great virtue of these frameworks of relationship lay in that uncommon complicity inter pares that would privilege shared experiences, closer to scientific exchanges than to any mere socio-mediatic attention-grabbing, but also, beyond the pure lucubrations of theory, in attempting in effect to present concrete proposals, images and situations for the future from a more open and innovative conception of the very ideas of city, landscape, context or, simply, habitat.

In spite of the fact that a number of recent international events –and the ghosts of one or more possible crises– would seem to counsel successive protective layers of scepticism, distrust and even *saudade*; in spite of the neo-traditionalist and ultra-conservative waves that continue to persist (and resurge) in many areas of society; in spite of the difficulties involved in continuing to defend the cultural values of innovation and creation in the face of a decision-making power bound up with a culture (hyper-pragmatic and hypo-daring) of the guarantee (in other words, of recreation and/or of retroaction); in spite, in fact, of a certain battle-weariness, I still feel there is evidence of a certain innovative spirit in a whole up-coming generation willing to defend an optimistic vision (not only in the conception but in the actual tackling of the space) from the point at which that term is seen as signifying not a vast lack of concern but a certain propositive ethics, less codified or ritualised than modern positivism, that aims precisely to optimize reality, projecting new qualitative actions on the environment, that is to say, on territories and urbanities, habitats and landscapes, private spaces and collective spaces, etc. And from the moment in which the idea of progress associated with that term –no longer as an absolute deterministic arrow but as an evolving will, as a shared intelligence– is still the most positive feature of our cultural capacity when it comes to outlining questions, meeting challenges, improving conditions and creating new and possible links –and spaces– exchange and harmonious coexistence.

I still believe there is a certain ethical conviction –more elastic and impure, less rigid or positional, less purist and dogmatic, more enthusiastic than the old critical resistance, more idealistic and ideological– in that commitment to keep on exploring the limits of what were until quite recently the established codes and, at the same time, to accept the essential substantive impurity of our time, with its accelerated conditions of exchange, interaction and mixture. That is what a multiplicity of voices and experiences seem to call for today: a generalized change of attitudes and paradigms that, in contrast to the idea of a redeeming urban reconstruction identified with the latter half of the 20th century, would appeal to a possible positivizing reactivation of the environment (a wider concept) based on the capacity of simultaneously combining information from various sources, generating synergies, and interactions (more than evocations or mere figurations), encouraging a transverse action between open fields of knowledge and creation (art, the sciences, literature, means of diffusion, anthropology...) necessarily freed of formal prejudices or prior disciplinary codes.

That paradoxical need to reconcile knowledge and proposal, theoretical reflection and practical involvement, vision and action, is the sphere in which the most committed and exposed experiences I am defending here move. At the core of that position we should not fail to posit the need to give, too, a certain degree of response to a series of doubts and questions that have arisen in recent times, not the least among which would be a line of critical reflection (synthesized with special clarity in the well-known text 'Fresh Conservatism' by Roemer van Toorn)[2] that would seem to reconsider, from a certain critical exigency, the truly provocative and propositive dimension of an architecture that, in spite of demonstrating a high degree of imagination and capacity for *bouleversement*, tends all too often to be confused with a simple effect of imaginative dilettantism, limiting its ultimate objective to a matter of mere appearance: that of bestowing freshness and casualness –or perhaps pure imaginative perversion– on the unrestrained neo-liberalism (and thus social conservatism) characteristic of the society of the late 20th and early 21st century.

The inherent message (not free of arguments and, of course, much more lucid than that of the all too familiar neo-traditionalist and pseudo-disciplinary critique) would be of the danger of confusing the demand for a reformulating methodological change (in the system) with a certain fresh and irresponsible collaborationism (with the system) in failing, in many cases, to throw into crisis (to denounce or reject) the underlying ideological framework in reality, attempting, in contrast, to make the maximum benefit and –uninhibited– use of its rules and potentials.
We have often been obliged to point out that the interest in attempting to 'resonate' with the current processes of development of contemporary reality (urban, social, cultural, productive, etc.) responds not to a mere speculative instrumentalization but to an activist will: that of conceiving new parameters of organization and/or restructuring posited beyond the traditional forms of what would have come to be thought of as disciplines of space. These parameters ought to take into account the diversity of relations, of flows and scales and, above all, of scenarios and

events as basic factors capable of constructing the developments of increasingly polyhedral organisms, in constant entropic evolution.

It is not a question, then, of pure opportunist cynicism but of a certain *pragmatic idealism* (pragmatic in terms of its acceptance of reality; idealistic in its will to endow it with a certain qualitative redefinition that this would transmit) intended to transcend the limits of that ambiguous *conservative progressivism* that has been dominant in Europe since the late seventies, particularly disposed to take refuge in the apparent endorsement of the already consecrated –experience or history as guarantees, the discipline as reference– as the basis of a certain consensual stabilizing order.

The entire contemporary debate could, in effect, be settled today between the longing for and stubborn defence of a resistant universe still subject to parameters of a fixed and stabilized order (the pondered as a guarantee of order) and often not free from a certain purist puritanism and the intuition (and acceptance) of a dynamic universe –definitively more unsettled and impure– that refers to more elastic and permeable trajectories, capable of combining variation and interaction, mix and change, and so also singularity and irregularity.
Perhaps it would be useful to recall here that the great economic crisis of the last third of the last century and many of the cultural, political and social movements that coincided with it –albeit less mediatized than current events– had decisive consequences not only in the global development of the planet but in a certain reorientation or readjustment of the thinking, management and conception of the urban. The idealism of development, the projection of the future, the pioneering ambition, the technological, spatial and/or formal researches and also the utopian dream –or dreams– of a new society (that is to say, a certain epic and optimistic vision of progress) thus led to a long period of operative prudence and revising of values (the revision of the past) that had been latent since the sixties and (in a context of new uncertainties) would end up replacing the risky idea of innovation with the most reassuring one of continuity, a backward movement in which we often still seem to be locked. Discretion and moderation, pondered management and possibilist profitability, reconstruction and/or recreation, tradition and habit, pre-existence or experience (as consolidated or consensually agreed assets) and a certain concentration on the local

context as the familiar framework of action would constitute the keys to a 'critical-realist' period that —with good and worse results— was to end up determining many of the most significant urban, educational, productive, creative and cultural references of the last thirty years.

Without denying the correcting values that this scenario would have brought with it, it is also worth noting the conceptual limits of an atmosphere inclined more toward recreating than proposing; more toward experience than the emergent; more toward brand image than the discovery of potentials; more toward training in the trade than to creative expansion, and more toward the code than the signified. The change of century and the advent of a new scenario of technological and social transformations, more interconnected, diverse and cosmopolitan, and also of a new conception of the idea of progress, no longer as the imposition of a new universal order but as the 're-activation' of reality itself have ended up evidencing the need for a return to innovation more as shared investigation in and by various disciplinary fields than as mere creative drive.

This situation illustrates a clear moment of change in architecture, defined between the last flickers of modernity (its 'squeezing out', in Federico Soriano's words) and the first manifestations of a new kind of logic —more, perhaps, than order— characteristic of a cultural era with new stimuli, challenges and rewards. '*We still work,*' as Federico Soriano has perceptively observed,[3] '*on the folds of the modern space. We have leaned out beyond the edge of continuous space, there in the infinite, and we have almost seen its back. We intuit definitions that are no longer geometric but topological. Similarly, we appreciate new classes of structures in which the way the loads (or flows) are connected is more interesting than the form of the solid pieces. The free floor plan is thus dissolved (as far as we can intuit) as a new process of conjugation.*'

2. NETWORK FRAMEWORK, OR WHY IS A NEW ARCHITECTURE NECESSARY TODAY?

The pages that follow aim to set out some examples of that new kind of projectual approach no longer identified with habits, manners, inertia or more or less particularist models but emerging from a new collective consciousness —related to the capacity for global exchange (and translated, at the same time, into local processes of investigation)— that seeks to respond with a new instrumental, conceptual and procedural, to the current conditions of contemporary reality. Why insist so much on this new glocal creative potential? Why refer so much to this will to innovate and investigate? Because, beyond identities and rivalries, references and competences, there can be recognized today in the creative field a new will to propose based on a profound change of visions and concepts, of concerns and formulations, that tends to link together shared attitudes and common objectives produced beyond the context, in various cultural spaces.

This is, in effect, a new network framework that can be defined more by the complicity of lines of research than by the strict following of 'dogmas' or specific models. A framework of action that would posit a new way of understanding the old notions of order, form and organization and, as such, a new way of understanding, among other disciplines, architecture itself.

A framework of exploration connected with a time of social, cultural and technological changes that it would want to favour others way of tackling new (and old) problems. A framework, then, that it would not seek solely to make up 'conjunctures'. Rather it would seek to recognize without complexes, with energy and precision but also with an absence of inhibitions, those key areas that would define contemporary reality itself. Infiltrating –and implicating itself– in it. Approaching the very processes and the factors that would determine it. Registering without inertias or prejudices the data of the environment itself and making the fullest inventive use of the new tools. Understanding 'the nature of things' so as to influence them.

We might think that there would be something ambiguous and uncertain in all of this, at a time when the limits between innovation, cynicism, progressivism, scepticism and resistance are tending to seem increasingly diffuse: poorly understood from the critical perspective of a distrustful Left (which has –paradoxically– found a prudent collective model in tradition), poorly thought of from the neo-liberal logic that sees in this attitude an overly idealistic tone, this involvement, at once innovative and qualitative, is nevertheless the great ethical challenge today. This is the same challenge that Sanford Kwinter identified in noting,[4] in contrast to the words of the British physicist Ernest Rutherford and his ironic definition of the qualitative as 'a quantitative evil': '*Only that desire to qualify reality itself (in aspect, in form, in knowledge)*

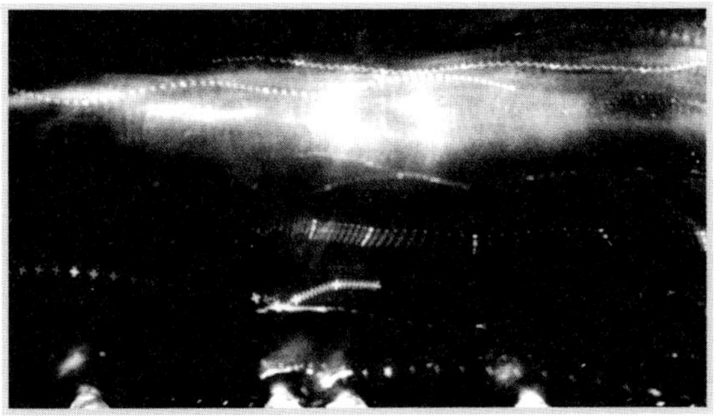

seems able today to pass through the glaucous film that envelops the numerical world, endowing it with a cultural and emotive meaning; it is a matter of conscience: a necessity and not, now, a betrayal.'

In the face of the new cultural challenges of our hyperpresent it seems timely to defend that disposition, at once critical and involved, capable not only of registering concerns about our environment but also of risking –and constructing– solutions for it.[5] To ask questions but also to venture responses. Now then: how does that reality we are alluding to present itself to us? To what conditions does it tend to refer? Probably to those of a more heterogeneous and complex environment, more dynamic and atonal, more dispersed and diffuse, more diverse and simultaneous and nevertheless more open to a plural interaction, that is to say, to exchange, contamination and mixture. To cohabitation and to miscegenation. To a certain progressive sensation of irregularity and impurity, more heterodox and paradoxical in its manifestations.

These recent decades have certified the evidence of a spectacular leap in scale in the definition of our spaces of relationship and living together –our habitats– connected with the increase in mobility and in remote communication, with the de-localization of exchanges and the capacity for the technological and material transformation of our environment, thus manifesting exponentially the dynamic nature of cities, societies and territories.That progressive simultaneity of messages, information and differential conditions that are not always cohesive but rather inter-connected makes it necessary to conceive a new kind of relational logic capable of orienting and articulating diversity in more heterogeneous and impure structures (that is to say, more sensitive to a possible n-dimensional interaction associated with a certain substantive incompleteness and indetermination) capable of translating, without formal predeterminations or pre-established terms, that possible 'agencied' coincidence of variable phenomena and events. A logic associated –really or virtually– with dynamic processes more than with static events; that is to say, with evolving structures, open to change and variation.

Evidently the city –in other words, its multiple definition as 'metapolis', its various manifestations and its structural mutations–have been a particular object of attention, thus revealing the new nature of a complex organism in accelerated transformation: a system at once dynamic and non-linear, that responds in turn to complex processes of operative interaction between networks of connection and layers of information. A 'multi-layered' structure, progressively heterogeneous and irregular –in local and global interaction– that nevertheless responds (with a higher level of complexity, that is to say, with a greater degree of synchronicity between different layers of exchange) to basic patterns of development related to the majority of 'spatio-temporal' distribution processes that govern our universe. This takes us to a treatment of the city and the territory formulated above and beyond the old paradigms of traditional compositional urbanism (fabric, surveying, construction, layout) but also far removed from the old yearning for disciplinary autonomy that have characterized the last few decades. A treatment that, to the contrary, simultaneously combines transverse influences and contributions borrowed from the world of art (Land Art, New Conceptualism, Situationism...), from physics and maths (chaos theory, diffuse logic...), from computing (data processing, programming...), from biogenetics (evolving patterns...), from thought (new literature, new philosophy...), from anthropology (interaction phenomena...) and elsewhere, no longer simply to propose other possible aesthetics –other figurations– but to explore, above all, a possible –and new– transverse nature between territories and scenarios. Architectures that could be described, in effect, as 'reactive fields within other (interactive) fields' and translate that paradoxical nature of an action posited at the crossroads, between scales and places, between tensions and demands, between limits and frontiers, transcending seals and dichotomies (nature and artifice, but also public and private, singular and plural, abstract and concrete, synthetic and expansive, etc.).

3. OPEN LOGIC: DYNAMISM, INTERACTION, IMPURITY

To speak of complexity refers us, today, to the dynamic and heterogeneous conditions of an environment –a time, a culture, a technology– destined to multiply information and exchanges, while at the same time favouring a growing sensation –and freedom– of displacement, at all levels and in all directions: in movements, in relationships,

in expressions and in the spatial manifestations of the processes associated with them, evidencing, as Paul Virilio has remarked, that progressive state of 'diachronic synchronicity' –of discontinuous simultaneity– between diverse and polyphase layers (paradoxical layers) of 'combined' events.[6] This is what the notion of complexity alludes to: to the capacity of simultaneously combining –activating and interactivating– a multiplicity of not always harmonious information in a single infrastructural framework of (inter)relation.

A defensive (or over-vigilant) vision of the architectural action –the most traditional, in fact– aims to work 'from' complexity in order to limit its effects, to 'essentialize' its manifestations: to calm the movements, to stabilize the trajectories, to purify the information. To prefigure –in order to control them– its own irregular dynamics. A more optimistic and positivist vision of the architectural action proposes to work 'with' complexity in order to mobilize and enhance to the full its combining potentials. Synchronous.

In the course of this essay I have commented more than once on the possible open and complex nature of the contemporary project. Its capacity to resonate better with the multiplied and dis-cohesive conditions of the time, proposing more flexible and fluctuating mechanisms capable of promoting a greater degree of freedom, dynamism and mixicity and of according in this way the suspense of the unpredictable. It is of this, in fact, that the new situation we are considering here speaks: of a more open conception of the order, of the form and of the action that refers to them. And in that acceptance of interaction and mixture, of the exchange and crossing of energies, we can detect one of the fundamental keys of contemporary culture, destined to replace the old notion of the essential, compact and monolithic identity of the things –and categories– with a more diffuse and impure quality. More hybrid: itself and many others at the same time: no longer a unidirectional and unequivocal arrow but an oriented and diversified bundle: capable of fluctuating, pirouetting and mutating –exchanging information– without this causing it to lose its particular condition. This would be, in any case, an attitude that would speak of more elastic and imaginative relations – and criteria: neither of 'impositions from' nor of 'integrations in' but 'interactions between'. This would posit the need to work with a new kind of operative logic capable of synthesizing that shift from the stable to the dynamic, from the additive to the combinatory, from the unitary to the heterogeneous, characteristic of our time. A more open logic that would be neither the classic (compositional) metaphysical continuity nor that of the modern functional (positional) objectuality but the strategic contemporary (dispositional) interactivity, capable of articulating and potentiating the diversity of our time.

Why should we invoke a possible open logic? The very term 'open' would effectively define that relational potential of a possible new architectural logic –defined in other spheres as advanced, reactive or informational– destined to favour more effective frameworks of interaction.

– A more open logic because virtually evolutive (capable of evolving, of changing and varying, beyond given states of configuration, according to dynamic processes that generate development).
– A more open logic because restless and animate. That is to say, because substantially dynamic. Sensitive to variations. To changes and to fluctuations. To mutations. Expansive and expanded.
– A more open logic, then, because more flexible (capable of fluctuating, of deforming, of adapting and transforming before and with the incidence of information).
– A more open logic because more indeterminate (or less predetermined, less prefigured, in its form and configuration). Because not sealed off or confined, but also because non-definitive (that is to say, because incomplete and unfinished).
– A logic, in any case, more open because more relational. More receptive and with more empathy. More permeable (and sensitive) to the demands of the environment, of the place).
– A more open logic, then, because more externalized and extrovert (capable of opening up to external scales, conditions and/or dimensions and at the same time of expressing or exulting (opening them up, too) its own internal dynamics and movements.
– A more open logic because more spontaneous and informal (in its evolution) and, as such, more joyous (more relaxed and uninhibited, more expressive) in its manifestations. Less severe. Less essential and single-minded. More impure and alterable, disposed to mixture, contamination and cohabitation. To exchange and interaction.

We could attempt to define that logic, which would adopt diverse and diversified forms – and modes.
– A more complex logic, then, capable of synchronizing simultaneous events.
– A more dynamic logic, capable of making events evolve.
– A more impure logic, capable of hybridizing events.
– A more generative logic, capable of instigating –and inducing– events.
– A more open logic, in short, capable of promoting scales, programmes, situations and trajectories, in other words, events.
This implies working with concepts more than with ideas. With strategies more than with plans. With systems more than with figurations. With trajectories (and environments) more than with objects. With fabrications more than with constructions. With synthetic registers more than with analytical studies. With dispositions and mechanisms more than with designs. With processes more than with incidents.
And this would allude to a strategic and tactical intentionality capable of guiding actions and making them more flexible or indeterminate to a time. Sensitive to movement, contamination and combination. In every case we would recognize, in effect, a positive assumption of diversity (and of the irregularity associated with it) that would be at the very basis of these potential.

1. On the one hand a diversity (or irregularity) that we might call agencied or related –relational– and would allude to combined processes of (re)appropriation, articulation and crossover between different families or systems of structural, morphological or technological codes.
2. On the other, a diversity that we might call generated –or genetic– and would allude, in effect, to the possible variable –of variations and variances– development (or evolution) of a single pattern (or family) of evolving and/or infrastructural codes.
3. And, last but not least, an agreed or shared diversity that could combine both at once, as joint partners.

Between the two actions –that of a combinatory or relational action that would tend to favour synthetic operations of crossover and encounter between informations and that of a genetic (or generating) action that would tend to maximize its generative and

fluctuating capacity, favouring the development of evolutive trajectories and systems of formal generation (and self-organization)– oscillate most of the investigations associated with that new consciousness that recodifies the dynamic processes and the structural diversity and irregularity that we have been considering here.

4. A NEW GAZE

If dualism has traditionally illustrated the conceptual division of the world into categories –the exact (or at least accurate) recognition of a reality on the basis of closed, unequivocal and differentiated classifications– today those formerly substantive categories that marked a certain deterministic vision of things are repeatedly faced with the undisciplined conditions of a time of slippages that proclaims, in all its manifestations, the brutal (and at the same time exciting) dissolution of those old dichotomic divisions that for years were the paradigms of our ideological and disciplinary baggage: 'exterior/interior', 'natural/artificial', 'public/private', 'order/chaos', 'determined/undetermined', 'formal/informal', 'ordinary/extraordinary', 'domestic/universal', 'particular/general', 'discontinuous/connected', 'open/closed', etc. configure new –and unusual– simultaneous experiences and, as such, new –and strange– mixed voices: coupled and dual terms as ambiguous as they are explicit; couples or couplings born of counternatural unions between once opposed categories that are nevertheless fused today in new cross-bred –bastard– realities that exacerbate the paradox situations by creating new –and more intriguing– meanings.
A reality of heterodox scenarios subject to ground conditions that are more heterogeneous, dynamic, diffuse, diverse, segmented, arrythmic, interconnected, contingent, cross-bred and artificial; in short, a strange and apparently chaotic (incoherent, unfinished and uncertain) reality that would reflect the overlapping nature of certain non-linear and increasingly abstract processes in which the paradox situations tend to multiply: in which large global structures articulate anecdotal (and often anachronistic) local iconographies, in the same way that unusual –new– situations or phenomena go hand in hand with surprisingly everyday behaviours or scenarios. Today we read our environment facing up to a new physical reality but also to impressions parallel to that reality: as in a manipulated field of incidences and incidents, real and virtual, we thus confront an ambivalently multiplied (definitively polyphonic, slippery and diffuse, because non-essential) reality that provokes disconcerting strangenesses in the face of a suddenly multifaceted environment.

Our orientation –and our action–now require a more hybrid gaze: hybrid because, precisely, artificial, synthetic and unprejudiced, multiple and polyhedral. A probably somewhat eccentric gaze; that of new –and curious– explorers equipped with a set of prosthetic approaches and objectives; mobile; retractable, polyfocal. A gaze no longer unidirectional –fixed or stabilizing– but simultaneous; capable of condensing –and linking– heterogeneous informations and stimuli –material and immaterial, figurative and abstract, diffuse and concrete, harmonious and dissonant– in new compatible registers.A compressive and compressing gaze, no longer destined to reproduce models but to recognize relationships, positing other possible conditions. No longer describing categories but reformulating them (interconnecting them) in new synthetic cartographies destined to formulate possible tactical–sometimes even counternatural– contracts between overlapping layers of information. A synchronous gaze, capable of superposing codes, messages and scenarios. But also a simulating gaze, capable of anticipating movements. A recodifying gaze, then, capable of encoding (inventing or interpreting new codes) and decoding (surpassing or dismantling old codes).

Merely visual (descriptive) instruments give way, then, to new processing instruments; the eye or the lens, strange multiple periscopes, sensors, radars and interfaces capable of capturing the close and the distant; the place and all places. The real and the virtual. Simultaneously. This, then, would be an alert and open gaze: attentive, as has already been noted, to perceptions, but also to phenomena; to situations and behaviours stemming from a transverse exploration generated in plural environments (experiences, investigations or scenarios).

A gaze no longer only visual but resonant and transferring, processing informations more than perceptions. A gaze more interested in the vectors of force and in connectivities than in tracing the detail. More interested in evolutive diagrams than in static and/or stabilized images. A gaze, then, subject to a definitively synaesthetic and reactive <i> space, as the musicologist Silvia Molina has indicated;[7] in other words, a space subject to synergies and synaesthesias as factors of global interrelationship:

'Not a space subject to eternal fixed laws. Nor a physical or visual space, full of scenes, echoes, absorptions or reverberations. Not a dimensional, tactile space. Instead, an intermediate space. A place for interaction. A reactive space. This is <i> space.'

If the principal condition of the old single-minded (purist, hierarchizing and codified) gaze of the discipline has been, precisely, that of applying (or recognizing) stable codes –be it from the evocation of experience or of memory (history), from the typification and serial rationalization of production (reason) or from the composition of meanings (representation)– today that gaze is progressively giving way to a new vision, decoded because unencoded: non-homologated, trusting little in assumed figures, in tried and tested models or in literal silhouettes but, by contrast, more receptive to those latent situations understood more as possible interactive keys than as recognized codes. A gaze, then, that is open and selective, negotiating and distorting, critical and active at the same time. A gaze not erudite but congenially forgetful (with effective –and timely– tactical amnesias), but at the same time vocationally holistic in the cultural sphere: no longer trusting in a merely eclectic vision of culture –an ornamental veneer or a compilation of bits of learning (as pure knowledge) but in a military and militantly geographical interpretation, attentive to those territories of exploration immersed in a propositive global framework, evolutive and entropic (proneist) and, as such, based on the movement of (and between) potentially new informations, with a view to action. A gaze synthetic because synaesthetic. Not an endogenous but an extrogenous gaze; not a pure but an impure gaze; not a stable but a mutant gaze; not a distant gaze –indifferent and trusting– but an involved gaze: infiltrated and intentioned. A gaze that is not only objective but, and above all, operative – cold and involved, induced and inducing; astute and at the same time (re)positivizing. Expectant and attentive, incisive and intentioned, infiltrated and tactical, this would, then, be an alert gaze –à l'affût– on guard, but also stalking, capable of recognizing in reality itself strategic criteria and tactical actions (decisions with a view to the action).

A gaze –like the chameleon's– susceptible to distorting and dividing itself, to projecting and of pro-injecting itself, thus simultaneously combining recognition and action.

5. ACTIVE WILL AND STRATEGIES OF '*DÉTOURNEMENT*'

In that 'astute and recodifying negotiation with the real' we recognize a new incidental will: that of mechanisms that maximize their will to active intervention in the environment through the explicit manifestation of their implicit –'geo-' or 'topo-'– strategic condition (recognition, diagnosis, response, simultaneously, as in a virtual geography or topography/topology of crossed information). This would, in effect, be an architecture that does not conceal its decidedly relational vocation –synthetic and synergetic– capable of recognizing and processing the surrounding reality, reformulating it with and from a new instrumental and operative apparatus. Redefining –re-evaluating and re-adapting, that is to say, manipulating– the codes of that reality, referring them to a new set –or catalogue– of non-inertial instructions, as efficient in their objectives as subversive (or manipulative) in their formulations. An architecture posited, then, as a 'de-standardizing' machine, as Frédéric Migayrou has described it –in contrast to the 'non-standard' logic of a substantially genetic investigation of form–[8] destined to *détourner* the lines of a certain prototypical (standardized and modern) and consensually agreed (evocative and postmodern) routine through a possible perversion of its own productive logics, favouring new anti-typological actions as singular as they are at the same time generic. This would be an instrumental definition grounded in the expedite and expeditious, decisive character of its own direct (synthetic) materialization, far removed from any solemn, rhetorical, essential or purified pretension of the form.

More than a figurative (pseudo-aesthetic) vocation, what emerge, then, is that operative will rapidly, instantly, cheaply and utilitarianly to condense –and accommodate– synthesized and contextualized information (conditions), potential (latencies) and actions (strategies). Systems and contingencies.[9] These dynamics are of interest because in such synaesthetic and syn-strategic action-architectures, the architecture and the reality in which this is inscribed appear condensed in programmatic decisions capable of fusing immediately cause and effect, question and resolution.[10] Demands and new organizations. These mechanisms would thus be formulated as abstract (generic) programmes of holistic information and specific (contingent) operations of logistic information: action map destined to reinform the system.

It would be interesting to highlight, once again, that will to positive 'incidence' on reality entrusted in one of reinterpretation and/or qualitative re-formulation of its own dynamics produced not so much from the confidence in a new imposed order, totalized, absolute, single-minded or prototypical as from the unprejudiced acceptance of the actual conditions —and situations— set out from.

From the infiltration and slippage of new movements —or codes— of evolutive formulation in (and between) the initial movements of the system; from the resonance with its own structures and from the utilization of its potentials; from that difficult combination of autonomy and interconnection, distance and complicity, abstract criterion and specific contingency, intention and alteration, determination and indeterminacy, which appeals to that slippery capacity of reformulating, fluctuating and tactical infiltration:[11] in line, then, with that diverse and at the same time concerted coincidence of assorted stimuli in mutual empathy that has been described here and speaks of diversity, of combinatoriality; of evolutivity and of interaction; of individuality and of capacity for articulation; of accommodation and of interconnection; of interlinkage and of absence of prejudice, in short, as factors (and parameters) of action[12] '[Contemporary] architecture and art aim to coincide with reality. It is not so much a will to abolish the profession, but more to liberate it from institutional-representative structures, from the extolling of autonomy and the tradition of critical marginalism. It is a plea for acting and experiencing. It is inspired by a utopian desire to connect with time and reality, both being understood as fragmented. [...] Increasingly art and architecture are breaking free of representation as generated and maintained by the system. Priority is given instead to real presence. [...] It is no surprise then that the phrase, relational work, is on everyone's lips. [The] new work of art is relational; its content is the interhuman experiences that it generates; every visitor becomes a spectator, discussion partner or next-door neighbour. The new art does not rely on any passive experience to restore contact with user and viewer; the keynote now is active participation.'

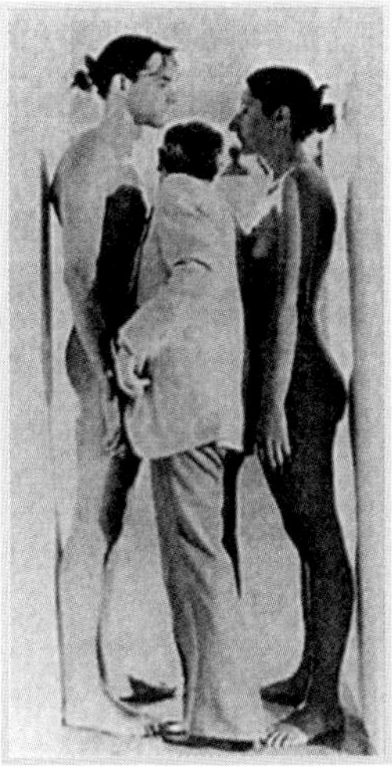

Sanford Kwinter, in an analogy that has become famous,[13] compares that dynamic action of slipping, sliding, infiltrated or usurped architecture with the slip or slide performed in sports such as surfing or skydiving, the delta wing hang-gliding, skateboarding or snowboarding, that are based on the challenge of being involved in a flowing environment.
Kwinter analyses such activities in depth, describing them as: *Techniques of movement combined in a rigorous and spontaneous action, in which the sportsman engages in an intimate relationship with the dynamic medium around him.*

Over and above the apparent cynical or collaborationist reading with which this metaphor has been interpreted by many critics, the most important thing about this syn-strategic will lies in that combined capacity for intuition and innovation: to feel one is an integral part of the wave, as surfers say, not only to flow with it but to try out new conditioned movements –incident operations– capable of exploring situations of resonance and limit, of intuition and innovation: to feel one is an integral part of the wave, not simply for to go with it or flow with it but to go beyond it ludically, to explore its inherent conditions of flow. In fact, more interesting than the figure of the surfer who lets himself go with the flow of the waves is the image of the swimmer that immerses and involves himself in and with them. A flow within another flow that adopts it and at the same time pushes and is pushed by it.

If the architectural debate of the last 30 years has tended to stress the autonomy of the discipline (reinforcing the more endogenous aspects of the form), it has also ended up favouring the very isolation of the architectural object –stopped and beached, disciplined because disciplinary– with respect to those possible stimuli –and/or demands– emerging from the actual natural or physical environment. Real or virtual A genuinely synergetic –and syn-strategic– reactive will would call not for an isolated or disconnected creative action but for an active and fruitful exchange as the product of a multiple and diversified experience in which the data provided by the information on the context (and beyond the context) would not have to be understood as definitive categories (accepted blindly) but as impulses or tensions that are interlinkable, interconnectable, couplable and instrumentalizable through timely agency-

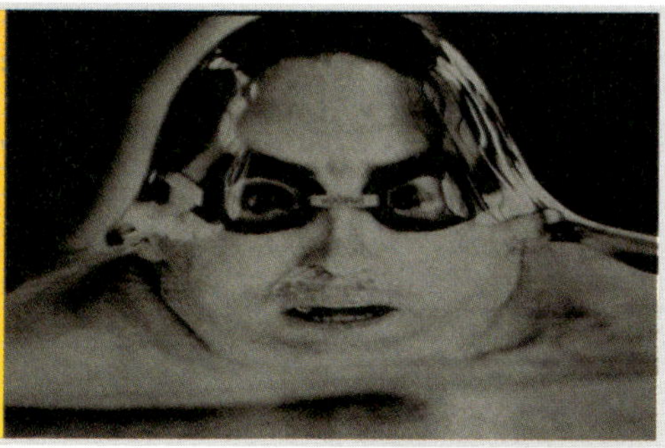

ings and displacements (understanding the term displacement not only as a dynamic movement but also as a de-naturalization of meanings). As an effective *détournement* –a qualitative diversion– of its less qualitative inertias, formulated, in any case, more from the convincing than from the entertaining.
Trusting in a more direct intuition, because freed of inertias, destined to favour unexpected agencyings, assemblages or montages previously ruled out as unusual.

And it is from this point of view that we would, in effect, defend that methodological possibility of favouring a genuine 'imaginative intuition' –to which, from different perspectives, Toyo Ito and Winy Maas both allude– rather than that will to refer to a hypothetical 'creative freshness' often understood as a mere label with an aesthetic veneer: *'It is a question,' as Toyo Ito has noted,*[14] *'of producing beneficial, unusual and also qualitative actions that, as in the story of the Emperor's new clothes, will be capable of generating explicit new messages, perhaps a little cheeky because free, but precise and straight, honest, courageous and true.' 'Observing (these action maps) we recognize an intuitive vision of society.' 'They would easily and somewhat eccentrically propose a tactical and indeterminate reappropiation of reality –of its behaviours and lifestyles– translated into open projects (with elastic and adaptable limits), thus penetrating its interstices.*
'This would not be a really critical critique (accepting any possible misunderstanding). In a society in which ideology has been turned into something diffuse or empty, the desire to project directly, without beating about the bush, and what is more, with projects that would embody and represent reality, would in itself be a posture loaded with critical reason.'

We move, then, in these fluctuating shifts between the basic conservatism of the social systems and the progressive and accelerated renovation that result from social reality itself and from the new individual behaviours (a duality that is, for example, evident in the own dichotomy that today opposes old inertias and emergent new movements). In that constructive game of social territorializations, de-territorializations and re-territorializations (as Yves Barel would call them)[15] we recognize that paradoxical new condition of operative multi-belongings and ambivalences it would be interesting for us to underline here: *'There is a paradoxical dimension hides in social change or in its forms: this change is presented at times as a continuity and as a break, favoured by agents of change that are at the same time presented as strategies of exploitation and collapse of the system itself.'*

If from a purist or resistant perspective reality appeared as an antagonistic, bastard medium against which architecture had to adopt defensive or redemptive postures, from that new will to active and synaesthetic (or 'synstrategic') infiltration analysed here it seems more interesting to note, in contrast, how architecture ought to favour clearer and more positive relationships with the environment: openings instead of defences, destined situate us in a real, mutable, changing and surprising universe. Dynamic and no longer static. Mapping (and multiplying) adequately, with clarity and forcefulness, data, emergencies and quotidianities that could be envisaged as harbingers of future phenomena and tendencies. Vectors as yet inhibited activated by uninhibiting actions; new relationships –and new combinations– that give rise to unexpected (re) configurations of the system from a kind of logic that would be posited no longer solely in the figurative terms of form but in the operative terms of activity, movement and/or exchange. That is to say, in the dynamic terms of an action map. It would be evident, then, that in this will or action, at once collaborationist and critical –agreed and distanced, resonant and transferent– we recognize many of the parameters to which Aaron Betsky referred in defining that 'critical pragmatism' that has characterized much of the most recent innovative production in Europe –and above all in the Netherlands– and has not ceased to manifest itself as an impure subversion of the modern logic as such in that move toward a new, more open and informal logic.[16] *'Critical pragmatism would define a concept that serves to describe a whole rich movement, above all in Holland, in which the architect would be converted into a surfer of the modern economy and of social systems, maintaining a balance between the movements of fashion and the desire to conceive a more human space, surfing the ocean of commercial structures and consumption that would mark the modern landscape itself [...] and whose star, the man who would have been slipped between the biggest waves, would be Rem Koolhaas.'*

It would, in any case, be interesting to highlight in all of this broad panorama a certain shared concern (activist and dynamic): that of an architecture destined to posit scenarios as linked as they are at the same time detached (more than unconcerned), capable, in effect, of resonating with the system and of transferring it, at the same time, toward other unexpected frames of reference. Rather than relationships of reflection (from *x* to *x*, isolated object) or symmetry (from *x* to y and from *y* to *x*, contextual object) what would be interesting, then, are those possible relationships of transitivity (from *x* to *y*, from *y* to *z* and from *x* to *z*, synaesthetic object) between realities and scales. The project would shift, thus, from being an 'entity' to being a 'transferent'. Destined to crystallize concrete landscapes projecting possible alternative landscapes. We move, then, in that pragmatopia that Andreas Ruby has described so well:[18] *'Located in the no-man's land of the modern dialectic, between utopia and pragmatism, pragmatopia would suggest an alternative territory of architectonic operativity. 'It resists the escapism of the utopia that incarcerates its vision in a space without place. 'At the same time it would go beyond the automatism of the pragmatic and its tendency to eliminate any idea conceived outside of the immediate action. The pragmatopia would propose a new plane of events capable of combining action (pragma) called on to 'take place' (topos).'*

6. PRONEISM, OR TOWARD A NEW OPERATING OPTIMISM

Today, in effect, as various authors would claim, 28 it seems there may be a new architecture on the horizon; beyond conventional appearance or the fixing of the object this would be an architecture positively involved with the adventure –or the avatar– of dynamic environments, the temporal dimension of processes and a qualitative vocation toward reality. An architecture conscious of the new dimension of a future time decidedly informal because informational. An architecture that, nevertheless, would seek to posit many things on the present; on everyday life. On its diversity and complexity. To give not only 'freshness' –as the critic Roemer van Toorn would put it– to an emergent new everydayness but 'vitality', and consequently a new and less severe, more ludic dignity to life. A new kind of 'revitalizing optimism'. Reactive and reactivating.

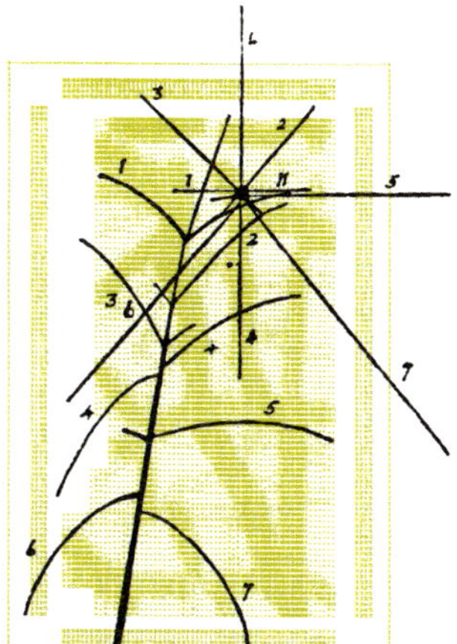

This would be a road full of traps (vanity, limelight-seeking behaviours, opportunism, even cynicism or greed), but these days it would tend only to demand a new kind of more positivist and optimistic operativity: full of integrity, joyfulness and the desire to work together: between investigation and pragmatism; between intuition and calculation; between forces and efforts; between actions and relations; as its open (and interactive) nature itself would demand. In any case this would, in effect, be a dynamic and revitalizing will that we have qualified on various occasions as 'reactive' by virtue of its relational and active vocation. A will that would claim an action and a gaze attentive to multiple emerging phenomena and to possible relations between scenarios and users, places and territories. An interrogatory action and gaze. With a combined vocation to understanding and proposal. A restless will in which what mattered would be hybrid strategies more than officiating specialities. Dispositions more than positions. Cartographies more than chronicles. Interpretations more than panoramas. Transverse searches more than multidirectional applications. (Undisciplined) alternatives more than (disciplined) inertias.

There would be no styles. Nor doctrines. There would be no models. Nor formulations. There would be criteria for action destined to synthesize possible combinations between hypotheses, logics and ventures.

– Ventures in terms of actions capable of advancing (concrete/local) dispositions and (generic/global) strategies.
– Ventures in terms of reflection capable of exploring new areas of interest with sufficient vitality to recognize the birth of other kinds of scenarios and stimulate the development of alternative options.

We could then –paraphrasing the musicologist Jean-Luc Hervé–[19] ask ourselves if that shared interest would not already define a clearly identifiable framework for action, to the point of giving rise to a homogeneous new set of investigations and proposals (as was the case in the 1930s and 1950s).

Because if the experiences contributed by each of the trajectories that refer to it can claim to be different and singular, the issues (and the way of apprehending the current situation) would, in effect, be similar.

- Rejection of a dry, gratuitous, pure or purified abstraction, and pursuit of a synthetic abstract efficiency that is more flexible, elastic and permeable, more alterable and impure.
- Explicit defence, in opposition to the 'back to ...' trend, of innovative responses that are as unusual (and spontaneous) as effective (and precise) in their materialization.
- Interest in rhythm and vivacity, animation and dynamics. Attention to (evolutive) processes more than to (episodic) events. To (formulating) strategies more than to (formal) designs. To (open) systems more than to (closed) figurations. Integration (in a conscious or intuitive way) of the local from the global (and vice versa).
- Transcendence of merely structural systems of organization (without, however, neglecting them totally) in order to reinvent (on the basis of a lucid reappropriation of the informal) new hybrid dispositions that are as systematic they are as singular; as (infra)structural as contextual.

This would, in effect, be the possible strength of contemporary art and architecture, and one of their greatest challenges: to produce new utterances posited from a new creative attitude born free of prejudices, more relaxed and un-subjected (more uninhibited; more unprejudiced and decoded; more detached and slippery; more denaturalized and liberated; more uninhibited and destabilizing; more disobedient and free of complexes, in short), trusting in the possibility of favouring more positive redefinitions of a reality suddenly sensitive to the collision of forces and references and, as such, approachable only from the conception of new relational mechanisms that condense the specific tensions of the local and those of other own energies inherent in the global contemporary space. Our challenge, then, would be to produce new and effective responses in line with the stimuli inherent in that glocal order, irregular and uncertain, generic and contingent, recursive and paradoxical, associated with the actual dynamic processes that define the interpretation and comprehension of contemporary space – and time. Complex processes defined by their high degree of indeterminacy, of interaction, of instability and of impurity, that is to say, by their own tendency to a certain informality associated with their intrinsic and increasing level of indiscipline. With their high degree of both synchronicity and ditony.

The current investigation would like to address the possibility of conceiving new logics, new structures and organizations, capable of articulating diversity better and of orienting uncertainty, of conjugating heterogeneity and celebrating complexity; from a strange paradoxical condition, midway between the given and the indeterminate, between order and chance, action and reaction, contract and indiscipline, the systematic and the contingent. Between collaboration and transgression. That would be the authentic cultural dimension of the contemporary project: its capacity to formulate 'new and surprising utterances': formulations understood as positive —efficient— eccentricities of the system rather than as extravagances. Formulations of possible 'others' produced out of 'impossible' unions. Trajectories generated in the system and beyond it. New operative paradoxes.

As we have already noted, it is only from the acceptance of that strange multiscalar cohabitation that architecture today can be understood. As a reaction mechanism, unprejudiced and positive; forceful and attentive to the individual, artificial but at the same time receptive to the particular demands of the scenarios in which it is necessary to act. A possibly strange mechanism, but also collusive, that is to say, potentiating: in resonance with the host body, so as not to provoke rejection, although no longer forcibly in harmonious symbiosis with it. That is, in effect, what this is all about. A more open conception (because non-predetermined, because more spontaneous and plural; because more relational and evolutive, but also because joyful and uninhibited). That of an architectural action capable of embracing the inherent and paradoxical complexity of our time, enabling the definition of a new scenario (real and virtual, global and local) oriented, in the last analysis, toward a new exploration of the very conception of our habitat, as individual and collective space, simultaneously.

An 'environment for interacting with more than a machine for living in'.
An environment not only decent but stimulating, active, changing, flexible; surprising and expressive. An environment associated with an architecture resolved to interact with the world. And it would, in fact, be of a more informal and extrovert architecture than that we are speaking of here: an architecture not only fresher but more joyful and stimulating, as van Toorn would, paradoxically, refer to it:[20] '*[An architecture] that aims to coincide with reality. [...] It is a plea for acting and experiencing. [...] It is inspired by a utopian desire to connect with time and reality. [...] Intellectual pes-*

simism would appear to have turned into its opposite - an optimism of action. Life is no longer thought of as a linear process, but as a complex totality that is full of contradictions. [...] Authenticity is no longer to be found in some sort of grounding; its permanence is of another kind. Authenticity is much more than the act of interpreting. Authenticity is a process of constant becoming.'

Open to the decisive use (strategic and plastic, operative and expressive) of colour, of light, of sound, of movement and of energy and of technology (not as a cold material but as a sensitive material); with a reactivation, in short, of the senses.

For the pleasure and the joyfulness of living and of relating and of qualitatively 'projecting' the individual, beyond the old familiar cultivated refining minimalism or the profitable commercial archetype; beyond, then, the mere resistant morality or the pure standard convention.Beyond cohesive unity or isolated autonomy. An architecture capable of celebrating and orchestrating diversity.

We would speak of a way of understanding architecture and we would speak of a way of understanding culture and society. Something rather important in recent times.

NOTES

1 The text 'Open Logic' will be published by Actar over the next few months.

2 See VAN TOORN, Roemer, 'Fresh Conservatism', in *Quaderns*, no. 219, Barcelona, 1998, p. 90 & ff.
The piece is a lucid approach not only to the dynamics of astuteness and opportunism that define certain aspects of our society, but also to the potentials for change within this society.

3 See SORIANO, Federico, 'Planta fluctuante', in *Fisuras*, no. 3 1/3, pp. 64/65.

4 See KWINTER, Sanford, 'The Hammer and the Song', in *OASE*, no. 48, 1998. p. 31.

5 A paradigm case would be the exhibition *Mutations*, orchestrated for Rem Koolhaas, with the help of, among others, Kwinter himself. See (various authors) *Mutations*, Actar, Barcelona, 2001.

6 See VIRILIO, Paul, 'Randgruppen', in *Daidalos*, no. 50, 1993.

7 See MOLINA, Silvia, 'Espacio intermedio. Visual-Virtual', in (various authors), *Entorno. Sobre el espacio y el arte*, ed. Editorial Complutense, Madrid, 1995, p 51.

8 The term was coined by Frédéric Migayrou. His initial idea was to devote two major shows to the concepts of 'Non-standard' and 'De-standard', but to date only the first of these has been realized (Centre Pompidou, 2003).

9 *'In the age of media and global production,' noted the architects njiric + njiric, 'architecture abandons its stylistic or canonic limits and enters the field of profane civic services.' From topological mappings, more than from typological concerns. Inverting in the 'field' conditions of our environment. But also incorporating sensual keys, colourist codes, incorporated messages; debating between the will to favour abstract concepts and possible actions.*
See the text-contribution by the architects njiric + njiric in the catalogue *ARCHILAB* no. 1, 1999.

10 See GUIHEUX, Alain, 'Action', in (various authors), *The Metapolis Dictionary of Advanced Architecture*, Actar, Barcelona, 2003.

11 *'In all of these cases we would observe an architectural attitude characterized by its permeability in relation to phenomena and to their dynamics of transformation. That degree of "infiltration into reality" would consequently depend on a more open understanding of architecture as an activity that not only involves a limited set of decisions but a decided co-participation of broader layers of incidence. Perhaps the only freedom left today would be that capacity to migrate between structures and to carry out a mutant practice that would operate in terms of the contingent more than the essential.'*
See ZAERA, Alejandro, 'The day after. A conversation with Rem Koolhaas', in *El Croquis*, no. 79, Barcelona, 1996.

12 See VAN TOORN, Roemer, op. cit.

13 *'The architect would no longer subscribe now to the erudite pact of volumes under the light: his –dynamic– writing would turn in a void, without an alphabet. 'The signs would no longer supply themselves a priori as symbolic reference but would reveal themselves in real time, riding bareback on a convulsed animal.'*
See KWINTER, Sanford, 'The Hammer and the Song', in *OASE*, no. 48, 1998. p. 31.

14 See ITO, Toyo, 'Architecture in a simulated city' in *Architectural Monographs*, no. 41, Academy Editions, London, 1995.
See also 'Architecture in the age of electronics', in *Quaderns*, no. 213, 1996, p. 157.

15 See BAREL, Yves, 'Le social et ses territoires', in AURIAC, F., BRUNET, R., *Espaces, jeux et enjeux*, Fayard, Fondation Diderot, Paris, 1986.

16 See BETSKY, Aaron, 'Landscape and the architecture of the self', in Quaderns, no. 220, Barcelona, 1998, p. 28.

17 See (various authors), *Reference OMA*, NAI, Rotterdam, 1995, pp. 36-37.

18 See RUBY, Andreas, 'Pragmatopia', in (various authors), *The Metapolis Dictionary of Advanced Architecture*, Actar, Barcelona, 2003.

19 See HERVÉ, Jean-Luc, 'De la forme aux images sonores', in *12 notas*, no. 1, 1997, pp. 160-164.

20 See VAN TOORN, Roemer, op. cit.

IMAGES

P 13 Trajectories of oscillation associated with a field dynamics.
Small optical discs inserted in a body in movement make it possible, when exposed to the right light and speed, to perceive the trace of the lines generated and the tensions deriving from them.' (from Étienne-Jules MAREY, 'Le vol des oiseaux', in Greg LYNN, *Animate Form*, Princeton Architectural Press, 1999).

P 15 Martha ROSLER, *Positions in the real world*, Actar-MACBA-Actar, Barcelona, 1998.

P 18 An intruder provokes a stampede during the Paris-Dakar-Cairo rally.
Photo, EPA/Patrick Herzog (in *El Periódico*, 9th January, 2000)

P 20 Hybrid gaze, multifocal gaze, strategic gaze (in *SD*, no.4, 1995).

P 21 The chameleon gaze. At once alert, ready and 'projective'.

P 23 Abramovic & Ulay. 'Infiltrations in dual bodies'. Performance.

P 24 (left) 'Surfing in a datascape.' Ramon Prat, poster for a workshop directed by Winy Maas (ESARQ-UIC, Barcelona, 1998).

P 24 (right) Swimmer in a flowing medium, the swimmer's head pushes the liquid membrane that at the same time covers and envelops the infiltrated body, illustrating a process of dynamic interaction between medium and mediator.
From an ambivalent condition of intrusion and complicity in an open medium —at once intrusive and reactive— capable of processing information and of re-elaborating it, of inscribing itself in a field of forces and of accommodating it, of fluctuating and re-impelling, of resonating and transferring, the change of paradigms of the contemporary mechanism can be interpreted.

P 27 Landscape of data and new natures.
Ramon Prat, graphic photomontage (in *Quaderns* no. 217, 1997/98).

Works

1. Actar Arquitectura
2. njiric + njiric
3. Neutelings Riedijk Architecten bv
4. NL ARCHITECTS
5. Périphériques
6. IaN+
7. WMA Willy Müller Arquitectos
8. Ábalos & Herreros
9. Lacaton & Vassal
10. Duncan Lewis
11. R&Sie... François Roche
12. Federico Soriano (S&Aa)
13. NO.MAD
14. Vicente Guallart
15. MVRDV
16. UN STUDIO
17. NOX
18. FOA

Synthetic logic would give primacy to the conceptual response in trajectories of synthesis as nuclear criteria (diagrams or ideograms).

Synthetic logic

1

Actar Arquitectura

Tornado Tower

Sociópolis. Hibrid Building

Pablo Picasso Square

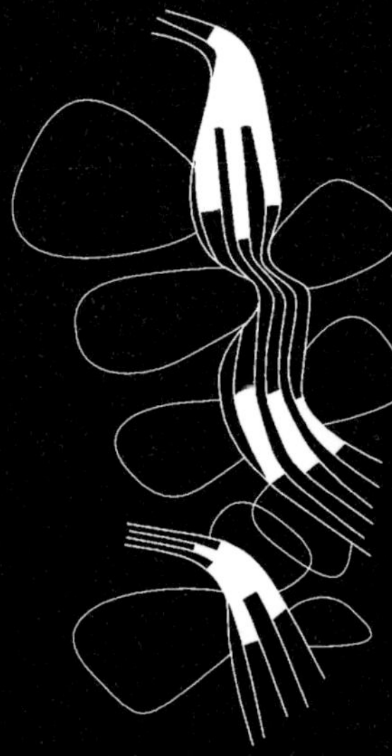

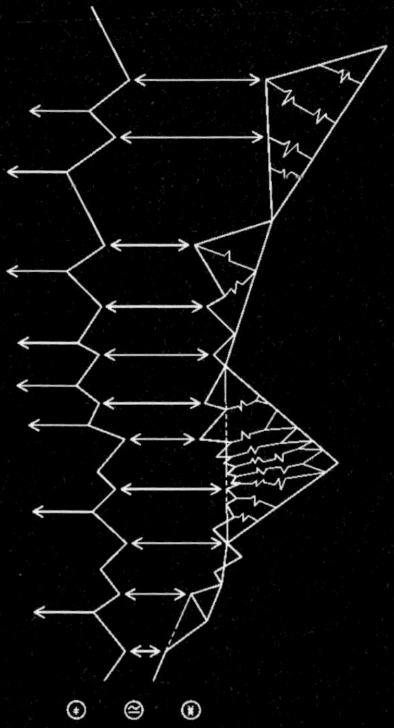

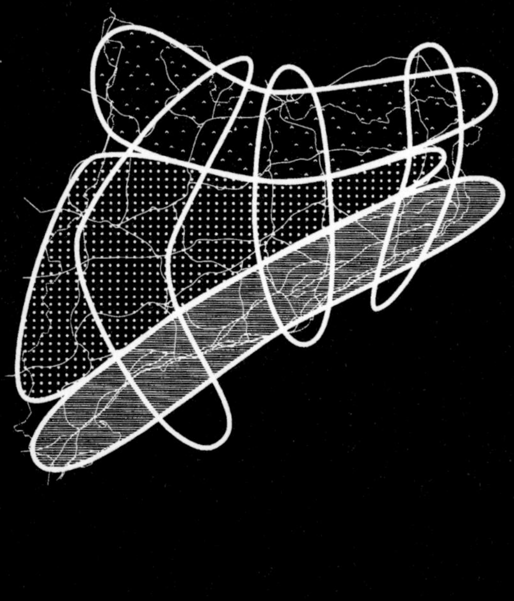

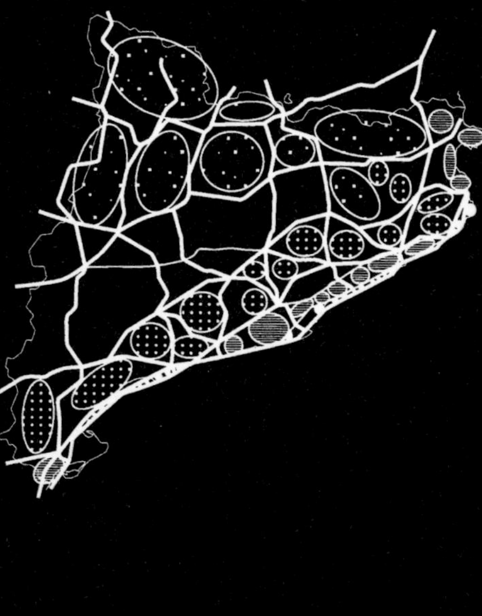

What is wanted is:

– A SYNTHETIC ARCHITECTURE

Capable of combining - and condensing - units of information, instead of purifying them. A compressive architecture (multi-layer) more than an essential architecture (unlayered). An architecture, then, that is multiple and multiplied. Complex, but not necessarily complicated.

– A DIRECT ARCHITECTURE

Conceived from a logic of action capable of generating forms and spatialities that - as compared to the complexity of the new scenarios - are far more effective, precisely because they are concise, incisive, decisive. An architecture at once relaxed and energetic; that would reveal its own conceptual definition. Explicit and efficient. Expeditious.

– AN, IN EFFECT, 'REACTIVE' ARCHITECTURE

'Reaction' and 'Activation' combined (interpreting the term 'reaction' as a cross between relation and action, at the same time). Capable of reacting to the environment and of activating new relations in it. Between flows and uses, scales and scenarios, processes and/or events.

– AN EXTROVERT ARCHITECTURE

By its nervous and 'vehicular' character. An architecture that would favour resonances and transfers, interactions and connections, with (and between) those events - and those environments - in which it is inscribed.

– AN EXPRESSIVE ARCHITECTURE

Rather than expressionist: engaged not in forcing the gesture but in expressing the action. That would 'express' links and relationships more than figurations. An, in any case, more communicative architecture. Transmitter and translator. Eloquent and convincing. Narrative and 'empathizing'.

– IN SHORT, A HAPPIER ARCHITECTURE

No longer elegant or austere but definitively uninhibited; spontaneous and flexible but also joyful and relaxed. Ludic and easy-going.

More 'animated' because virtually dynamic.

More 'open' precisely because informal.

A more stimulating and optimistic architecture. Resolved to interact with the world. Open to the decided use (strategic and plastic, operative and expressive) of colour, of light, of sound, of movement and of energy; open, then, to a celebration of the senses.

An architecture committed to that pursuit (more or less deliberate) of pleasure, of desire, of stimulus and exchange - of a joy as much communicative as expressive - that would favour, today, a new alliance between architecture, creation, technology, art, culture and communications media that seeks to promote new and unexpected transversalities made up of mixes and transfusions - crossovers and hybridizations - that are all the more suggestive and effective the more unusual and surprising they are at the same time.

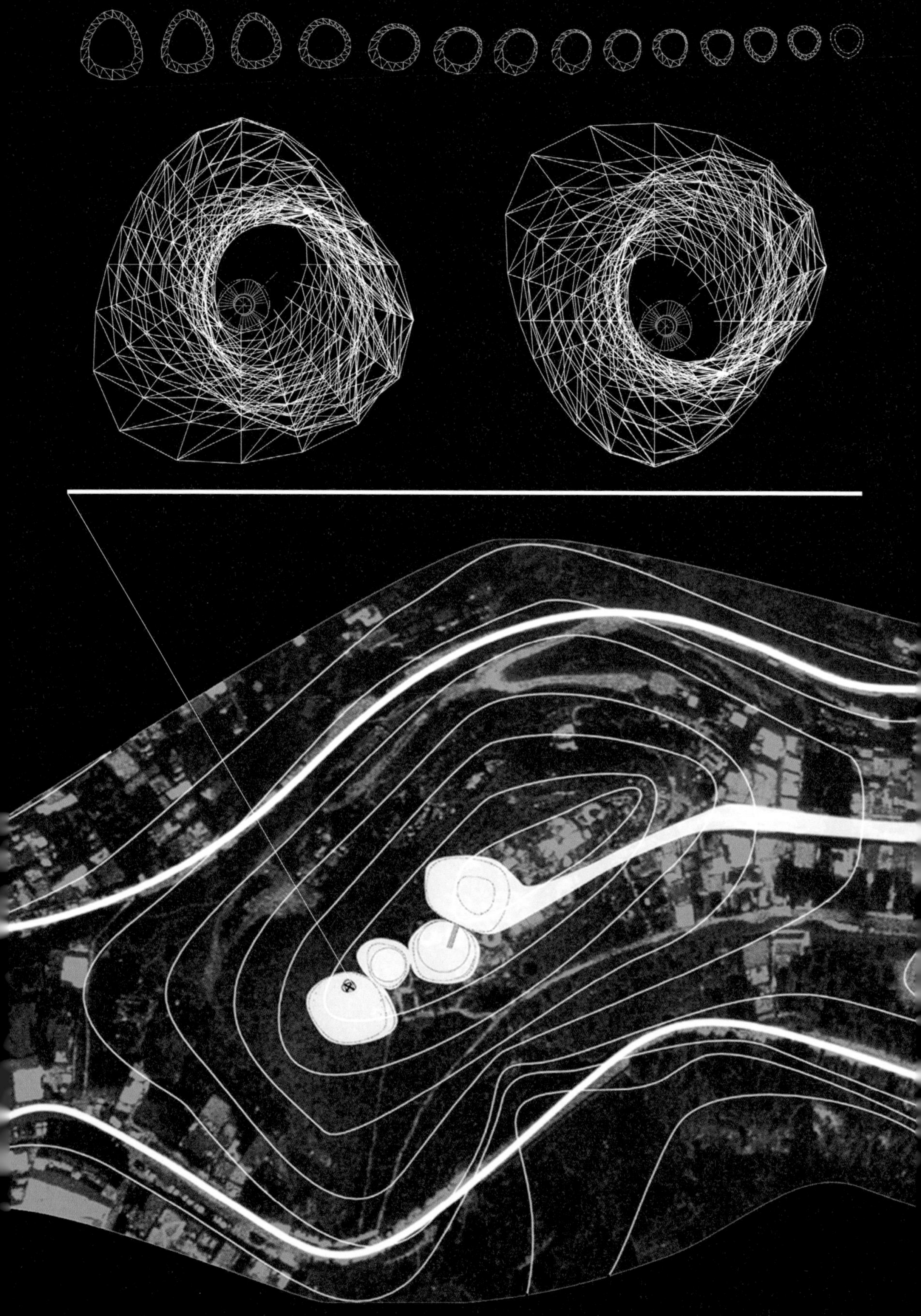

Actar Arquitectura (Gausa, Raveau, Gelpí, Santos)

1 *Tornado Tower*

LOCATION Barcelona DATE 2001 PROJECT restricted competition, 1st prize SURFACE AREA 2,000 m^2 ASSOCIATE ARCHITECTS Cecil Balmond & Charles Walker – OVE ARUP COLLABORATORS Carlos Sant'Ana, Flavia Cancian, Roland Stutz, Vicky Lenz

The transparent skin is at once the structure and support of the technical platforms and the vertical communication systems. Once built in perimetral terms, the tower is a huge transparent void that contains and holds up the seemingly centrifugally sucked-in elements (the antennae). The tower has no wish to become a metal artifact, but seeks instead to be like some meteorological phenomenon (the tornado). It's more a complex geometry than a static element.

The structural skin is more or less dense according to the tower's section in plan. The different sections in height vary according to the visualization of the technical elements to be supported. The elevators and vertical communications cores are adapted to the design of the inner part of the skin.

The structural concept is that of a steel tube with bracings. The tube has an amorphous shape that opens outwards as the height increases. It is foreseen for the structure at the top to be like a lightweight steel filigree, as open as possible to reduce the gusting of wind and the gyratory effect at the base. The entire structural load resists thanks to the steel framework, which acts as a carcass. The surface is triangular, in order to support theload plane. The carcass is reinforced by a set of diaphragms formed by lightweight cables. The diagonal direction of the support lends the tower the appearance of a spiral or of a tornado.

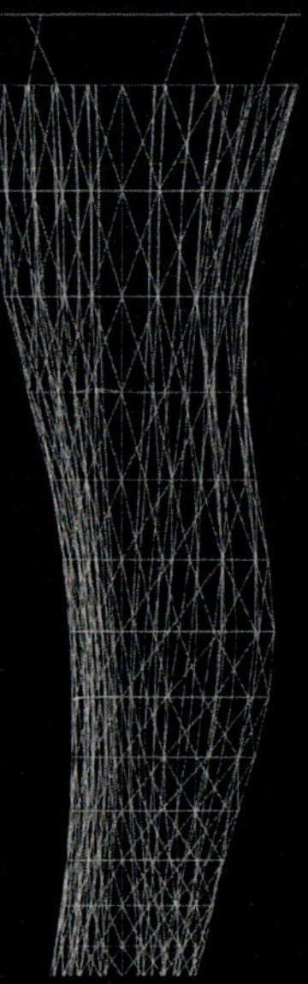
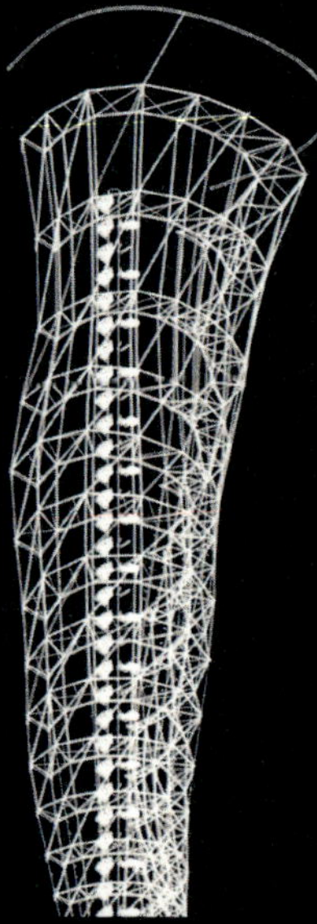

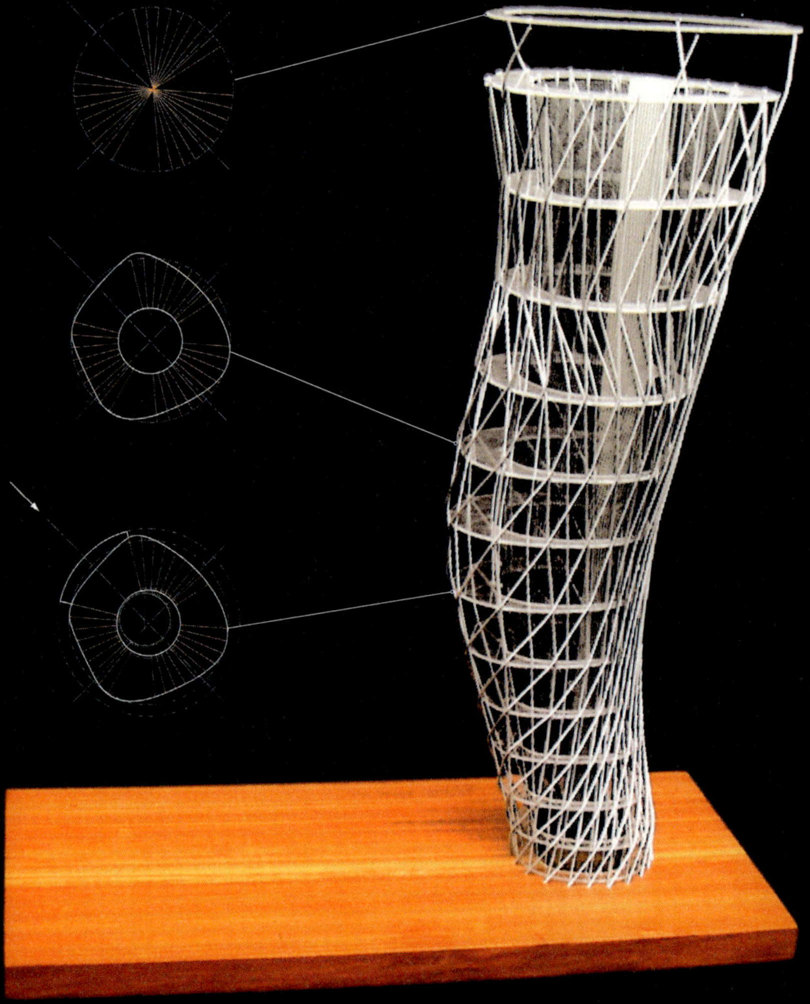

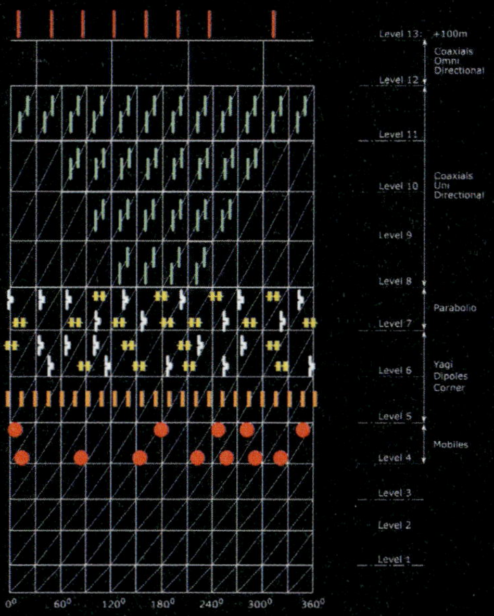

String of Antennae on Cylindrical Tower

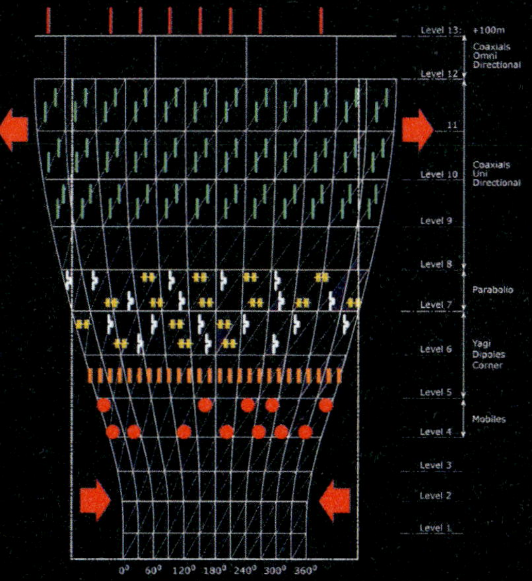

Distorted Tower Shape to Maximise Usable Surface

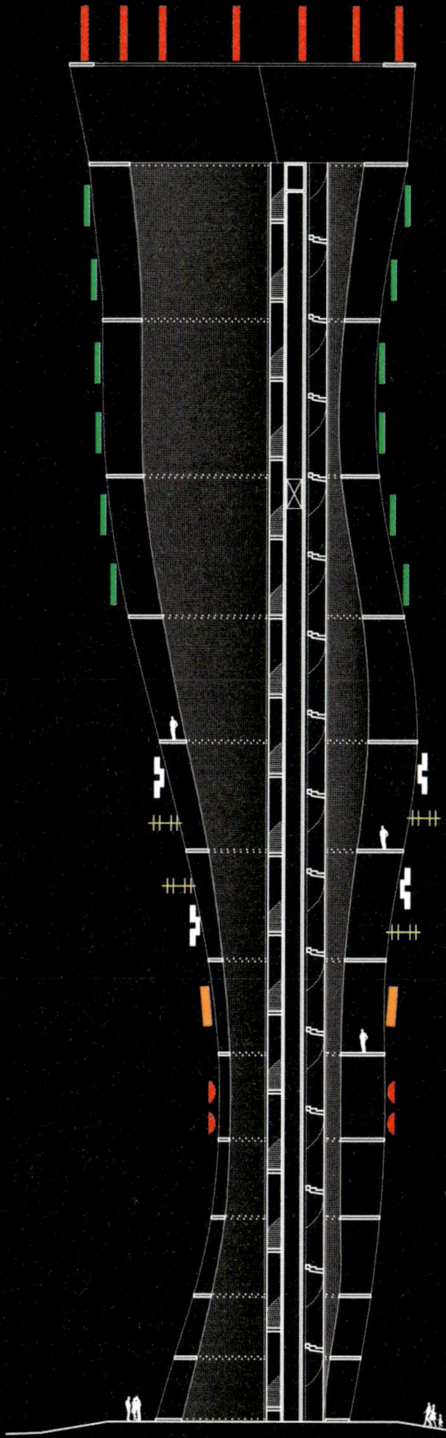

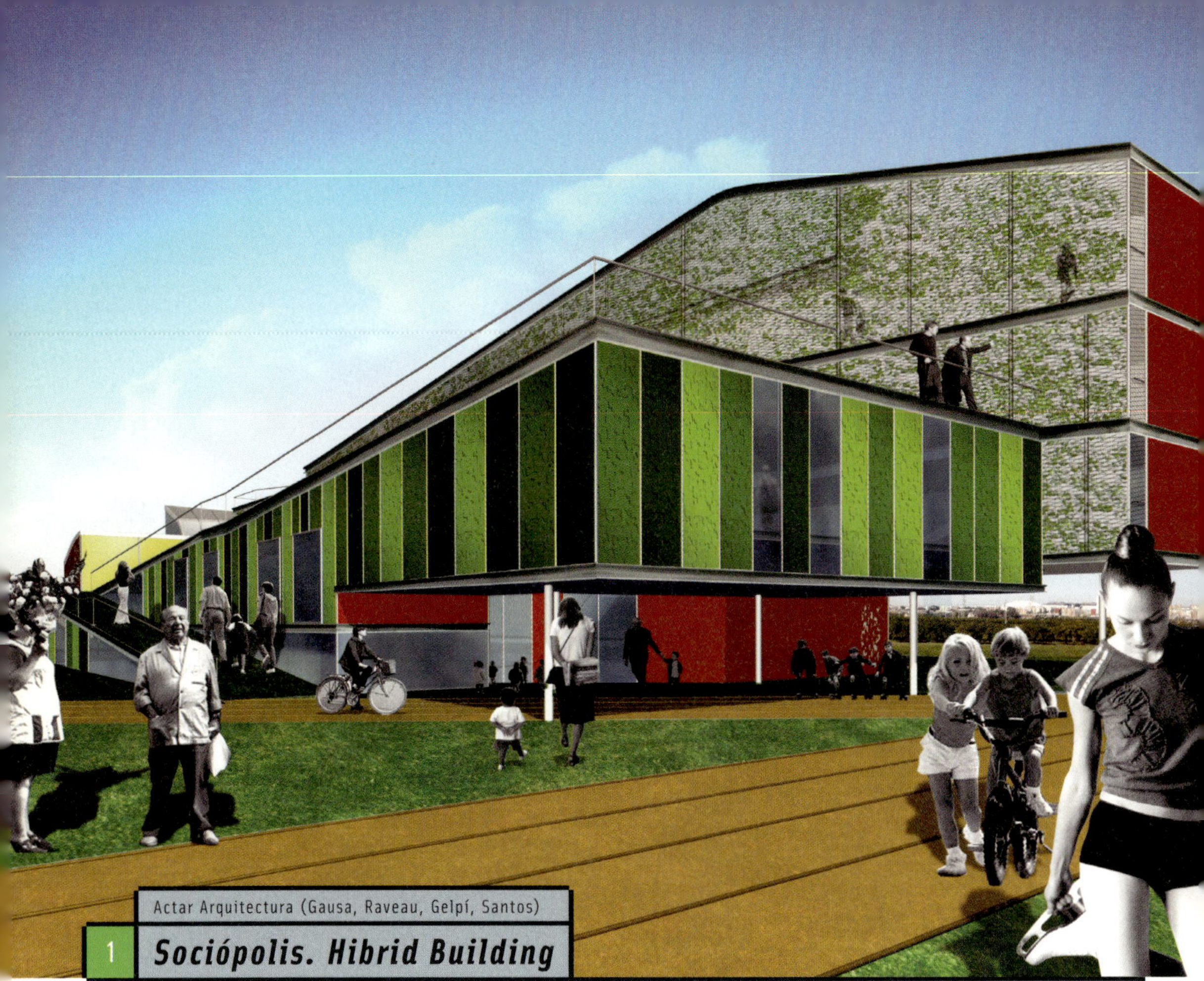

Actar Arquitectura (Gausa, Raveau, Gelpí, Santos)

1 Sociópolis. Hibrid Building

LOCATION Valencia DATE 2003 PROJECT international consultation SURFACE AREA 2,500 m² COLLABORATORS Elise Reiffers, François Martín, Vicky Lenz, Patricia Simoes, Francesca Demarchi, Kazuyo Nishida

The complex proposed here is presented as a great "social and residential culture". The maximum slope of 8%, appropriate for a setting planned beyond traditional architectural barriers, turns into a basic generating element when it comes to shaping a connective, landscaped geography among ramps and rooftops, which likewise permits a fluid access and routing to most of the levels of the complex, combining public and private spaces, articulating them around a great central landscaped patio which focuses the activities of the center for autistic children. The latter forms part of the complex while simultaneously possessing its own independent and interlocking logic. The dwellings face towards the outer perimeters, while the routing and access spaces are planned around said courtyard. A system of residential modules, flexible yet regular, enables the spaces to be adapted via slight variations to different situations of conviviality, privacy and exchange.

The handling of facades and roofs optimizes the chosen condition as a hybrid landscape: the investigation of ceramic constructional elements based on abstract plant motifs evolved with the actual industry of the areaæbacks up the conceptual gamble of the scheme.

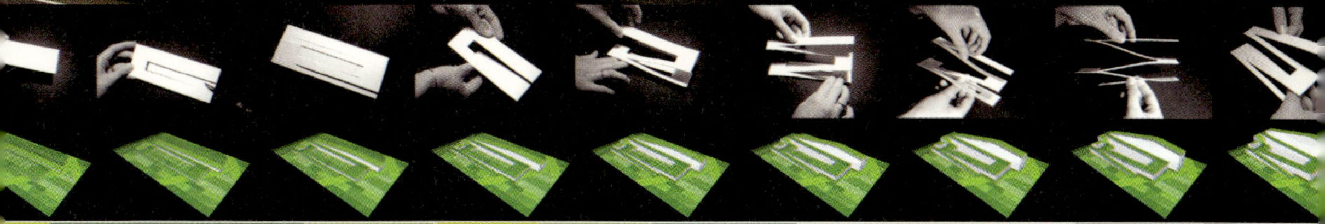

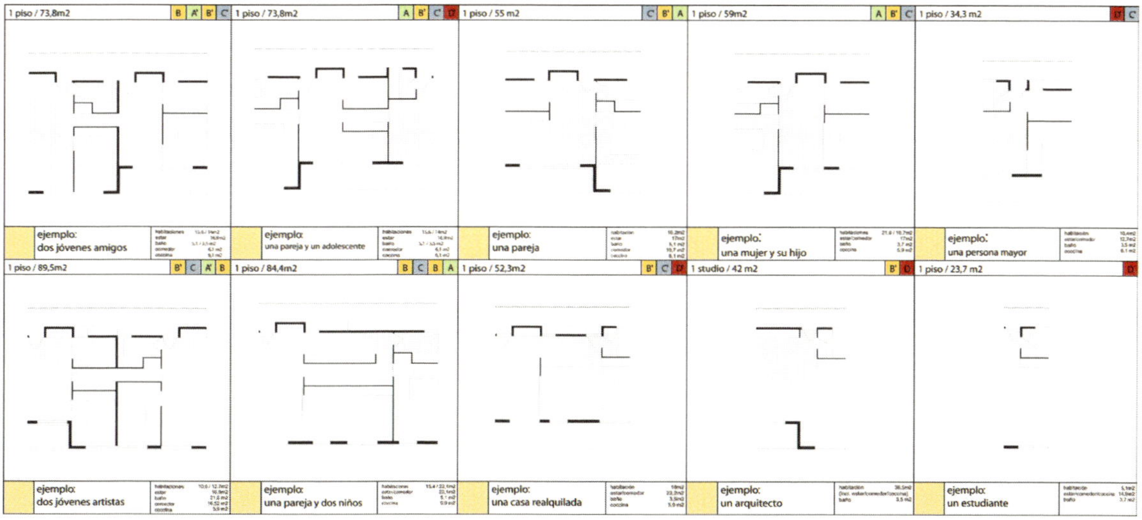
1 piso / 73,8m2
ejemplo:
dos jóvenes amigos
1 piso / 73,8m2
ejemplo:
una pareja y un adolescente
1 piso / 55 m2
ejemplo:
una pareja
1 piso / 59m2
ejemplo:
una mujer y su hijo
1 piso / 34,3 m2
ejemplo:
una persona mayor
1 piso / 89,5m2
ejemplo:
dos jóvenes artistas
1 piso / 84,4m2
ejemplo:
una pareja y dos niños
1 piso / 52,3m2
ejemplo:
una casa realquilada
1 studio / 42 m2
ejemplo:
un arquitecto
1 piso / 23,7 m2
ejemplo:
un estudiante

vegetación artificial
paneles de fachada exterior:
paneles cerámicos tipo "craft"

vegetación natural
paneles de fachada interior:
malla metálica con vegetación trepadora

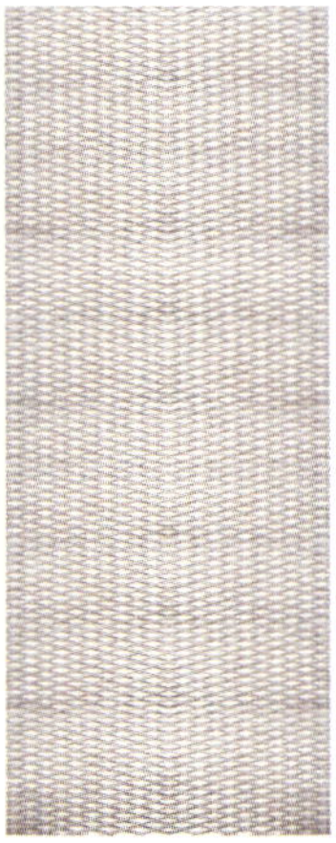

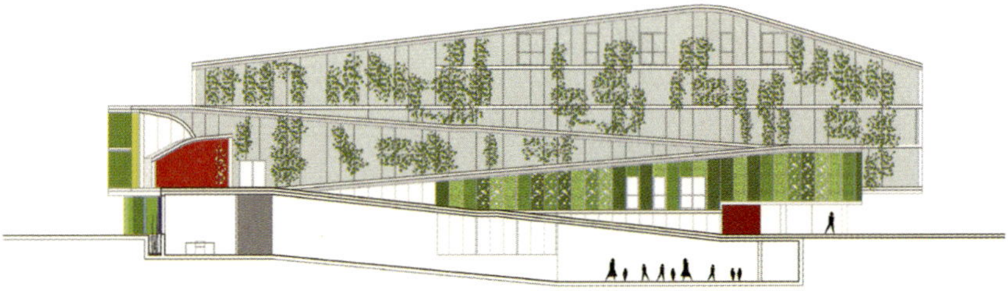

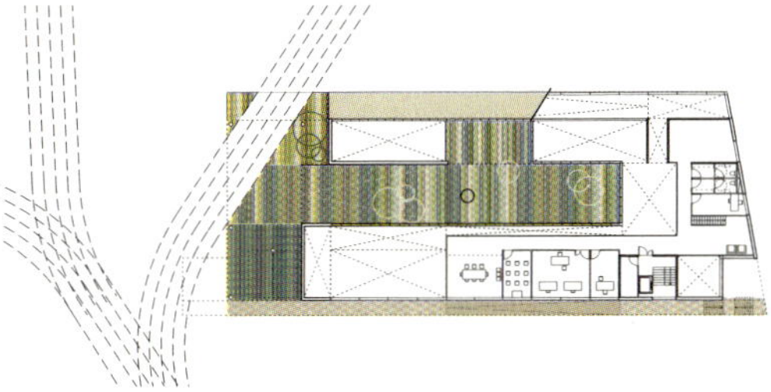

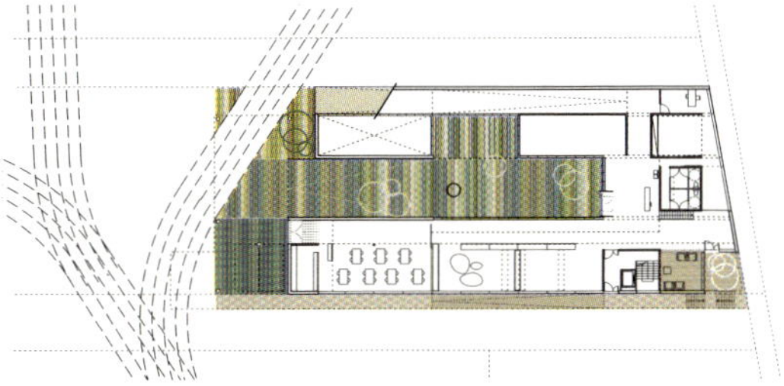

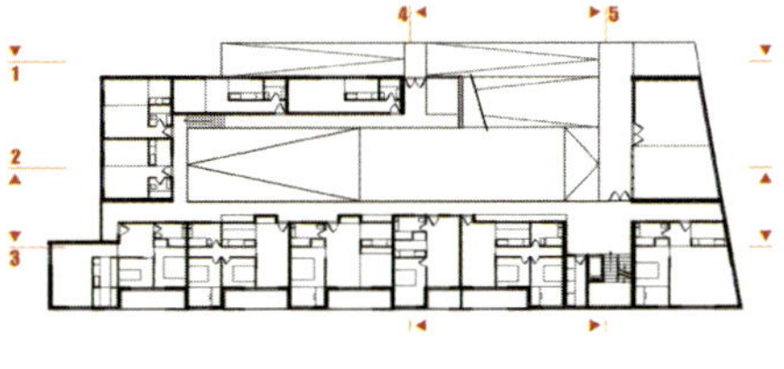
4
5
1
2
3

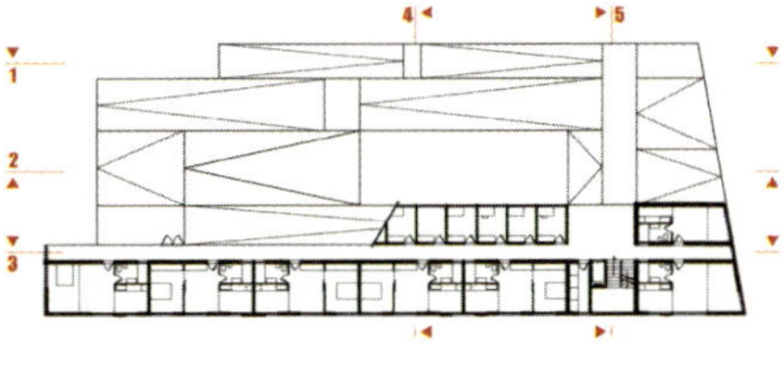
4
5
1
2
3

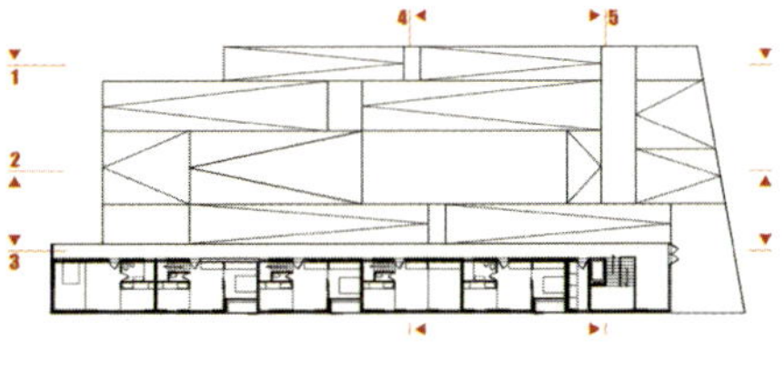
4
5
1
2
3

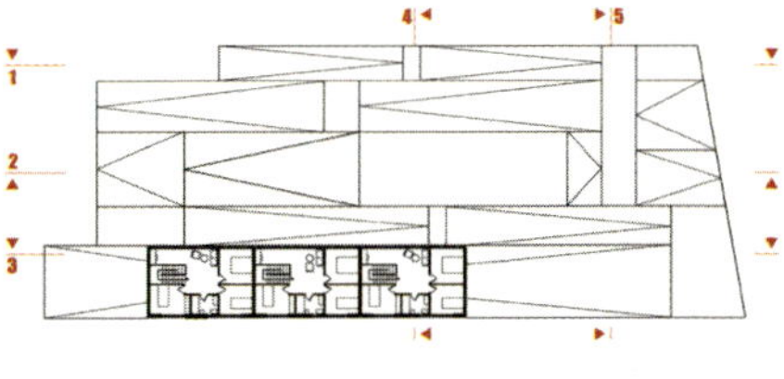
4
5
1
2
3

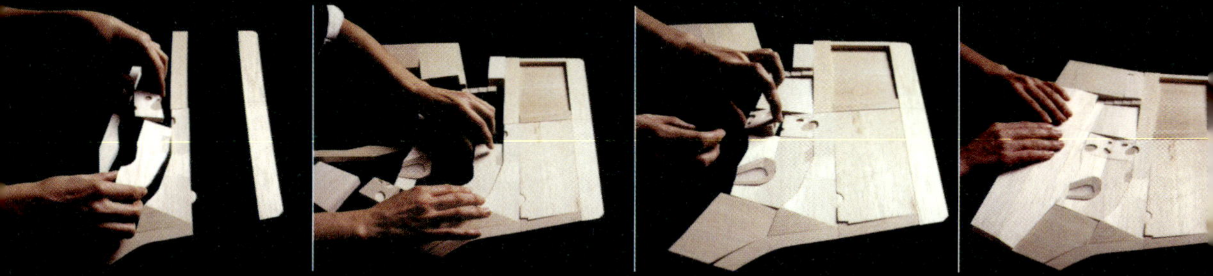

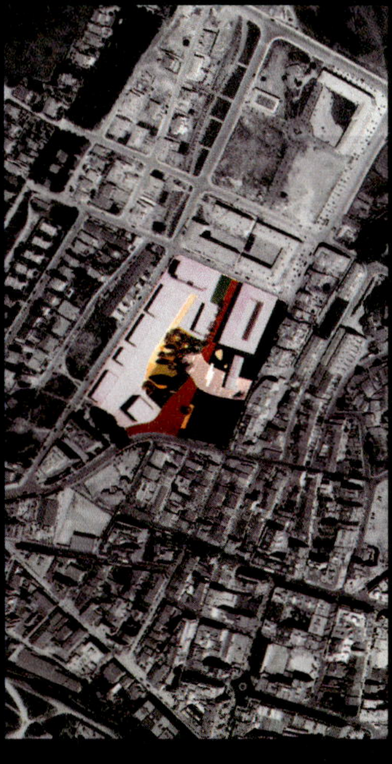

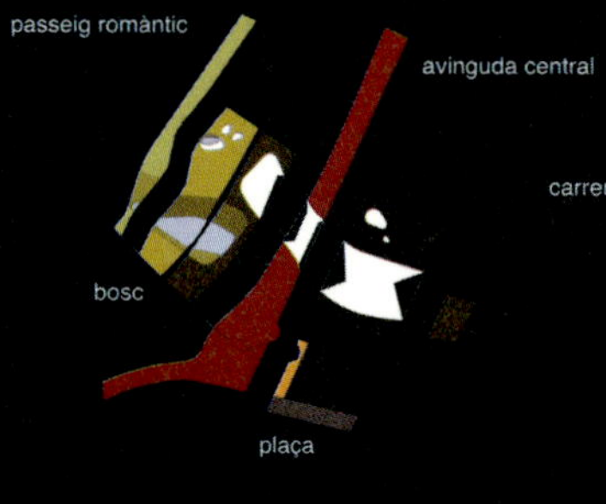

ESQUEMA DE BANDES

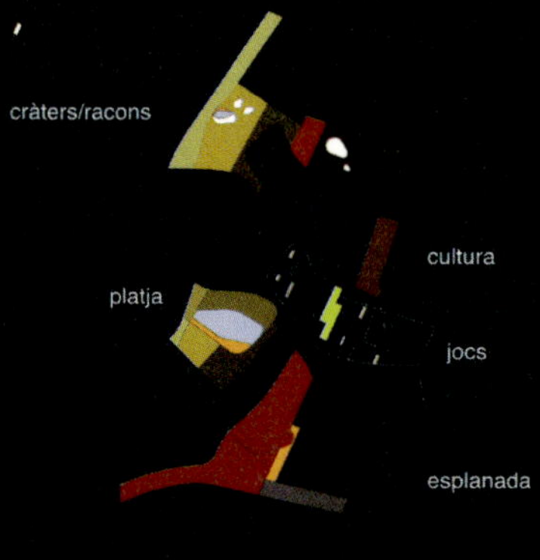

ESQUEMA DE ZONES

Actar Arquitectura (Gausa, Raveau, Gelpí, Santos)

1 *Pablo Picasso Square*

LOCATION Montornés del Vallès DATE 1998-2004 PROJECT competition, 1st prize SURFACE AREA 15.300 m² ASSOCIATE ARCHITECT Ignasi Pérez Arnal, AxE Arquitectura i Entorn COLLABORATORS Vicky Lenz, Kazuyo Nishida CONSTRUCTION COMPANY Requena SL ENGINEERING AND ENVIRONMENT Gerccat STRUCTURAL ENGINEERING Jorge Blasco CONSTRUCTION MANAGEMENT Jaume Bellavista PHOTOGRAPHS Laura Cantarella

The project resolves a huge irregular void by converting it into a great new connective space for the town. Rather than a unitarytotalizingdesign, one seeks to propose a system which might enable the diversity to be articulated: to organize the new space and at the same time to valorize its potential as "a place of places": one place, many landscapes.
The intervention plans an intersection between a longitudinal system of "typological" strips (street, square, avenue, woodland, path) and a transverse system of functional stains (an esplanade for communal activities, games, a pool-cum-beach, clearings and craters of individual activity) based on calligraphic interventions conceived by means of continuous pavements of different colors and materials that aid and abet the gradation produced from external urban space to internal woodland.
This overlapping of weave forms enables the imbalance of existing spaces to be systematized without foregoing the specificity of each of them. In effect the scheme, which is economical in both budgetary and formal terms, seeks to maximize the color, the textures, the light and shade, the sounds and the spatialand specialcharacter of the location itself.

NO FEAR

2 njiric + njiric

Baumaxx Hypermarket
McDonald´s Drive-In
MSU

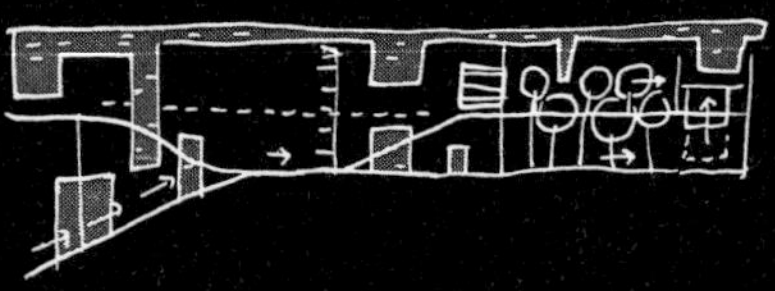

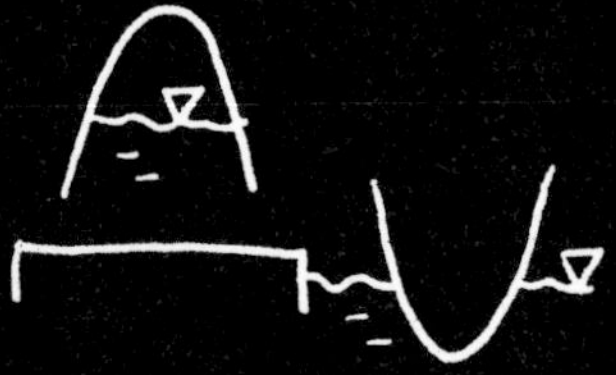

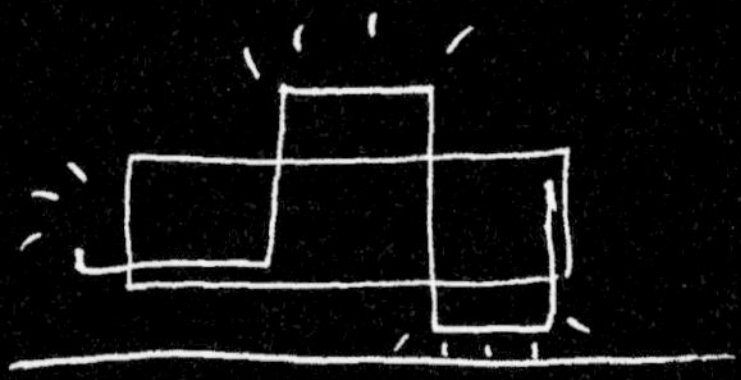

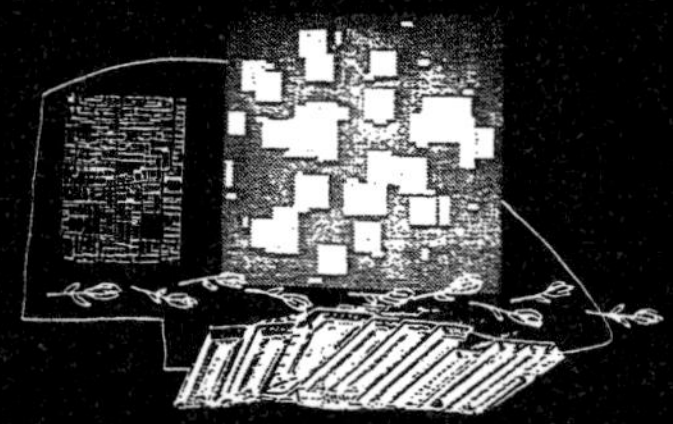

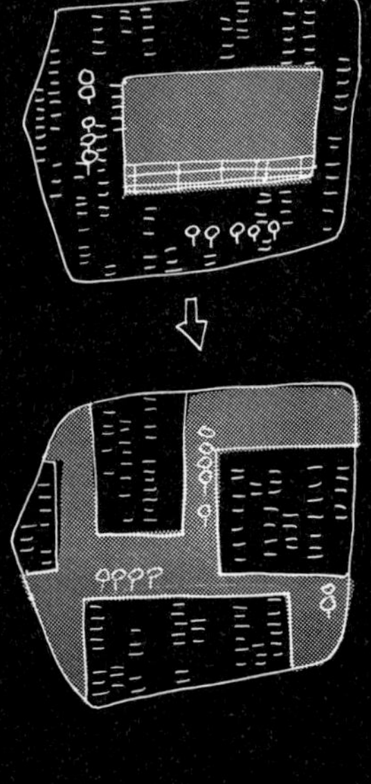

The end of Modernism

Understanding architecture today inevitably leads to a series of diverse positions, ranging from utopian to pragmatic, from ordinary to heroic, from engaged to relaxed, often looking beyond the boundaries of the very discipline. New issues like conditioned contemporaneity, design as substraction and deliberate rhizomatic choices, point towards the end of modernism as we knew it, but we feel fine.
Based on events and images, the supermodern architect interprets the present tense, thinks through visual icons, enhances defaults, manipulates reality, and is sceptical towards all-embracing theories and autonomy of architecture.
Beyond misused terms like "landscape", "infrastructure" or "ecology", there is a true interest in architecture as an operative discourse.
The dawn of the new century shall witness the end of classical perspective and 3D-space, a final rejection of formalism, the end of aestethics, a shift towards non-authorship and termination of urban planning. A new condition of deeper architectural thinking beyond Y2K shall bring a cultivation of themes like ordinariness, fragmentation, time-related process, social welfare and mass culture.
The form will be generated, rather than designed. It was The Author who produced The Object, it is The Interdisciplinary that defines The Process.
Combinations of analogue and digital will proliferate. Imaginative, client-oriented reprogramming will be appreciated as a reliable strategy.
The "faith in fakes", the exclusion of architecture from every practice grounded on morphology, composing with readymades, taming infrastructure, mixing corporate brandsand shaping of consumer's culture, shall be the points of departure for the profession. An architecture "just there"...

njiric + njiric

2 Baumaxx Hypermarket

ARCHITECTS Hrvoje Njiric, Helena Njiric, Alan Kostrencic, Goran Tomas, Miljenco Stanic, Sinisa Glusica, Ivana Knez, Koraljka Brebic, Natasa Franciulla LOCATION Tabor, Maribor (Slovenia), 1997-1999 CLIENT Baumaxx Slovenia CONSULTANT Bogdan Budimirov STRUCTURE Buero DI Franz Karisch (Völkermarkt, Austria) GENERAL DEVELOPER Stuag AG (Austria) PHOTOGRAPHS Damir Fabijanic, Ramon Prat

An urban concept of reversing the figure / ground ratio of American hypermarkets. A celebration of traffic performed by cutting the regular parking patterns into the irregular plot contour should be strengthened by the green roof substance, as a new, publicly accessible, elevated ground. The negative reaction of the developer turned the former concept into the new perceptual reality – no trespassing. The landscape is thus to be observed / mentally consumed / remote-controlled. The surreal nature of the fireplace on the roof terrace of the Bestégui apartment by Le Corbusier is equalled by the virtual status of the landscaped zone in the Hypermarket.
All inward-facing planes are entirely glazed, all perimeter ones are mute, but user-friendly. A green roof as a common denominator and a recreated artificial topography. Four billboards "anchor" the vast slopes of the House to the site and turn towards the streams of traffic.
Colour "classification" is an attempt to handle architecture by ordinary, if not banal, criteria – size, smell or colour. By assigning colour as a consumption-profiled term to the projects we are trying to resume the manifold facets and secret ambitions of each of us to an understandable communicative platform, but also not to limit ourselves with a couple of sizes. On the contrary, different shades of a single colour could transmit the subtle expectations of a particular design, even.

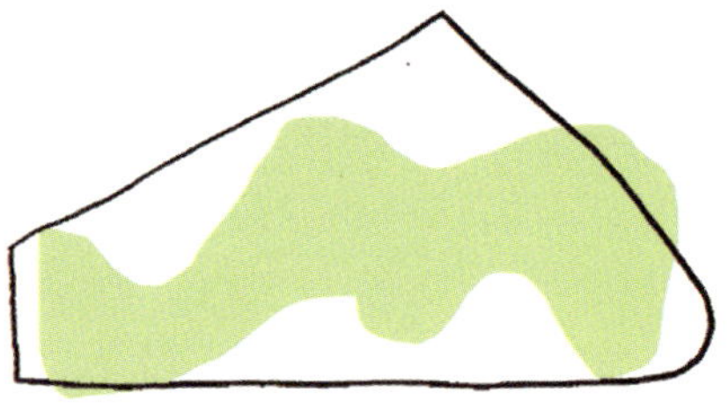

1

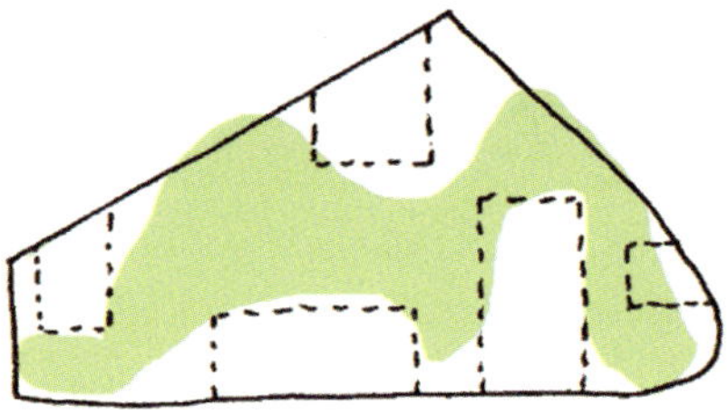

2

3

4

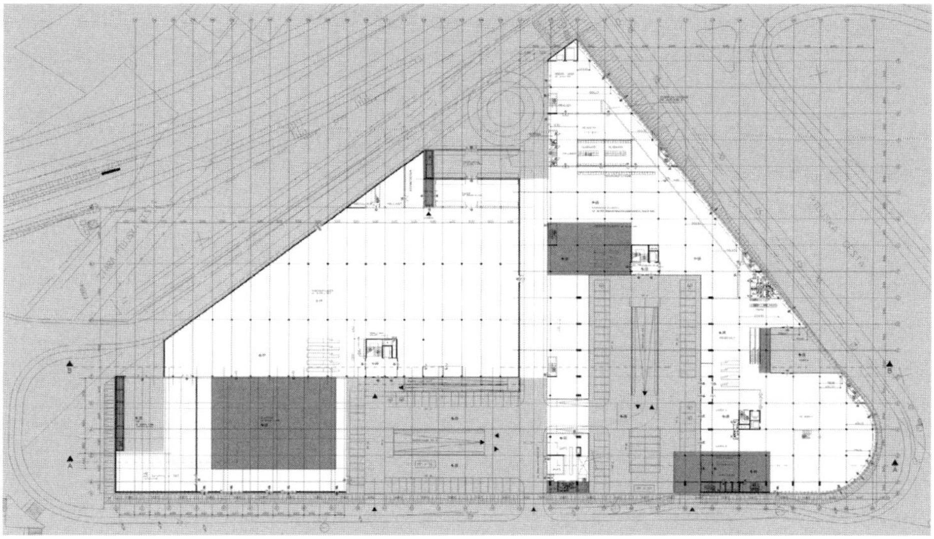

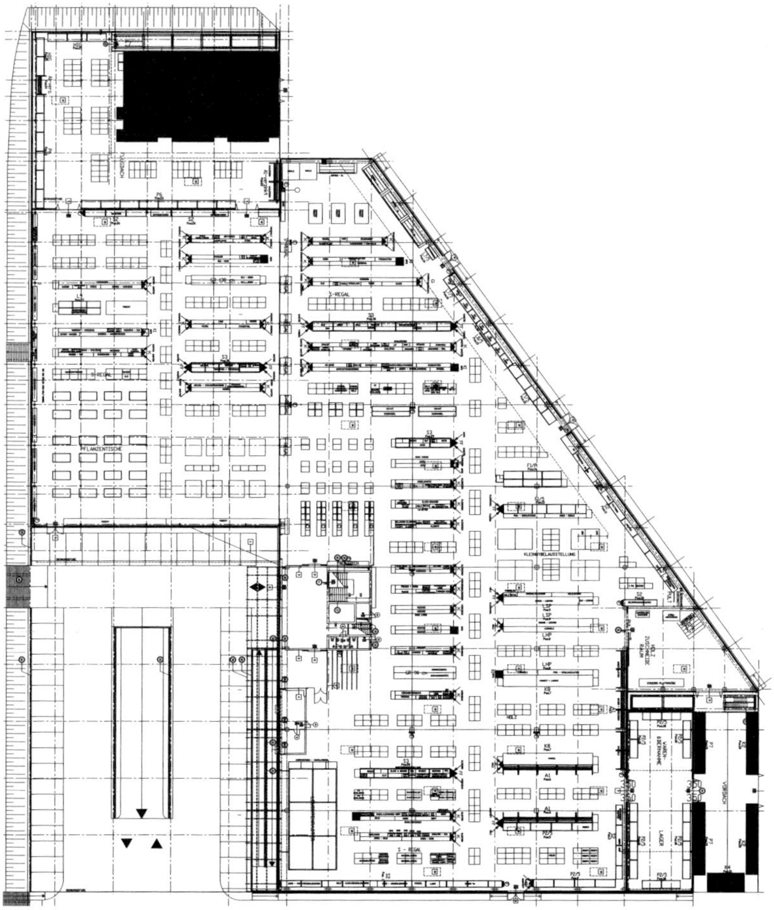
S-REGAL
PFLANZENTISCHE
S - REGAL

njiric + njiric

2

McDonald's Drive-In

ARCHITECTS Helena Njiric, Hrvoje Njiric, Alan Kostrencic, Iva Bedenko, Miljenko Stanic LOCATION Maribor (Slovenia) 1998-2000 CONTRACTOR McDonalds d.o.o. Slovenia/Mario Gregori STRUCTURES Ing CAD/Vedad Dracic, Varazdin SITE SUPERVISION Velt d.o.o. Vlado Veltruski, Maribor SERVICES Lenassi d.o.o./Mitja Lenassi, Ljubljana; ProFi d.o.o./Bojan Germovsek, Ljubljana CONSTRUCTION FIRMS Lenassi d.o.o. (Ljubljana), Elektra d.d. (Maribor), Kograd gradnje d.o.o. (Maribor), Alu Projekt d.o.o. (Kamnik), Pulko d.o.o. (Sp.Duplek), Proneon (Vrhnika), Karba MGE (Ljutomer)

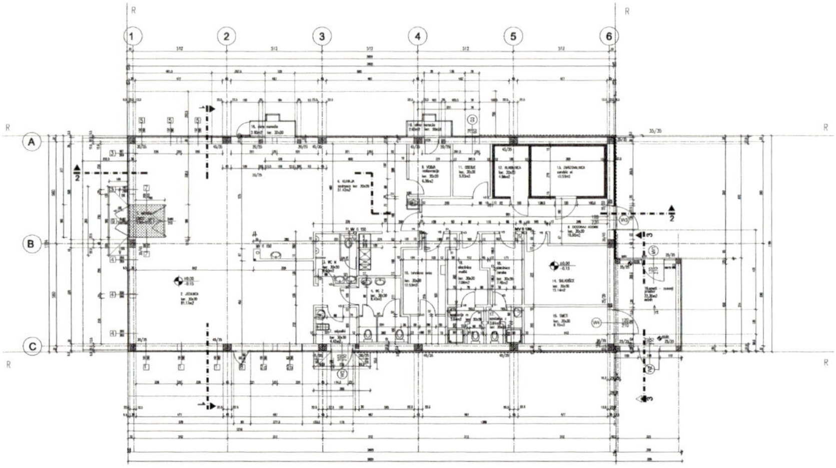

McDonalds Drive-In Restaurant in Maribor, Slovenia is an attempt to reformulate the existing, globally used typology, to reiterate the semiotics of the American and fast-food stands in general, still maintaining the corporate guidelines of the client towards a new possible standard. It was initially conceived as an ordinary McDonalds shed, topped by a fenced basketball court, but finally built without a sports' function, due to shortage of time to get a permission from the McDonalds' Chicago Headquarters. The cage-like roofscape, now devoid of function, takes on the legacy of conceptual art as a point of departure: Duchamp's caged sugarcubes, Giacometti's Palace at 4.00 AM... The virtual «playground» becomes a coded signal for a drive-in public, deriving its aesthetic from inflatable ephemeria and accentuated by floodlights whose intensity varies according to the cash-flow in the restaurant. The «non-profitable» character of the whole upper part of the building thus blends with its fast-income base.
The 9m high Golden Arches tackle the theme of bigness and its acceptability: the client went for the biggest «M» in the central Europe at once. Among other «applied» icons, a recycling logo on the rear elevation, expresses the corporate re-use policy, but maybe comments the (re)productive nature of junk food as well.
The choice of materials opposes the usual McDonalds' fake domesticity: wire mesh and corrugated eternit on the outside, synthetics inside. A reduced interior setting should accomodate a broad range of clientelle, rather than insisting on outdated family-visits concept. This paradigm shift is attempted throughout the house but succeeded only in fragments. The inevitable fate of the architects is to negotiate and compromise as long as it takes.
Even the not-very-comfortable chairs in the restaurant should contribute the accellerated digestion. The kitchen clock is not of this world: an artificial timing, structured in the ten-times-six-minutes rhythm, defined by the criteria of the Big Mac life-span: every unsold item should be thrown away in 3x6 minutes. Shouldn't every McDonalds shed be dismantled in a 3x6 years ?

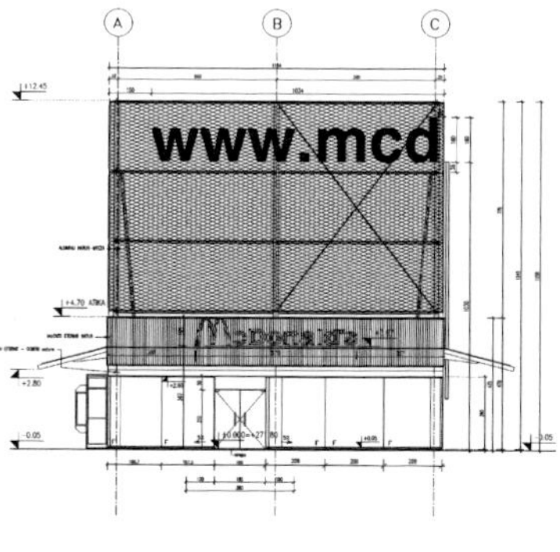

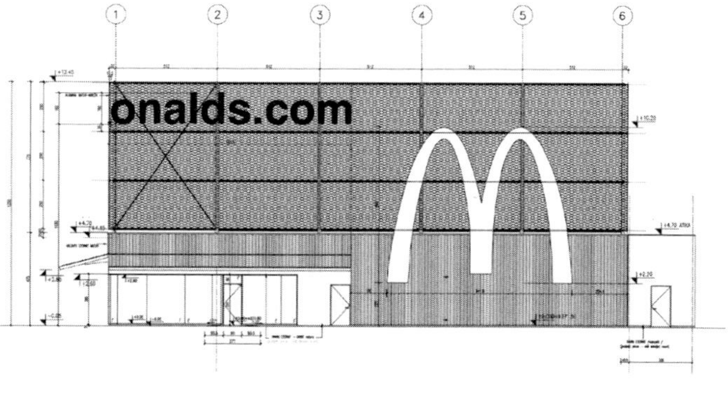

njiric + njiric

2 ***MSU, Museum of Contemporary Art in Zagreb***

ARCHITECTS Helena Njiric, Hrvoje Njiric, Iva Bedenko, Alan Kostrencic, Petar Miskovic, Mladen Freskura, Hannes Sorger LOCATION Zagreb (Croatia), 1999 COMPETITION 2nd Prize

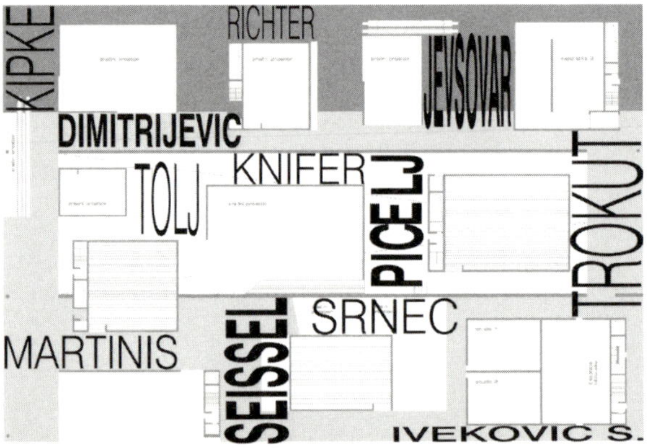

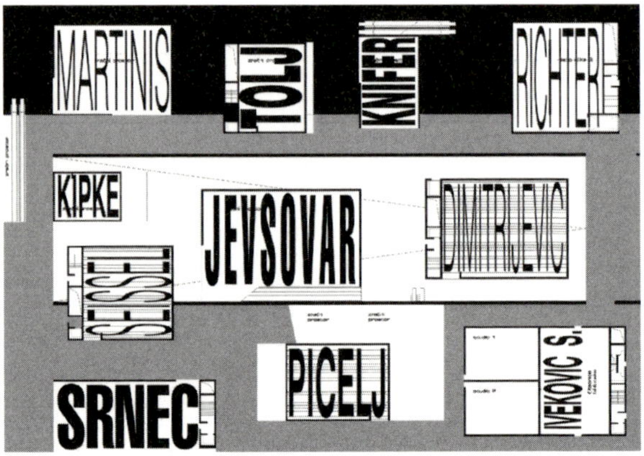

A new Zagreb museum of contemporary art, the MSU, is to be built on the main street of the city. We considered it as an urban procedure for an extended exhibition area: a field where art enters the public domain and limits between the House and the City cease to exist. A series of billboards, blending artwork (like the one by Jenny Holzer) with commercials, stress the project's chief concern: to find a suitable mode of art consumption on the threshold of the new century and a relation of the artistic to the other features of open urban space. A new typology, one familiar from supermarkets and shopping malls, is being examined. As the latter are considered to be a genuine public space today, such a hybrid might reduce the institutional character of exhibiting art.

The basic structure of the house is thus a conglomerate ordering of:
1 museum
2 shopping centre
3 mechanical garage

The conceptual framework is based on reworking the 19th-century museum typology, while simultaneously questioning the 20th-century modernist legacy of authorship and operating with readymades. The enfilade of rooms is inward-bound – it closes in on itself, forms a series of interiors, folds and twists into a continuous spatial sequence.
Aside from its commercial possibilities, the "Bilbao Effect" is an indication of how to exhibit art today. A series of specific geometries is favoured by contemporary artists themselves. "My curves are not mad," says Richard Serra, when delightedly adjusting them to the irregularities of the building. The proposal for the new MSU is such an anti-container-like understanding of the Room, a set of implosions, yet within a strictly controlled envelope – a "Boxed Bilbao."

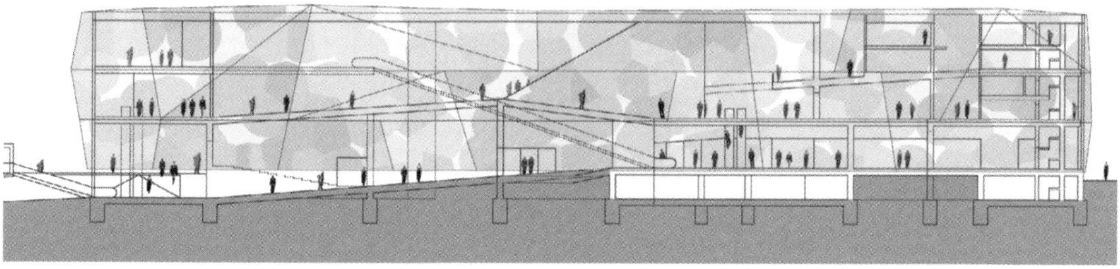

nivo +7.00

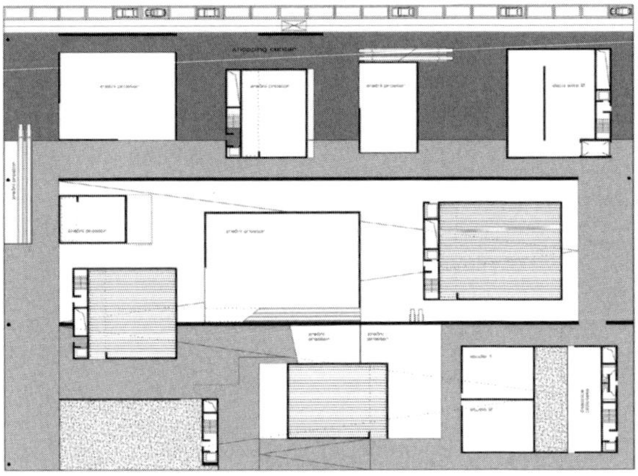

nivo -2.00

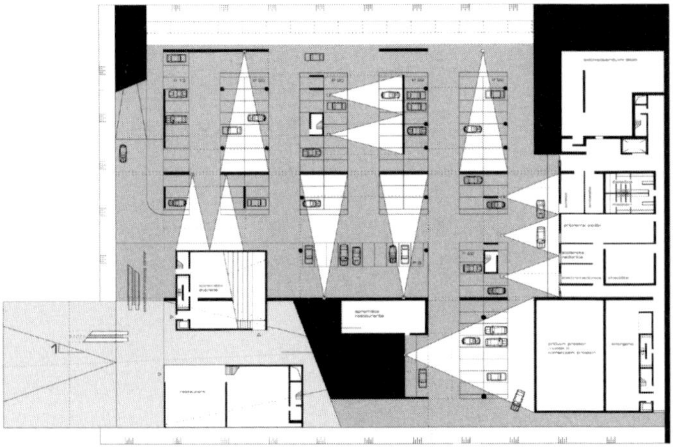

nivo +1.30

3

Neutelings Riedijk Architecten bv

Veenman Printers Headquarters
NAA, Nederlands Audiovisueel Archief
Concert Hall in Bruges

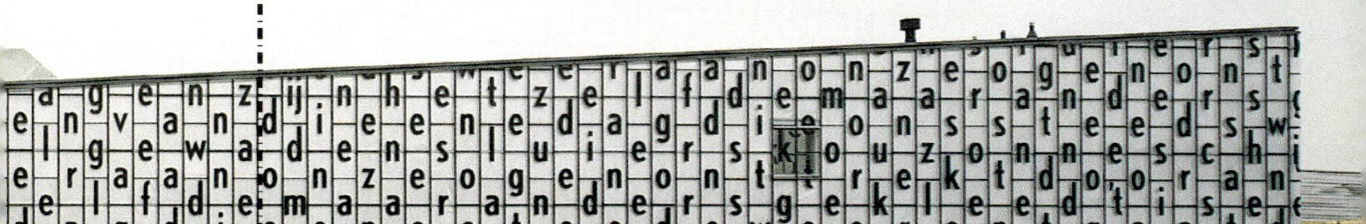

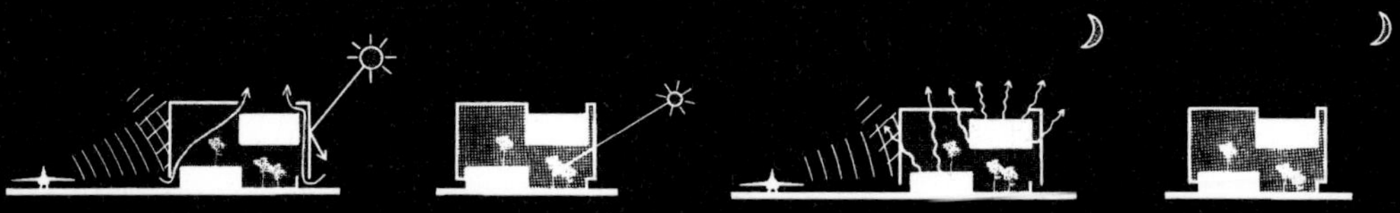

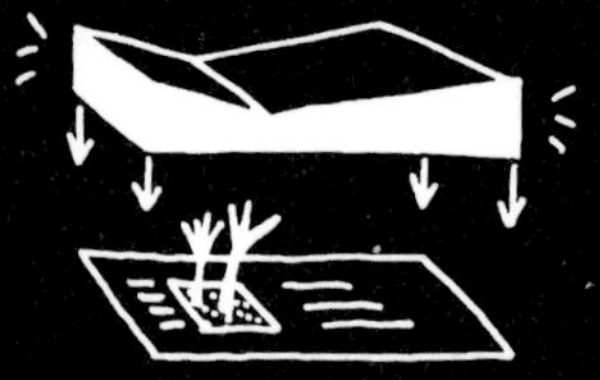

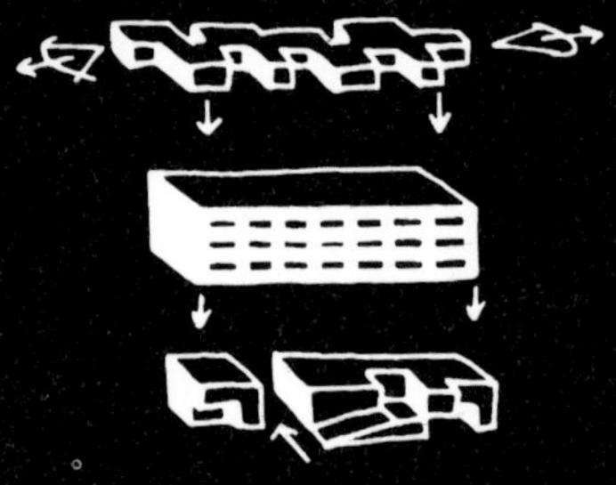

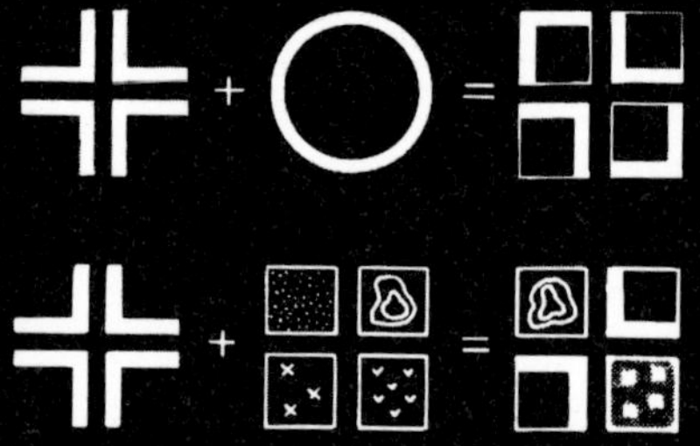

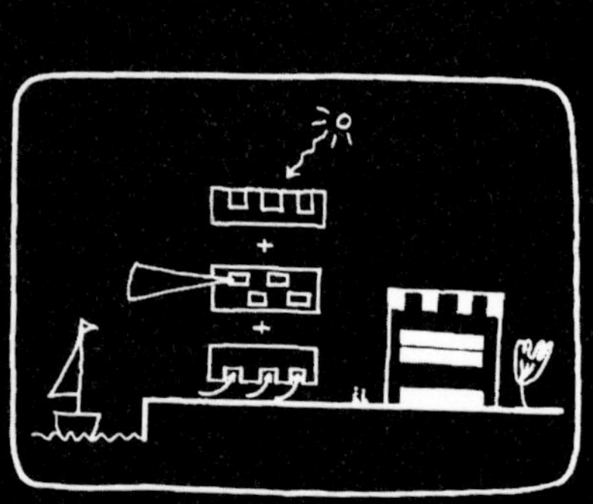

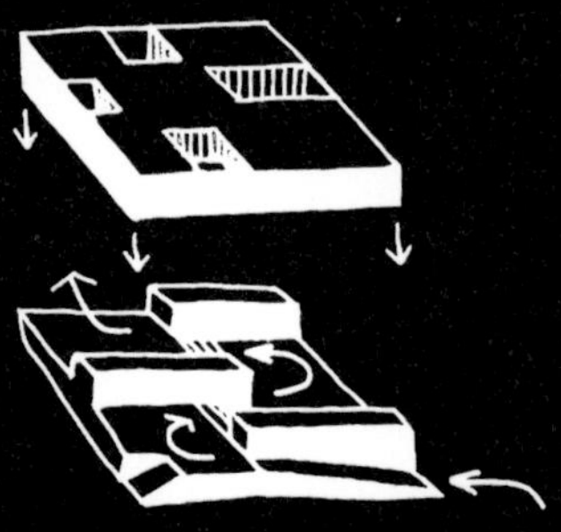

Laziness, recycling and wit

1

Professional clients in particular regard building as an end in itself and the only way to create added value. For example, a splendid office building on a charming site, barely twenty years old but now empty because the tenant no longer exists due to reorganisation, is no longer 'performing' as an estate agent might say. Only complete reconstruction and a contemporary curtain frontage would bring about a successful turnaround in the building's ability to attract tenants. In such a case it takes a major effort to convince the client that might also pay to do nothing. This situation arises with private clients but unfortunately is also spreading to whole towns.

2

Under the banner of durable building, local authorities in the Netherlands nowadays draw up lists of building materials which may or may not be used. The selection is based on a complicated calculation of the energy content of the life cycle and the reusability of the material. Oddly enough, these lists neglect the best possible way of achieving durability, i.e. by not building at all or by reusing an entire building. Laziness can be an important ecological instrument.

3

The third way of taking advantage of laziness is by recycling typologies and concepts. Architecture seems to be one of the few disciplines in which new developments seem not to rely on earlier achievements, but rather on their rejection. The reason for this seems to me to lie in the neglect of earlier concepts on the basis of style, an architectural taboo never stated explicitly but always immanent. The reuse of powerful types in a contemporary version is a more effective and less wearying approach.

4

The fourth way of taking advantage of laziness leads to the methodology of sculptural mathematics. The most exhausting sort of design process is one in which each version requires a conscious decision. We therefore make it our practice to start off with a simple basic mathematical concept within which the programme is to be organised. Once this basic concept has been properly set up it can guide us through the whole process. Subject to this powerful layer of rationality, we are free to do things that are completely irrational. This is a highly rewarding arrangement for the architect, who is able to do more or less what he wants, since intuition and taste need no justification. The use of this method results in unforced diversity, strong character and a simple system.

Neutelings Riedijk Architecten bv

3 *Veenman Printers Building*

ARCHITECTS Willem Jan Neutelings, Michiel Riedijk LOCATION Bedrijventerrein Frankeneng, Ede PROJECT 1995 EXECUTION 1997 COLLABORATORS Willem Bruijn, Dirk van den Heuvel, Andy Woodcock CLIENT Veenman printers, Wageningen CONTRACTOR BCE Bouw, Ede INTERIOR DESIGN N.R.A., Rotterdam INTERIOR DESIGN CONTRACTOR van Gils projecten, Emmen LANDSCAPE ARCHITECTURE West 8 landscape architects, Rotterdam TECHNICAL CONCEPT ADVISOR Bureau Bouwkunde, Rotterdam ENGINEERING ABT Adviesbureau voor bouwtechniek, Velp SERVICES DWA Installatie- en energieadvies, Bodegraven TEXTS K. Schippers, Amsterdam PHOTOGRAPHS Christian Richters

The new building for Veenman Printers in Ede consists of two parts: the printing works with the necessary stockroom and an office area. The site is in a typical business location amongst a lot of fairly randomly dispersed buildings of mediocre quality in which the office section is always differently articulated and materialised from the production section. In order to avoid this traditional distinction between white- and blue-collar workers, we opted for a continuous elevation wrapped, as it were, around the building. In addition, the building is organised around a courtyard garden from which the various departments are in visual contact with

one another. This courtyard garden (designed by West 8) forms a counterpoint to the neighbouring business premises and creates a pleasant work climate that is in touch with the changing seasons. The facade is composed of three sections: a black, concrete stone plinth, a row of windows in the plinth, and above this a glazed section. The latter consists of glass panels through which it is possible to see the light-reflective insulation. The glazing is mounted in a simple framework deriving from greenhouse construction. The glass is printed with text by K. Schippers (layout by K. Martens). The building has a V-shaped roof. The section is such that the areas requiring a lot of headroom are located under the highest sections of the roof. The volume is indented at two spots: the main entrance, which is marked by the load-bearing company logo, and the dispatch entrance. These, together with the V-shaped cornice line, add up to a striking volume that can be recognised from the motorway.

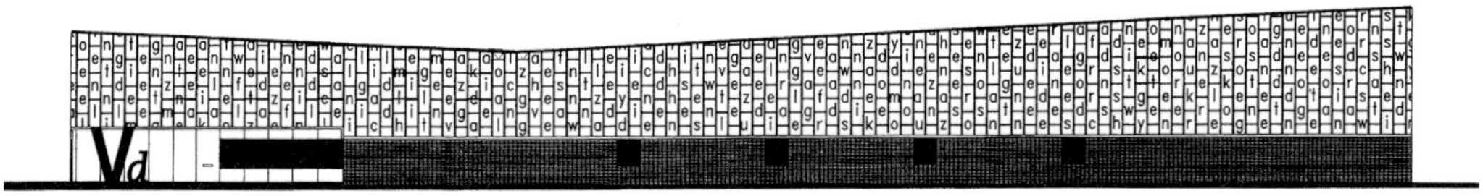

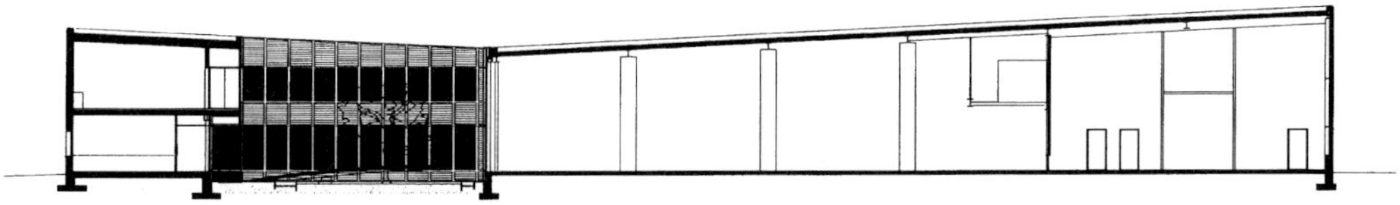

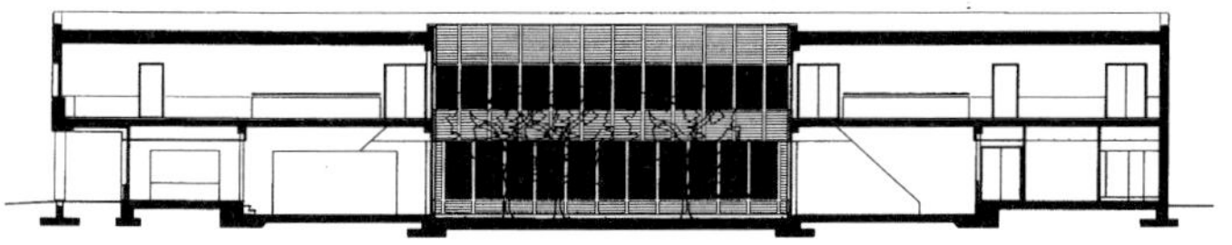

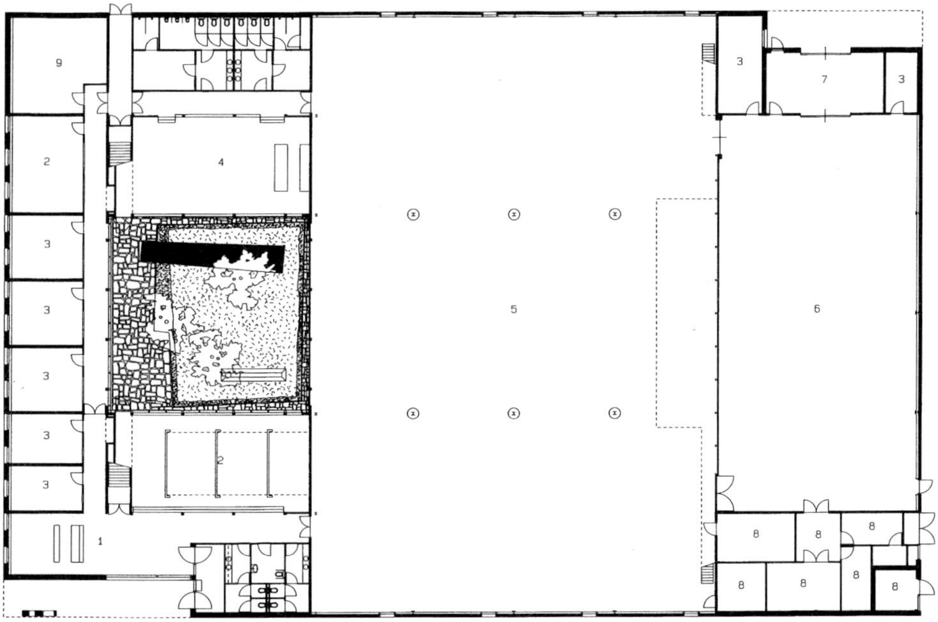
9
3
7
3
2
4
3
3
5
6
3
3
2
3
1
8
8
8
8
8
8
8

Neutelings Riedijk Architecten bv

3

NAA, Nederlands Audiovisueel Archief

DESIGN TEAM Willem Jan Neutelings, Michiel Riedijk, Joost Mulders, Wessel Vreugdenhil, Lennaart Sirag, Bas Suijkerbuijk, Arjan Mulder LOCATION Hilversum (NL) DESIGN 1999 START CONSTRUCTION 2001 CLIENT Nederlands Audiovisueel Archief, Hilversum TECHNICAL DESIGN AND BUILDING CONSULTANCY Bureau Bouwkunde Rotterdam STRUCTURAL DESIGN Aronsohn Raadgevende Ingenieurs, Rotterdam BUILDING SERVICES ENGINEERING Ketel Raadgevende Ingenieurs, Delft BUILDING PHYSICS CONSULTANT Cauberg-Huygen Raadgevende Ingenieurs, Den Bosch COPYRIGHT PHOTOGRAPHS Neutelings Riedijk Architecten bv PHOTOGRAPHS OF THE MODEL rob-thart.nl

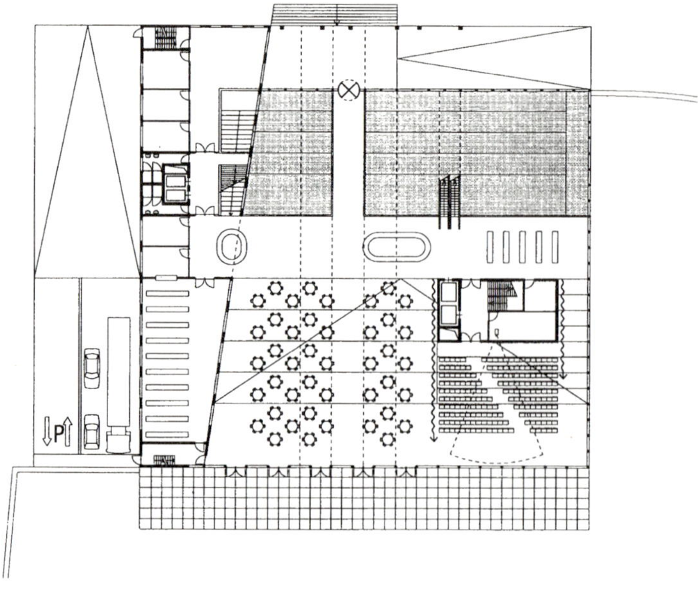

The NAA (Nederlands Audiovisueel Archief) houses all the audio-visual material produced in the Netherlands since the early days of Dutch radio and television. Our building divides into five distinct elements: archives/stores, museum, offices, client reception and services. Together, these parts bound a central well at the building's heart. Here is the building's public area, consisting of the main reception hall, restoration facilities and video auditoria. This large central space binds all the components of the NAA together.
Considering that something like half of the required programme encompasses storage and archive rooms with rigorously stipulated climatic conditions but no need for daylight, we decided on a horizontal division into two. The part below ground contains the archives/storage vault and that above it the museum and other uses requiring natural light. Bridging the gap between these two areas are the public spaces, client reception and services.
The central well conducts daylight to the lowest levels of the vault. At the entrance the void is evidenced as a deep canyon that brings the sheer size and scale of the archives/storage vault home to visitors. One of the canyon's sides is a flush wall; the other rises in a series of inverted terraces. These contain the rooms for receiving clients plus annexes serving the archives and stores;
the archives and stores themselves are concealed behind the flush canyon wall.
The central well culminates in an enormous void where both museum and offices show their best face. The inverted cascade of the museum levels registers as a wall sculpture that shapes and gives scale to the internal space of the building.

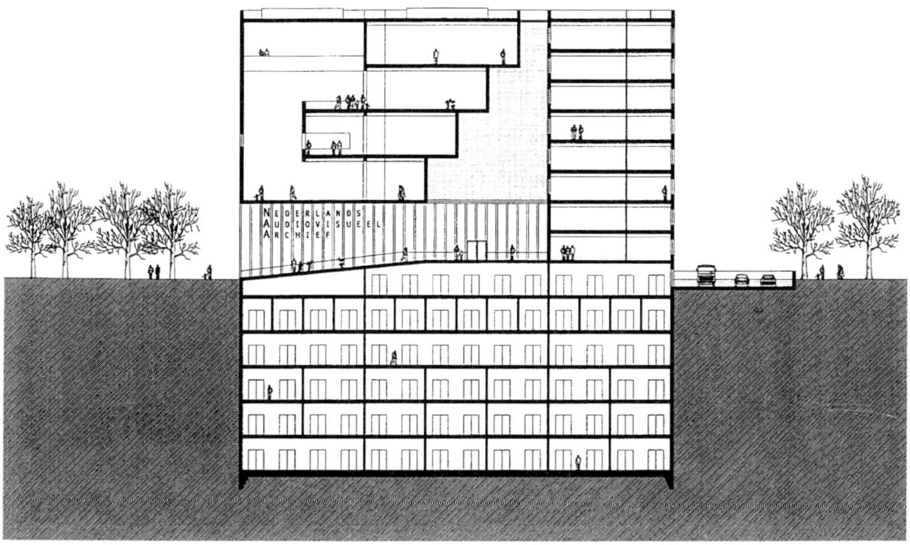

Neutelings Riedijk Architecten bv

3

Concert Hall in Bruges

ARCHITECTS Willem Jan Neutelings, Michiel Riedijk LOCATION Bruges, Belgium INVITED COMPETITION DESIGN 1998 (Prize Winning Competition Entry) COLLABORATORS Joost Mulders, Ute Schneider, Tania Ally, Bas Suijkerbuijk, Arjan Mulder, Dimitri Meessen, Marc De Bruijn, Lennaart Sirag, Wessel Vreugdenhil TECHNICAL DESIGN Bureau Bouwtechniek bvba, Antwerp ACOUSTICAL ENGINEER Adviesbureau Peutz & Associes BV, Zoetermeer SCENOGRAPHIC ADVISOR Raadgevende Ingenieurs Prinssen en Bus bv, Uden STRUCTURAL ENGINEER Aronsohn Raadgevende Ingenieurs bv, Rotterdam PHOTOGRAPHS rob-thart.nl

Such a building must necessarily have a strong individual character and must distinguish itself by its scale and presence from the sea of houses that comprise the old city. The site for the concert hall is two-sided: one side stands in the medieval city, one on the underground urban motorway leading to the outskirts.

The concert hall therefore offers two facades, one facing t'Zand, like a piece of sculpture in the square, and another facing the tunnel, like a gate standing before the city. The base of the building stands in the empty area between the existing car park and the tunnel, making the building totally independent of existing underground structures. Above the base stands the flytower, with the halls jutting out on two sides. On one side hangs the large hall, curving up over the tunnel. On the other side hangs the small hall, sloping up into the park, like an entry porch and platform providing a spectacular panorama of the old city.

The large hall is designed like a perfect barrel. This shape combines the best possible acoustics with great degree of intimacy, and follows classic models such as La Scala in Milan.

The barrel shape of the hall and the floor of the foyer form the two skins of a complex spatial framework, whose connecting bars run through the space like

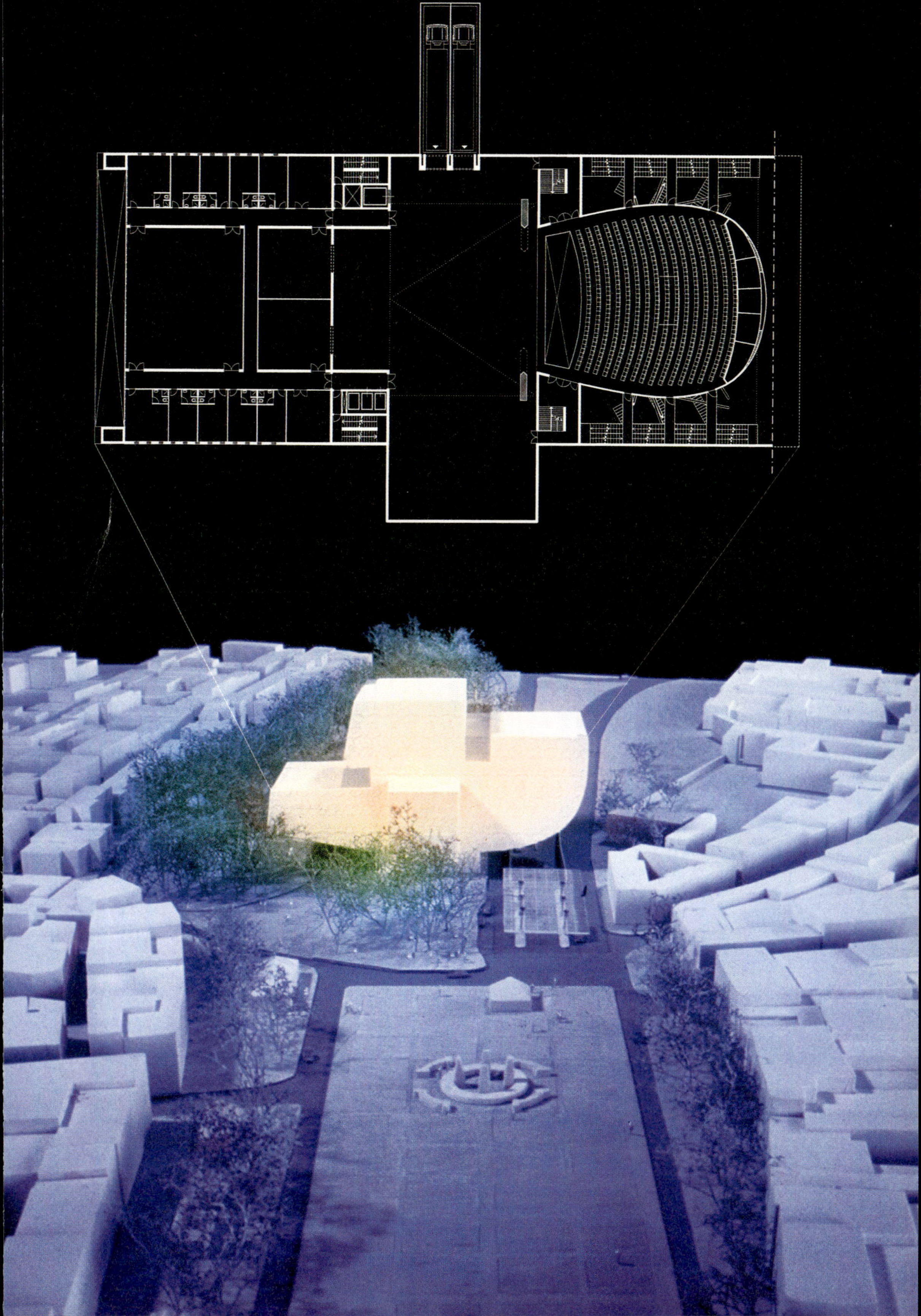

long slanting sticks in a game of spillikins. Glass domes set into the floor of the foyer provide peepholes giving an exciting view of the moving lights of vehicles in the tunnel. Zenithal light falls from the glass roof between the great hall and the exterior wall.
The closed sections of the exterior elevations are constructed of pigmented sand-coloured concrete panels bearing an abstract openwork decorative pattern. Behind them lies an amber-coloured metal coffer plate providing proper protection against wind and water.
The building as a whole looks like an enlarged view of a piece of lace work, a contemporary version of the filigree work produced by stonemasons for mediaeval cathedrals. In this sense the frontage seeks to achieve both an architectonic and an iconographic link with old Bruges.

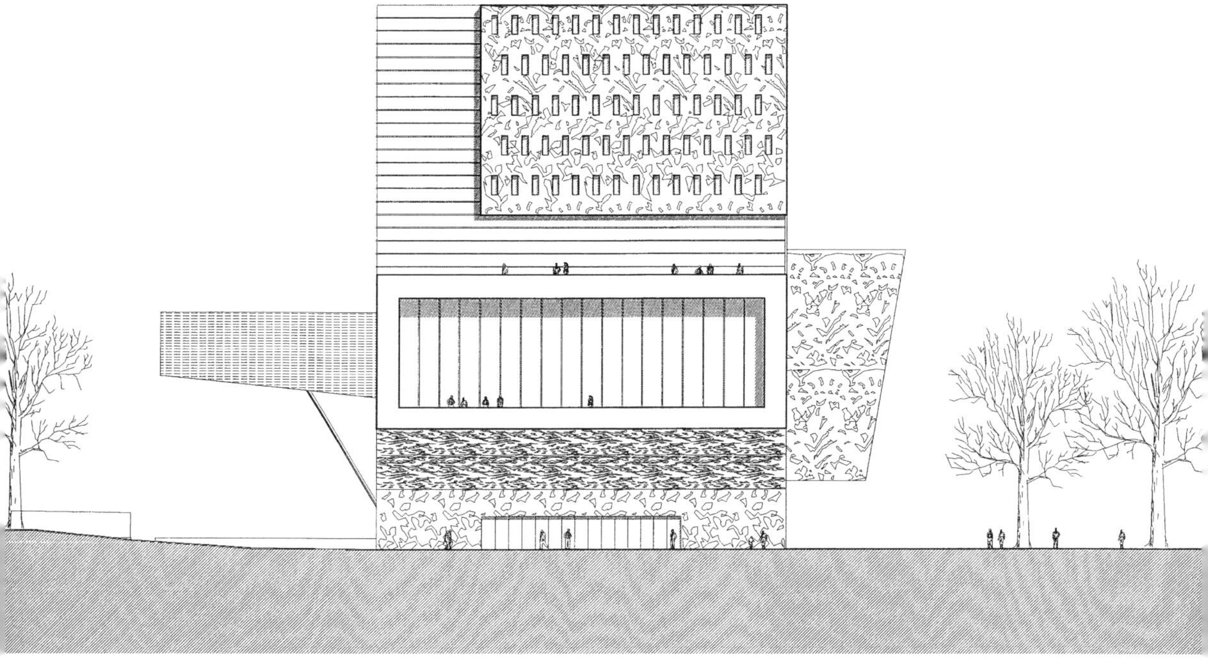

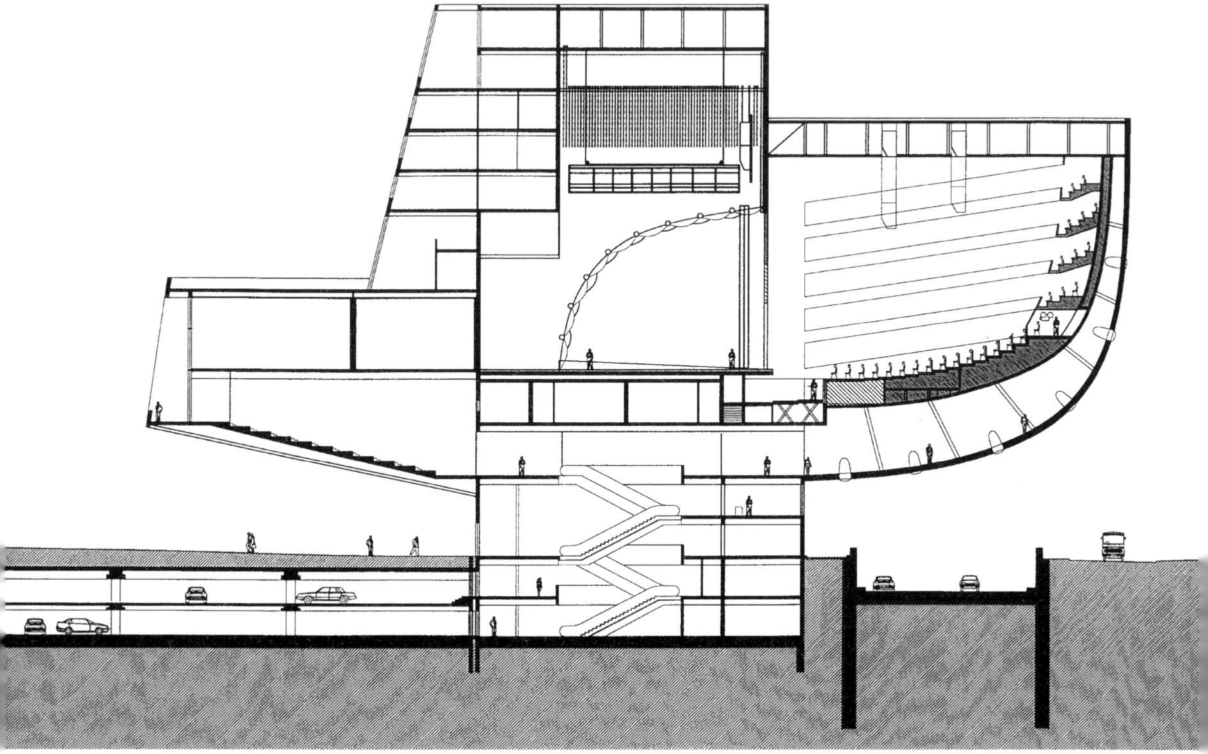

Direct logic would place more trust in decoding operations and actions, in which new icons and signifieds would have priority.

Direct Logic

Pizzeria

4 NL ARCHITECTS

Basketbar
YBuilding - Flower Tower
Sky Cemetery NT
WOS 8

WAH NAM HONG SUPERSTORE
3 LAP RACE
CAR 11 RUNNERS 22

Circuit City

At this moment illegal street races are immensely popular. Large groups of car freaks meet each other in secret locations. They are extremely well organised. The mobile phone and the Internet are crucial in planning their operations.

The authorities are worried and try to stop the races where possible; a cat-and-mouse game takes place that generates even more excitement. According to the racers their game is perfectly safe, but several casualties have been reported in the slipstream of the events. The races are generally held in peripheral business districts, harbours and warehouse areas. At night the spacious infrastructure is deserted and as such perfect for drag races.

When designing these business parks it might be a good idea to consider the activities that are normally just a derivative of the real function of these areas in an early stage. The hypothesis is that a reciprocal relation between both types of use could come into being: a situation of mutual benefit.

If a soccer stadium can provide an identity, can help boost the image of an average business area, as in the south-east of Amsterdam where the Ajax stadium became a fulcrum for intense urban expansion, the same could be true of a race circuit.

The proposal is to optimise the infrastructures of new business areas for driving fast. At weekends and in the evenings "illegal" races can take place. And during the day the circuit is a wonderful driveway along which you can park. How would Monte Carlo have looked if during construction the ideal curves had been used?

Official races can be organised several times a year that will have a positive effect on the surrounding businesses. The glamour that comes with motor sport will reinforce the "dynamic character" of the entire district; real-estate values will go up. Identity, the commodity that is fundamentally lacking from this type of generic environment, can be derived from the additional function: infrastructure becomes logo. Circuit City invites you for a test drive.

NL ARCHITECTS

4 BasketBar

COLLABORATORS Caro Baumann, Sybren Hoek, Kirsten Huesig, Nataly Lavi, Friso Leeflang, Jennifer Petersen, Misa Shibukawa, Rolf Touzimsky, Richard Woditsch CLIENT Universiteit Utrecht Huisvesting, Aryan Sikkema INTERIOR DESIGN BOOKSHOP Broese Henry Betting INTERIOR DESIGN BASKETBAR De Drie Musketiers STRUCTURAL ENGINEERS Adviesbureau voor Bouwtechniek bv ABT Velp / Rob Nijsse MECHANICAL ENGINEERS Ingenieursburo Linssen bv BUILDING MANAGEMENT Berenschot Osborne CONTRACTORS Bouwbedrijf Van den Hengel bv INSTALLATIONS Van Losser bv Rijssen PHOTOGRAPHS Luuk Kramer, Jeroen Musch

The campus of the University of Utrecht is growing into something that might be called a city. The urban plan by OMA consists of a compact cluster of University-related buildings, leaving the intrinsic qualities of the existing landscape intact or even reinforcing them. As soon as student housing became possible in this area nightlife became an issue as well: a local bar was needed. The Café will serve as the informal centre of the campus, as a relaxed meeting place for professors, researchers and students. It will be positioned right under the Van Unnik Building, the 80-metres-high logo for the University as a whole. This massive building is constructed with the Jack block system: a surreal

construction method that builds the top floor on the level of the ground, then jacks it up and constructs the next floor, again on level zero. The last act is lifting all 21 storeys to construct the ground floor: a bizarre gravity-defying operation that sends Baron Von Münchhausen back to school. The Uithof Café is a 15 x 15-metre extension of the existing bookstore. The remarkable horizontality of that construction is extended with the oversized roof of the new cafe. The complex appears as if flattened by the big block. Since the floor height of the shop is not appropriate for a grand café, the floor of the bar is sunken into the ground to a depth of minus 1.2 metres. This perfectly coincides with the height of the counter: you enter on top of the bar. The lowered position allows a new perspective on the public square: an urban conversation pit. The large roof of the café provides the ultimate location for a basketball court, whence BasketBar.

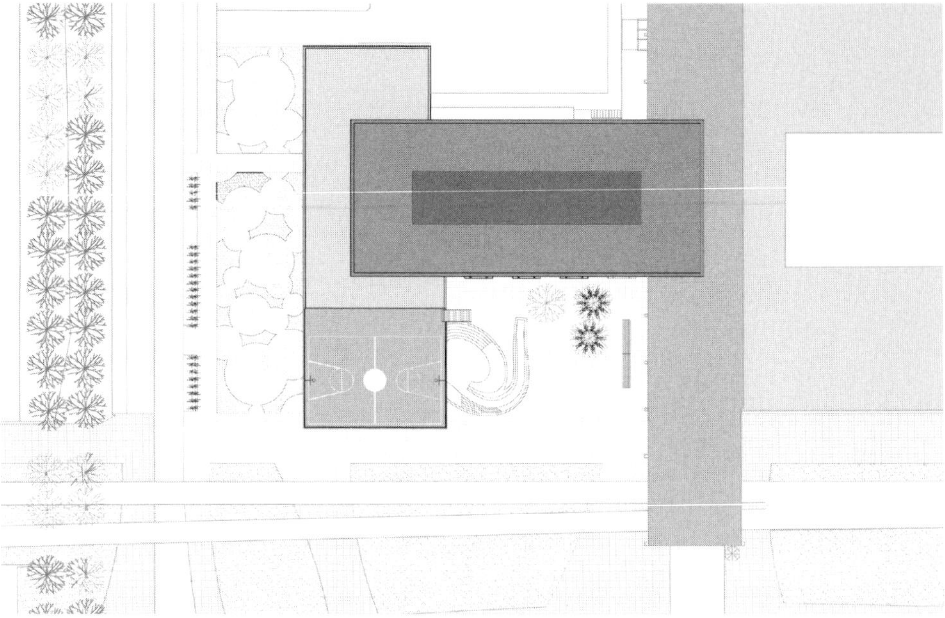

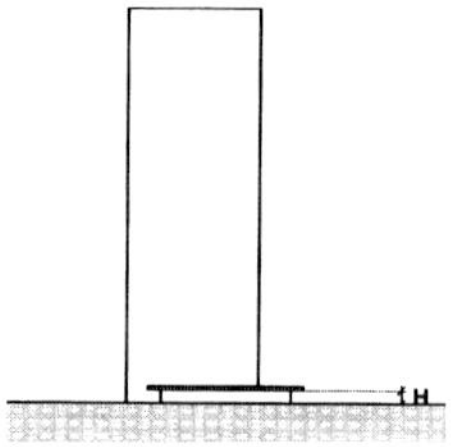

H = 2.60 m The existing bookstore with a flat roof: it´s beautiful

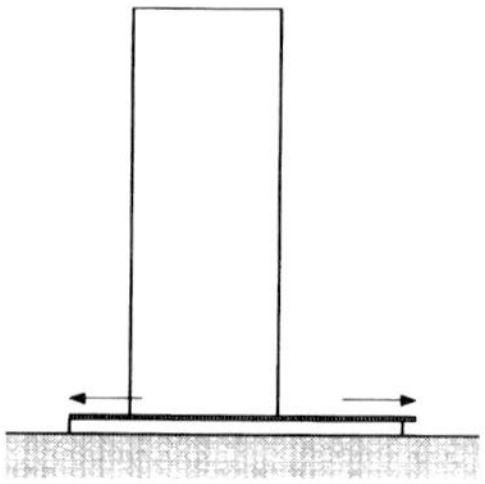

H = 2.60 m The new cafe + bookstore extension flatter = more beautiful

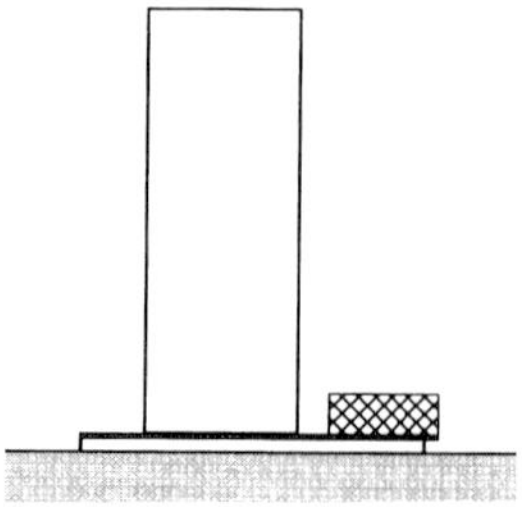

H = 2.60 m The roof becomes big enough to fit a basket court on top.

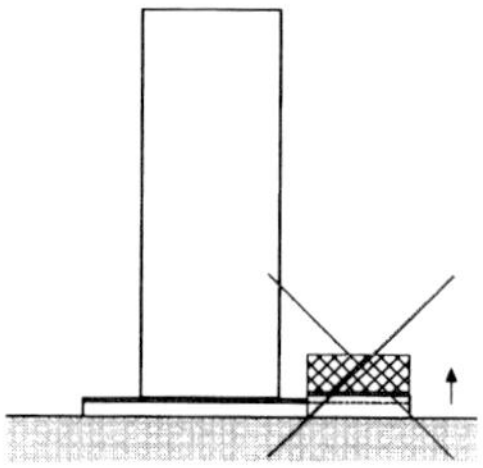

H = 3.80 m The cafe needs clearance to become "grand", but a broken roof frustrates elegant flatness.

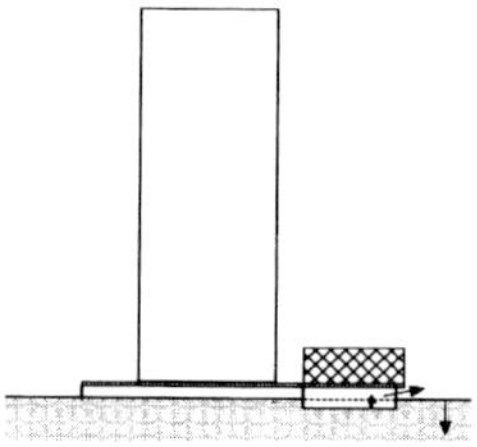

H = 3.80 m The roof remains flat. The bar floor sinks in the ground: intimacy comined with an extensive view. Bar = Catwalk

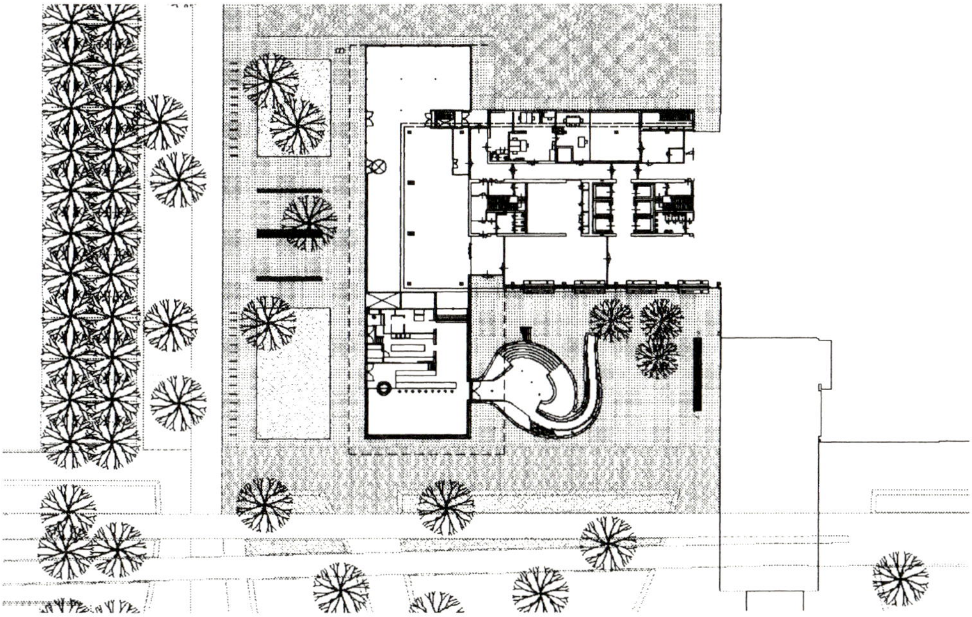

Je dag begint met het AD.
Algemeen Dagblad

NL ARCHITECTS

4 YBuilding – Flower Tower

ARCHITECTS Pieter Bannenberg, Walter van Dijk, Kamiel Klaasse, Mark Linnemann EMPLAZAMIENTO Westelijk Stations Eiland Amsterdam PROYECTO 1999 CLIENTE Departamento de Urbanismo de Amsterdam (DRO Amsterdam) COLABORADORES Alessia Allegri, Caro Baumann, Kirsten Huesig

The Westelijk Stations Eiland is the last 'undiscovered' island in the stream of the ambitious waterfront redevelopments on the south bank of the River Y. The investors of the so-called Harbor Building, one of four landowners on the 'island', are looking for possibilities to double the existing floor area with at least 12,000 m^2. The dimension of the site, height restrictions and the monumental character of the building by Dudok make any extension problematic. This proposal suggests to 'clone' the existing building. The result is manipulated, stretched and deformed in order to provide enough daylight and to maintain the important views. Y Building colonizes the 3D space outside the site boundary. The buildings are arranged like flowers in a vase: confined at the bottom, released at the top. The Harbor Building has a peculiar hidden property: there are two elevator shafts, two staircases, two mechanical shafts, two toilet groups and two pantries on each floor. The slab in fact consists of two towers that are kept together by one facade: twin in one skin! In the cloned building these towers are partly set free: a Siamese Twin-tower.

NL ARCHITECTS

4 *Sky Cemetery NT*

ARCHITECTS Pieter Bannenberg, Walter van Dijk, Kamiel Klaasse, Mark Linnemann
COLLABORATORS Kirsten Huesig, Sarah Moeller, Nadav Monselise, Yoko Taguchi

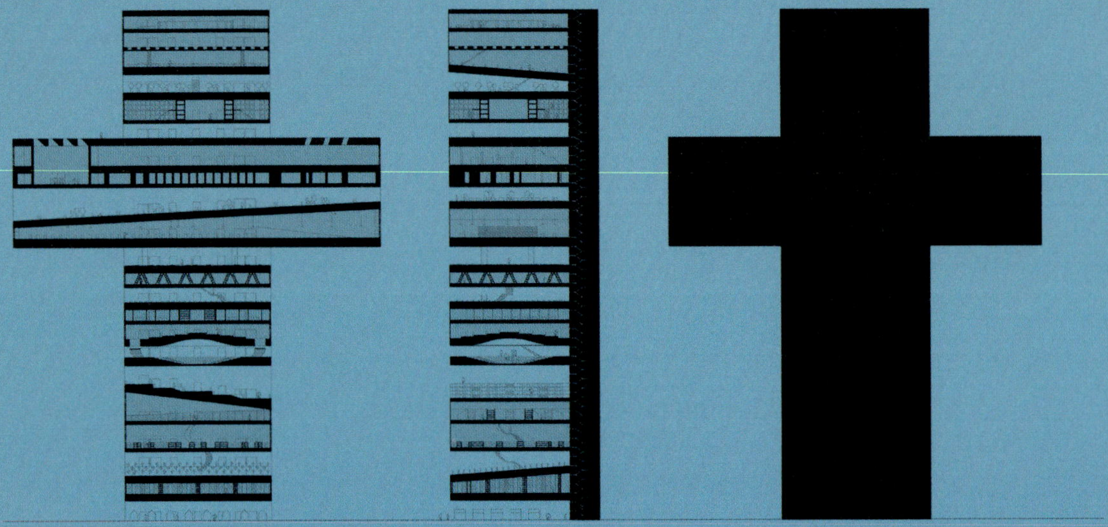

The cemetery is the last cultural field not to be explored by postmodernism. Ceremonies are customized, diversified and individualized according to people's personal wishes, but somehow the concept of the burial ground itself remains unaddressed.

Sky Cemetery NT is an attempt to fundamentally rethink the planning, organization and orchestration of burial grounds and crematoria. Sky Cemetery NT is an amassing of atmospheres, to the point that critical mass is reached. By using the most successful logo of all time a powerful gesture is created, familiar but at the same time strangely new and multilayered: the cross as an immediate symbol of its content.

Sky Cemetery NT is an almost infinite accumulation of alternating indoor and outdoor spaces, of artificial climates, of various atmospheres, and of typologies, traditional and advanced (or not yet extant); a graveyard on top of a columbarium, or a catacomb suspended in the air (like a basement in the attic). Buried halfway to heaven.

Ever since the Dark Ages cemeteries have been precluded from the city center for hygienic reasons. Pushed out onto the margins, they became the first peripheral program, in a way. Now that this dichotomy no longer exists – the periphery became center and vice versa – a strong highway look could be a boost for this new identity and the memorial would be absorbed by the urban substance.

Sky Cemetery NT can become the center of gravity of a society's collective memory. Thus far, most of the valuable details about the deceased's life and achievements disappear with him or her into the grave. In order to survive, the cemetery needs a virtual extension. The "spirit," or at least a biography of sorts, could be downloaded into a database. Sky Cemetery NT will become an archive in which information may be stored on a voluntary basis. Someone's accomplishments, facts, failures or funniest home videos can be consulted. In that sense Sky Cemetery NT will become a destination for people in mourning, but also for tourists and for researchers.

Mausoleum becomes Museum, Cemetery becomes Archive: Sky Cemetery NT is a black box made of white alabaster.

4 WOS 8 (Warme Overdracht Station nr. 8)

ARCHITECTS Pieter Bannenberg, Walter van Dijk, Mark Linnemann, Kamiel Klaasse; in cooperation with ir. Djin Sie (Bureau Nieuwbouw Centrales UNA N.V.) LOCATION Utrecht PROJECT 1997 EXECUTION 1998 CLIENT Energieproduktiebedrijf (energy production company) UNA N.V., Bureau Nieuwbouw Centrales, Utrecht COLLABORATORS Quirijn Calis, Florian Idenburg, Eliana Mello, Michel Schreinemachers, Ruud Visser ENGINEER DHV AIB BV, Amersfoort CONTRACTOR Van Zoelen B.V., Utrecht PHOTOGRAPHS Daria Scagliola, Stijn Brakkee, Teake Bouma

WOS 8 is a Heat Transfer Station (Warmte Overdracht Station) for the latest extension of Utrecht, which is the new city Leidsche Rijn (the largest Vinex development in the Netherlands). WOS 8 is a transfer node where energy from the power plant is dispensed to several distribution loops serving future housing areas. WOS 8 will service a total of 11.000 dwellings, employing a technology that consists of a central heating system on the scale of an entire city. WOS 8 has been online since November 1998.

The size of WOS 8 was determined by the minimal functional dimensions of the pipe system in the interior as well as the forces of realty economics limiting its size to the smallest possible.

Our client, the Energy Production Company UNA, essentially asked that we design a skin. Polyurethane was originally developed for parking roofs because it

was strong, flexible, waterproof, durable, attractive and chemically inert (no pollution of earth and ground water). It is easily applicable by spray gun or paint roller. A polyurethane membrane enables architecture to become seamless and building parts such as doors, which might refer to scale or size, disappear. WOS 8 is accessed only three times daily (in eight hour intervals) when the meters and the gaskets are checked. This type of unmanned utilitarian buildings is an easy target for vandalism because these complexes are typically the blind spot of urbanism. The facade is programmed with a number of activities that intend to make the building attractive. Since climbing is fast becoming a national sport in the Netherlands, a series of climbing grips have been inserted under the polyurethane skin. Applied in Braille, they read, "the Blind Facade." A so-called Doorscope (a large door-spy) is placed around in the main door. Normally used to see who's delivering pizza, the "doorscope" is installed in reverse and instead displays the entire interior on a little screen. Standard issue, but still amazingly beautiful road reflectors are plugged into the east facade and sprayed over. Some pop through the skin and spell the name of the building: WOS 8.

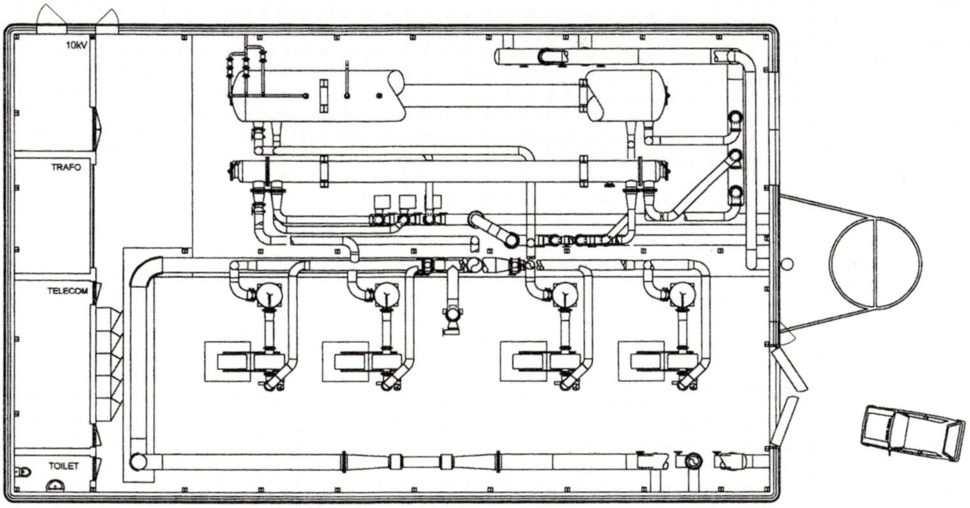
10kV
TRAFO
TELECOM
TOILET

5 *Périphériques*

Café Musiques
Pink Ghost
Towers for Echigo-Tsumari

contents
IN-EX

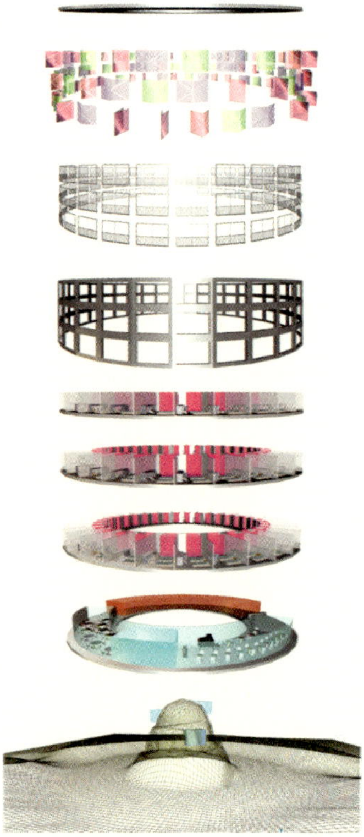

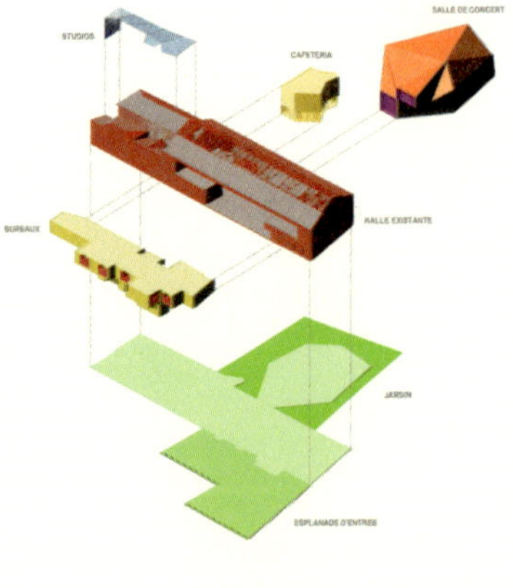
STUDIOS
CAFETERIA
SALLE DE CONCERT
HALLE EXISTANTE
BUREAUX
JARDIN
ESPLANADE D'ENTREE

Why Périphériques? Because!

Périphériques Architects is strongly committed to a status of architecture producers, to broadening the field of architectural activities so as to encompass publishing (IN-EX projects), writing and mediating. Underpinning our approach at Périphériques is the desire to revise the rules of professional practice and architectural design. It is both a pragmatic and subversive approach that we have adopted in order to appropriate what we call "hyper-reality." For this purpose, we develop strategies aimed at reinvesting situations with a new attitude in order to endow them with aesthetic and functional qualities that deviate from the norm. In an economic and cultural context that imposes standardisation at all levels of space production, we strive to transform the assignment by diverting it so as to revitalise, modify and recycle it and ultimately to make something unique using standard building components. In this way we can focus the economy of the project on the aesthetic sphere, defy production modes, and propose more, even when we are asked for less. These are some of the principles inherited from the concept of "customisation," which we define as the third possible way dear to Colin Rowe in the current architectural context. Also, we think radically that projects can only be specific to the context (urban, programmatic, economic, formal, et cetera); whence an experimental architectural language devoid of formal taboos. Indeed the urban landscape (or environment) has become a pre-existing "hyper-form" that we endeavour to infiltrate, to slip inside the way a "surfer does who creates an intimate relationship with the dynamic environment surrounding him" (Sanford Kwinter). Since we are "condemned" to build and thereby to pursue this continually developing urban-territorial situation, our goal is to transform this existing situation into a system that is at least "as good" as it was before our intervention, restoring to this "context" a new fresh quality, far from the "contextualist" philosophy of certain practitioners, but also far from Rem Koolhaas' famous "Fuck the context!" Many of our projects are located in peri-urban areas, in those peripheral areas that have become the building ground of generic architecture (the zero degree of architecture, says Paul Virilio), with the entertaining, exhibitionist and idolatrous thrust that has come to characterise huge commercial zones, development sites, or renovated city centres. This aesthetic and urban landscape, this mixture of ugliness and vulgarity, of the empty and the large scale, is our architectural material. With it Périphériques endeavours to propose, without cynicism, critical, reactive, efficient buildings in which the accent is placed on "ambiences" and "atmospheres" rather than "beauties" and "spaces."

Périphériques

5 *The Music Café*

ARCHITECTS Trottin & Marin-Trottin, Paillard & Jumeau + Jakob & MacFarlane SITE Savigny-le-Temple PROGRAMME 1 restaurant, two rehearsal and recording studios, 1 concert hall for 300 people and a Hip-Hop dance room COMPETITION 1997 EXECUTION 1999 CLIENT Ville de Savigny-le-Temple (France) COLLABORATOR B. Douliery NET FLOOR AREA: 1,200 m² BUDGET FF 7.5 M (exclusive of tax)

The Music Café site hinges two contrasting spaces. The first is the urban north: station, car park, roundabout and business park – the unstructured banality of the outer suburbs. The second is the "countryside" to the south, where a dense copse of poplars separates a pond from the railway. Woods and fields stretch as far as the eye can see, while bulrushes and water lilies provide cover for bird life. The scene is one of nature that has survived the onslaught.

We have adopted two different architectural approaches to reflect this marked dichotomy in the two landscapes surrounding the Music Café site. On the town side, we have responded to the signs with a sign of our own in the shape of a basic volume – a box whose essence is portrayed through the finish of its outer shell. The architecture is defined by light, in the same way as the commercial outlets and their signs. The pond is both a visual element and a retreat; by means of an architectural device, we have therefore created an architectural camouflage that enables the building to blend into its environment.

One of the scheme's interesting features is that it can be divided into several different entities:

B The billboard

C The concert hall

D The restaurant

are three independent programs which, grouped together, form a whole.

The "billboard", which houses the foyers and lounge areas along the entire length of its coloured facade, interacts with the town like a sign, revealing the activities taking place in the Music Café. Clad in a galvanised-steel facade fitted with translucent and transparent coloured glass panels, the building is lit differently by day and night.

In contrast to the "billboard" which fastens a commercial image on to the town, the concert hall and restaurant blend into the countryside. The concert hall is clad in reflective stainless steel sheeting, thereby transforming the shape of the surrounding countryside; the restaurant however, plays at camouflage: its concrete is staggered in alternating glossy and matte segments.

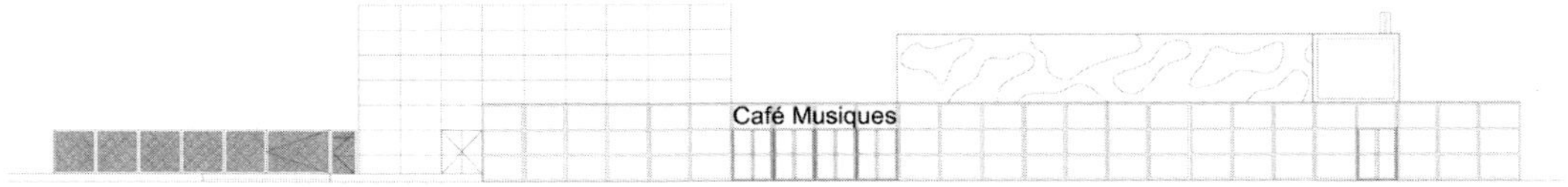
Café Musiques

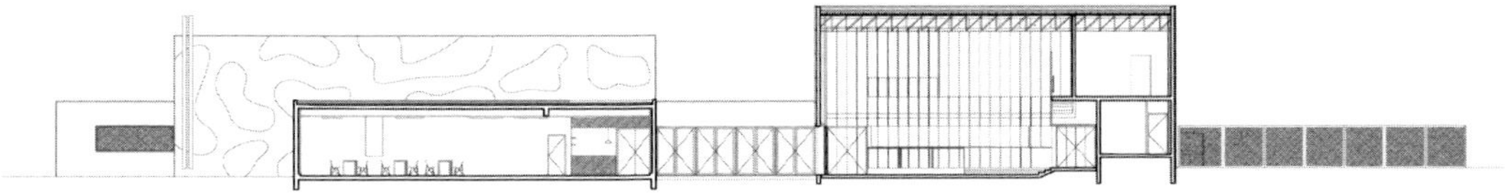

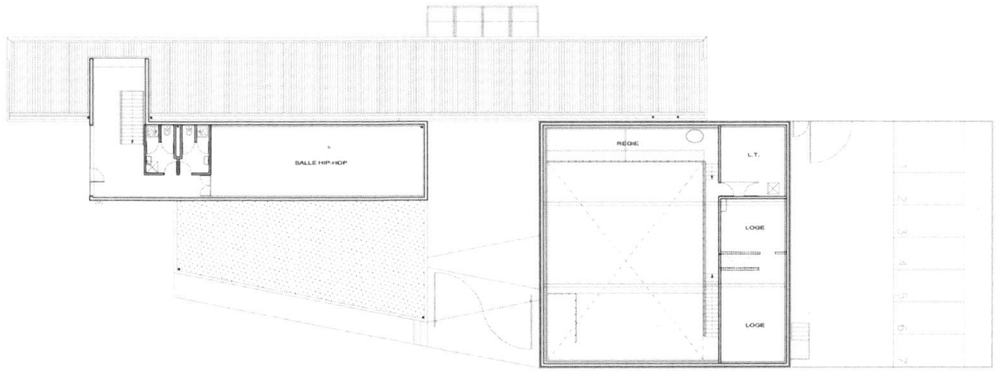
SALLE HIP-HOP
REGIE
L.T.
LOGE
LOGE

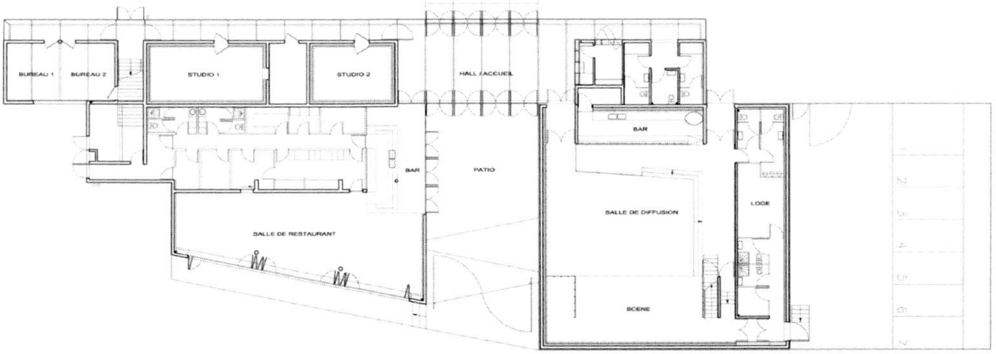
BUREAU 1
BUREAU 2
STUDIO 1
STUDIO 2
HALL ACCUEIL
BAR
PATIO
SALLE DE RESTAURANT
BAR
SALLE DE DIFFUSION
LOGE
SCENE

Périphériques

5 **Pink Ghost**

ARCHITECTS Marin-Trottin+Trottin & Paillard + Jumeau PROGRAM Transformación temporal de la plaza Furstemberg como salón exterior, París LOCATION París, Francia EXECUTION 2002 CLIENT Comité Saint Germain des Près COLLABORATORS S. Raissi, J. Pascual FLOOR AREA 100 m² BUDGET 15.300 EUR (con impuestos)

Within the framework of the second Saint-Germain-des-Près / Parcours / Paris-Soho contemporary art exhibition organized by the Comité Saint-Germain-des-Près, which ran from 28 May to 18 June 2002, Périphériques Architectes were invited to intervene on the Place Furstemberg. A "plastic" intervention of "transformation" is involved, one having to do with an attitude of "preservation" of the central part of the square. "Pink Ghost" is made in pink-colored resin and, along with the entire surface of the square, envelops the four trees and lamppost up to a height of 2.5 meters. Once dismounted in Paris, the pink phantom was remounted in the French Pavilion at the Venice Architecture Biennale as a memoir of the square and of its new usage.

Périphériques

5 3 Towers for 2003 Echigo-Tsumari Triennale

ARCHITECTS Marin-Trottin+Trottin & Paillard+Jumeau LOCATION Echigo-Tsumari, Niigata, Japan EXECUTION 2003 PROGRAM Vantage point and camping area CLIENT Art Front Gallery, Tokyo COLLABORATORS Henri Kangas, Stephane Raza, Mitsuru Hamada FLOOR AREA 200 m^2

Within the framework of the Echigo-Tsumari Art Triennial in the north of Japan the Art Front Gallery, which organizes this event, has commissioned an intervention from us. We have proposed three projects which play with the landscape: the snow in winter (with a layer up to seven meters thick!), the vantage points and the trekking the visitors do. In this expo, the works are spread out over a series of wild and depopulated valleys.

- Cloudoo is an igloo or a cloud. It climbs according to the season up a ladder-cum-mast of polished stainless steel and plays with the snow and the tops of the trees. Inside this bubble a spartan chamber invites the visitor to spend an "experimental night" there.
- Flamingo is a vantage point overlooking the site. It displays the hieratic attitu de of a strange animal.
- Vertical Camping is the proposal that is to be built. It combines the two above functions in a tower covered over with a brass mosquito net (offering protection from the abundant mosquitoes in summer). Each of the six decks in grating can accommodate campers for the night.

6 IaN+

Dada Headquarters
Tomihiro Museum

Architecture in new-ecology

ARCHITECTURE AS A LIVING SYSTEM

Architecture becomes a support to the territory transformation, a system which organizes and defines relations between subjects. It works in perspective, it's not a closed system, but it is open and flexible, ready to accept modifications.

ARCHITECTURE AS INTERFERENCE WITH REALITY

To design relations means to provoke interferences, or variations of state, able to stimulate different spatial organizations. Architecture produces interferences, it doesn't only define space, but it creates conditions for this kind of space to develop and root on territory.

ARCHITECTURE AS TERRITORY

Territory is a relational space between landscape and human beings experiencing it. Territory defined through this process is a high-complexity system in constant development. It stays in a state of apparent order while its normal state is chaotic and full of conflicts. In this way architecture itself constantly develops.

ARCHITECTURE AS PARTICIPATION

Every project is based on three elements: forces involved, zones and interzones. Zones result from the analysis of activities and flows. The main character of zones is their functional homogeneity. Edges between zones turns into interzones of relations, while superimposing zones produce interzones of exchange. Interzones are design models with no leak of energies. Minimum and flexible interventions are localized inside the interzone, following a soft strategy which can be modified by external events.

What we call interzone is a texture able to fit with in every possible transformation taking place in the urban spaces. This transformation, acting for a best answer to get the best possible life, involves the concept of participation: institutionalised participation as much as spontaneous participation. Architecture is an auto-eco-organized system.

IaN+

6 Dada Headquarters

ARCHITECTS Carmelo Baglivo, Luca Galofaro PROJECT 2001 MODELS Marco Galofaro
COLLABORATOR Laura Negrini ENGINEERING CONSULTANT Stefania Manna

A new-economy company needs a head office for its Florence branch. Presenting oneself to the competition provides a good occasion to revise the typology of work stations. In a network environment like this kind of company's, private space gives way to social. Work teams are constantly exchanging information, knowledge and experiences and so they need open spaces that favor direct communication.
In order to favor the nomadic behavior of the employees it is necessary to reduce rigid, predefined areas. The work space does not enter into contradiction with domestic space, as in the past. If we spend so much time in the office we have to redefine this space. Office + DOMESTIC space = Dada space. A flexible space seems to afford greater freedom, but obliges any spatial mutation to reiterate itself with a repetitive schema that does not permit work activity to be undertaken in the way the requirements of the information age demand. Dada space needs to be changing and continually reversible and it must constantly yield among the different phases of work activity.
Permeability replaces the concept of transparency; what is involved here is not vision but the movement of activities. An area has to contain different states of permeability in order to permit different states of contact. Transparency allows for visual exchange between the public and the private. During its evolution Dada space needs to be modified and, if necessary, it must assume a form completely different to the one before; the sole space that allows for continual transformation is an empty space from which all forms are generated.
The main feature of Dada offices is a new concept of open space in which the two-dimensional elements of separation between different work areas are replaced by three-dimensional elements which, in dividing and combining at the same time, affect contiguous areas by their presence. They have different sizes and accommodate different activities of leisure, meeting, individual work and information exchange. They enrich the open space with specific activities that were previously relegated to different areas of the building.

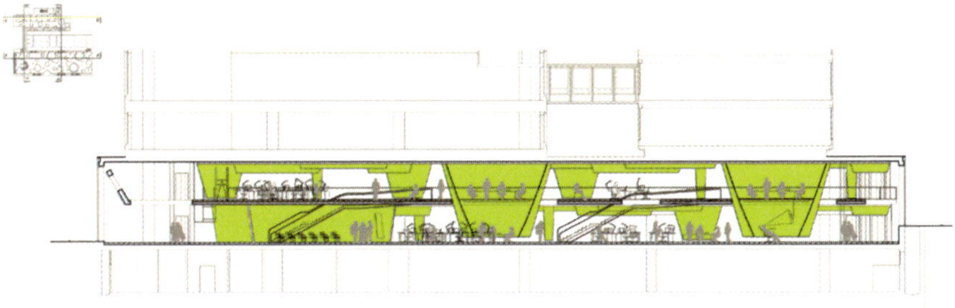

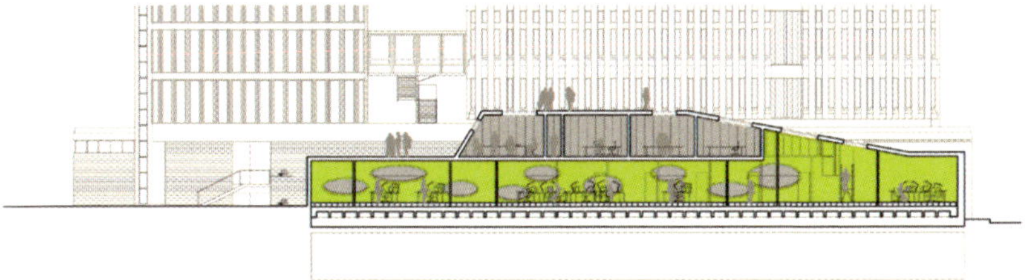

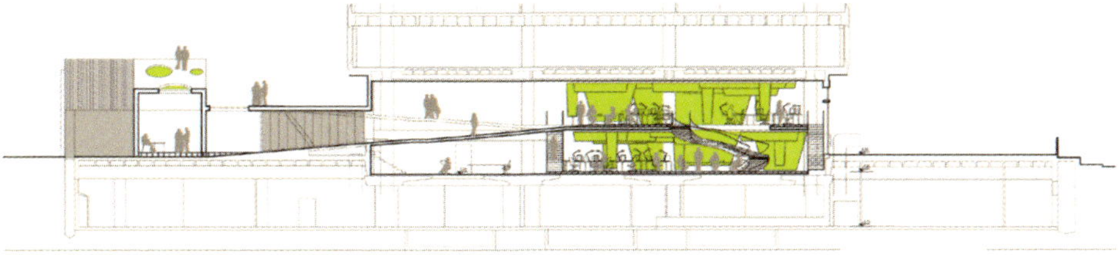

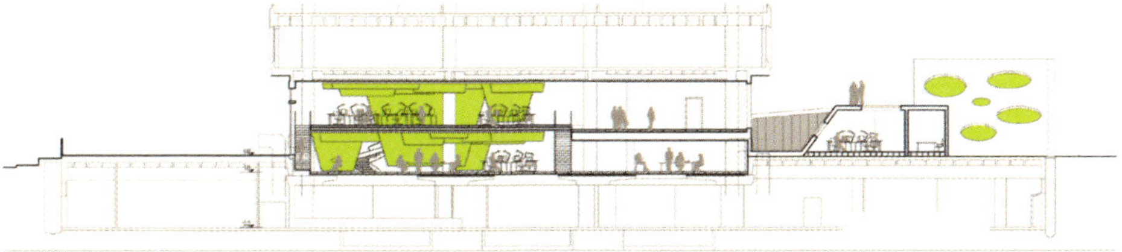

Via Paolieri

Via Paolieri

The museum wishes to recreate the ideal conditions for being in contact with art by means of contemporary architecture. The conceptual thinking of an architect confronts poetic and artistic work in a space in which architecture becomes an expression of the person and of their art. The museum is the synthesis of three elements: museum / nature / artwork. The transparency of Hoshino's painting and the power of the landscape they depict are the basic elements involved.
A prismatic glass beehive plays host to the museum rooms. The glass partitions filter the light of the landscape around the village of Azuma, the main subject of Hoshino's work. The light is able to give meaning to the passing of time and the changing of the seasons. The empty space under the building is a basic part of the museum: it hosts a garden in which it is possible to be in contact with the Azuma landscape prior to visiting the exhibition. The glass and brick halls create a sense of oneness between the poems and the outside scenery. A flight of stairs leads into the museum, built on a single level in order to facilitate the movement

IaN+

6

Tomihiro Museum

ARCHITECTS Carmelo Baglivo, Luca Galofaro PROJECT 2002, International Competition LOCATION Azuma, Gunma, Japan MODELS Marco Galofaro

of the visitors. In the museum we find rest areas and a patio facing the garden below, in which seasonal flowers are on show. There are two exhibition halls: the larger one permits visitors to contemplate a single oeuvre at their leisure, while the smaller one contains videos, photographs, texts and objects.
All the special facilities are organised in the access area to the museum on the second floor: a room to study *shi-ga* works, a conference room, offices and the archives with a small library. A bar, bookshop, exhibition space for children's works, and the promotional area are located in a public space at the end of the exhibition. All the storage areas and the installations are located below garden level, in order to facilitate humidity control and the correct working temperature.
The old museum will be pulled down following construction of the new building. The honeycomb structure allows the museum to gradually occupy the entire area available, as per need.

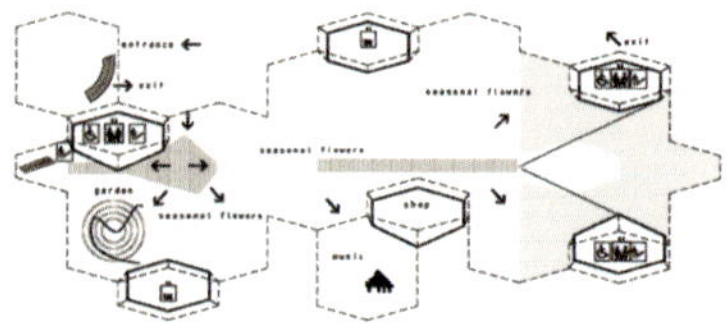
entrance
exit
seasonal flowers
seasonal flowers
garden
seasonal flowers
shop
music
exit

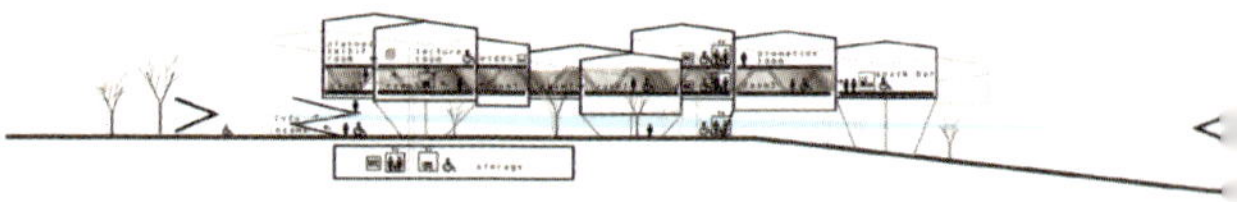
storage

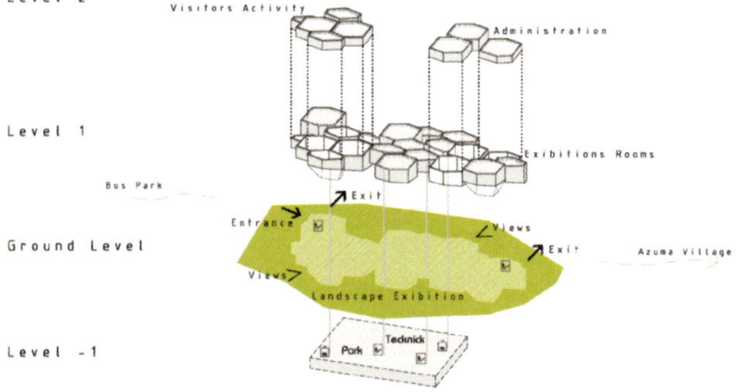
Level 2
Visitors Activity
Administration
Level 1
Exibitions Rooms
Bus Park
Exit
Entrance
Views
Ground Level
Exit
Azuma Village
Views
Landscape Exibition
Level -1
Park
Tecknick

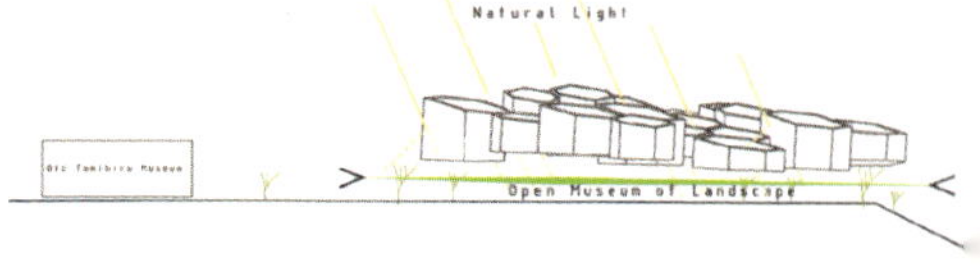
Natural Light
Open Museum of Landscape

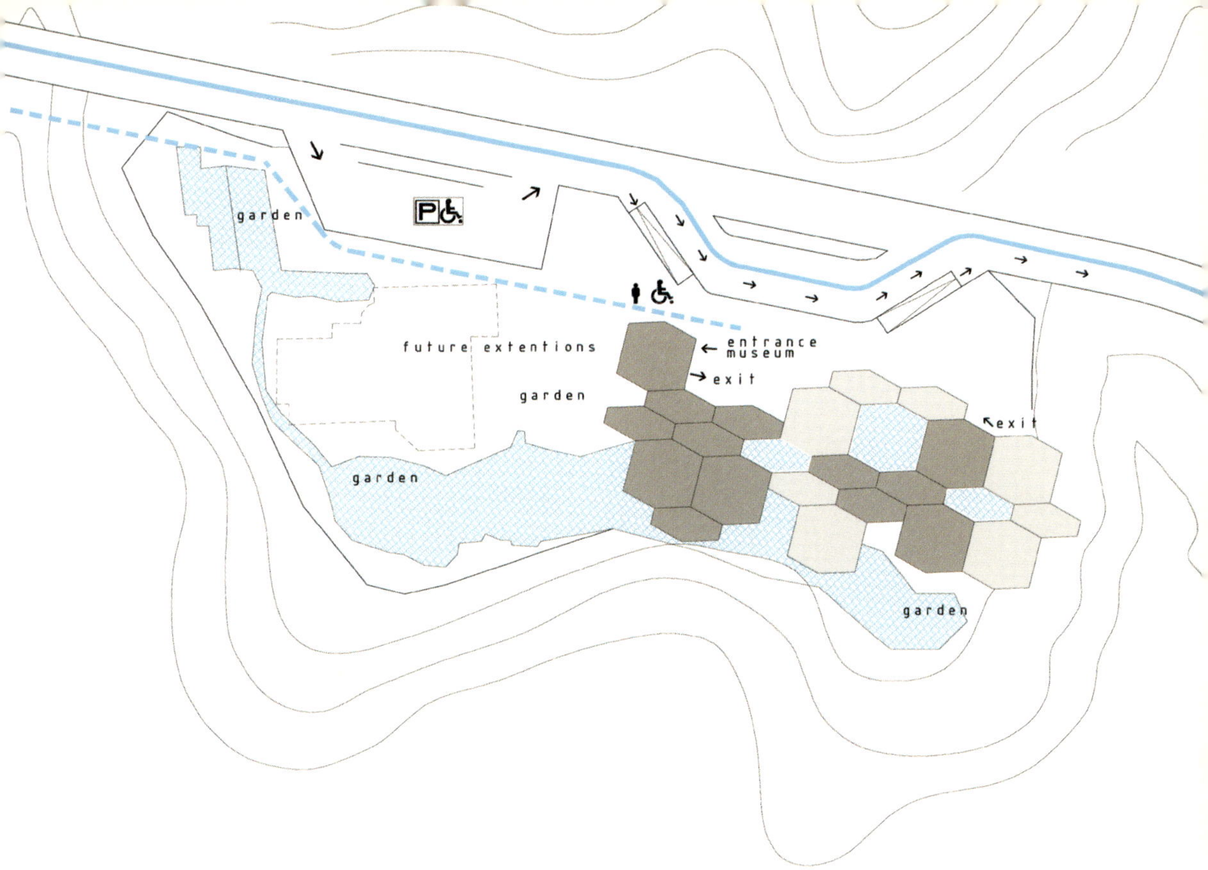
garden
future extentions
garden
entrance
museum
exit
exit
garden
garden

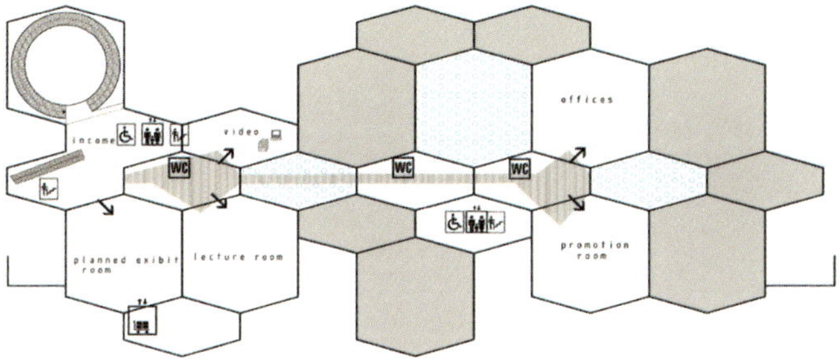
income
video
offices
WC
WC
WC
planned exibit room
lecture room
promotion room

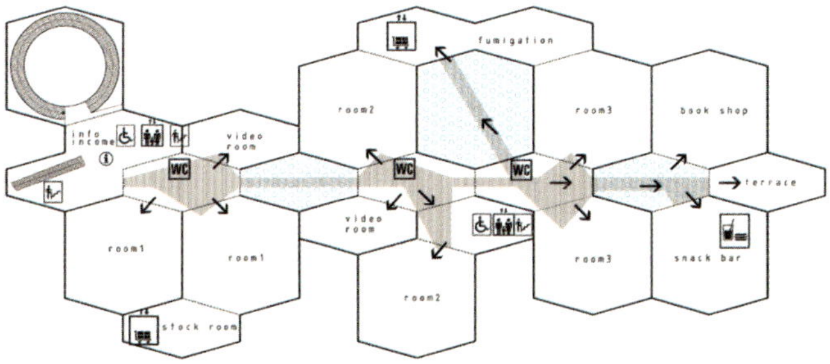
fumigation
room2
room3
book shop
info
income
video room
WC
WC
WC
terrace
video room
room1
room1
room3
snack bar
room2
stock room

Productive logic would work with composite construction materials and techniques; that is to say, with catalogues of prefabricated components.

Productive Logic

7

WMA Willy Müller

Flower Market
House in La Floresta
Waste-management plant

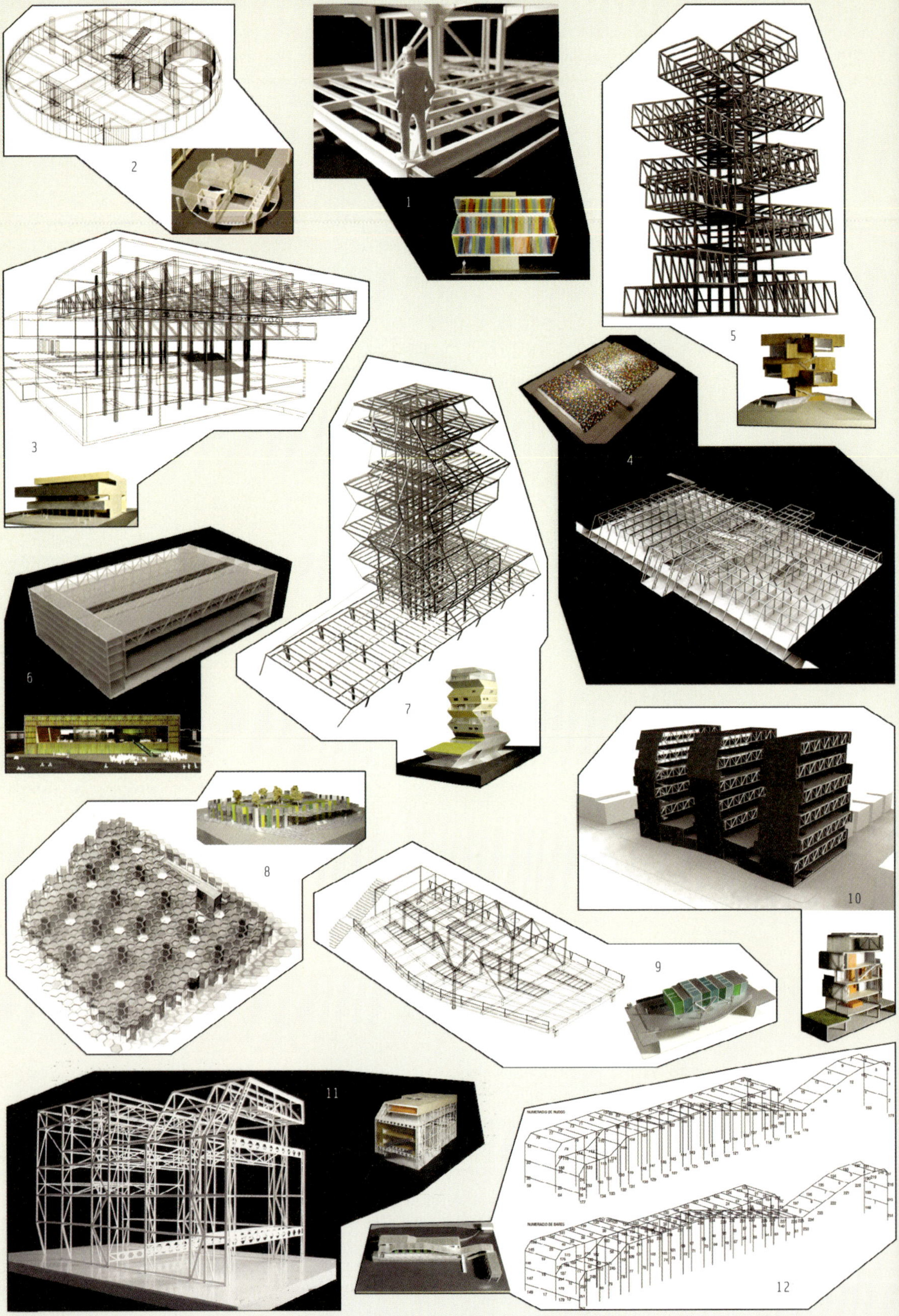
2
1
5
3
4
7
6
10
8
9
11
12

It is a question of size

One of the phenomena most typical of metropolitan areas is the speed at which vast spaces are acquired by the major industrial and service sectors: after almost a century of permanence and integration these spaces gradually disappear from the historic centers and quickly reappear in mutant territories around the city, only to disappear once again within the phenomenon of delocalization in every shorter periods of time, without the possibility of being fully integrated in the landscape. The life of cities seems slow in unfolding, but their concentration speeds up peripheral phenomena: the turbulence is noticeable in the places furthest from the center. These spaces are sufficiently close to the center to receive the scalar impact of the size of the needs of these urban concentrations, but at the same time sufficiently far away to avoid the reach of the regulatory norms which shape and create city space, in an evident conflict of interests.

We have worked for some time in this mutant, untamed and functional territory, a territory at once disproportionate and practical, and clearly hostile to architecture. We incorporate new architectural scales and we believe that the solution isn't about working in dribs and drabs but about an optimistic, go-ahead attitude in the defining of these new territories, referents that no longer distinguish between categories like center or periphery.

This may possibly be the territory that is, paradoxically, more mistrustful of the particular intervention yet which accepts the overall challenge with more interest. It's a question of scale.

1 Pile System. 2002
2 Peugeot showroom. Mataró 2001
3 Navarra General Library. Pamplona 2001
4 New Flower Market in Barcelona. Mercabarna 2002
5 Eco Center. Pusan, Korea. 2005
6 Arts School. Cádiz 2005
7 Pile Tower, Sociopolis. Valencia 2004
8 New Market. Sant Adrià 2004
9 Restaurant Bridge. Mercabarna 2000
10 Beam System. 2004
11 Cultural Centre. Santa Pola 2002
12 Recycling plant. Mercabarna 2001

WMA Willy Müller Arquitectos

7 *New Central Flower Market in Mercabarna*

ARCHITECTS Willy Müller (principal architect), Fred Guillaud (associate architect) LOCATION Mercabarna, Zona Franca, Barcelona EXECUTION 2003 INVITED COMPETITION DESIGN 2002 (First Price) COLLABORATORS Sérgio Pinto, Joana Lages, Anne-Irène Valais, Caterina Morna, Christof Larbig, Jetske Kox, Rupert Maurus (3D models) SURFACE AREA 29,000 m² COST 8 M € DEVELOPER Mercabarna STRUCTURE ADVISORS Ingenieria Raventós INSTALLATION ADVISORS Greccat

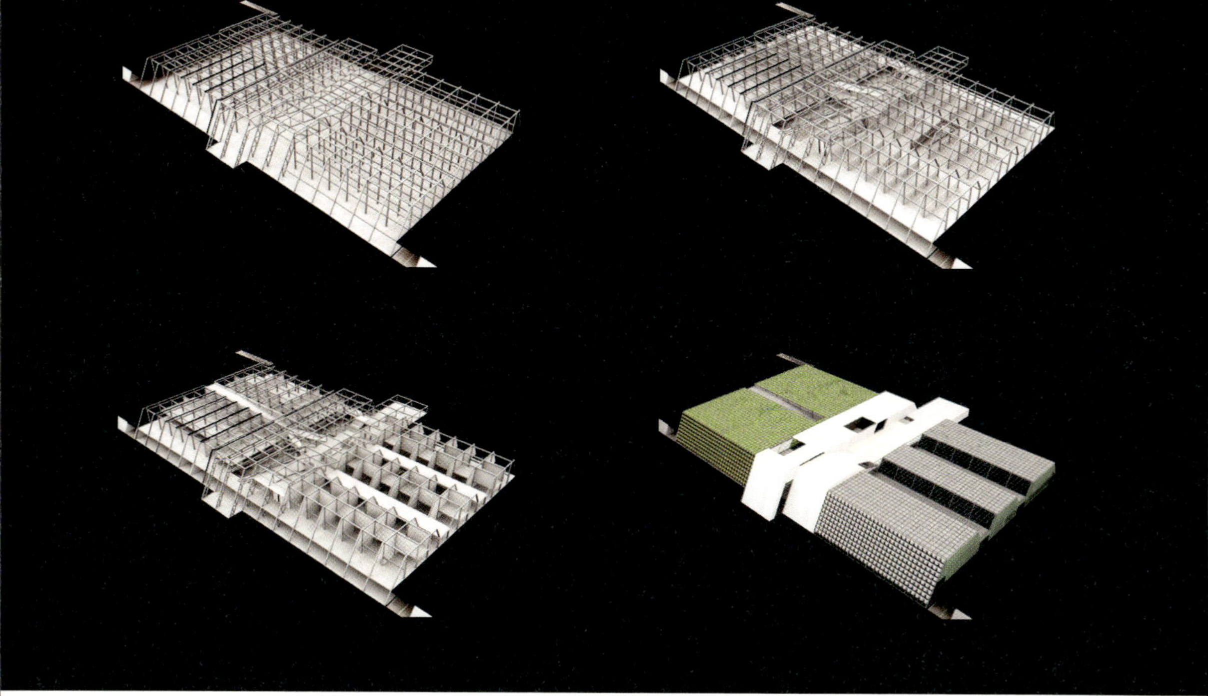

We distribute the Market on two main floors of activities interconnected by a huge central void: on the lower level is the market for cut flowers and on an upper one the markets for plants and accessories.
Around this central space, which we will call the Forum, we locate different public services like the quick-service bar, the bank, and the information control and security departments, and on an upper level the areas of the program that have to be closer, such as the administration and trade-union offices, the florists school and the restaurant, which is located in the big protuberant volume so as to grant this the possibility of functional autonomy. The distribution of the spaces is the outcome of a spatial grid based on the relationship between the structural modules (of 8 meters) and the slighter modules with a sales or street frontage (of 6 meters). This 8 x 6-meter grid forms the market's spatial armature. This model structural skeleton is deformed or adapted according to the different market typologies stretching out along the longitudinal section.
Finally, we conceive the roof of the building as a means of endowing this center with a new image. This great outer skin fuses the concepts of wall and roof into a single element that the integrated volumes transform into a great raiment of colors, into an authentic *impression* of a flower market.

WMA Willy Müller Arquitectos

7

House in la Floresta

LOCATION La Floresta, Sant Cugat del Vallès PROJECT 2001 EXECUTION 2002 COLLABORATORS Frédéric Guillaud, Caterina Morna DEVELOPER Marí-Ballester CONSULTANTS THB Consulting CONSTRUCTION THB Consulting SURFACE AREA 120 m² COST 102,000 € PHOTOGRAPHS Giovanni Zanzi (site), WMA (models)

Level -1

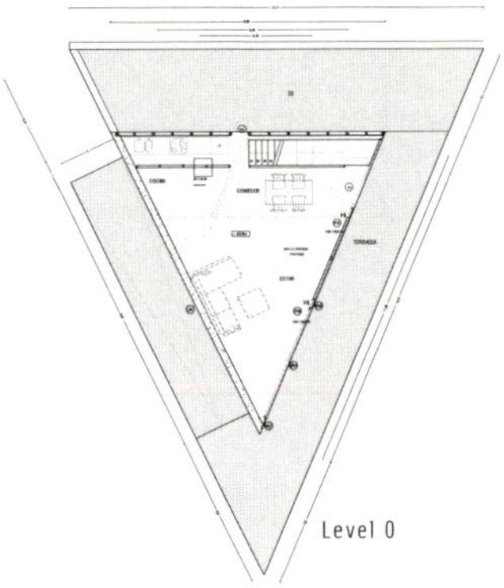

Level 0

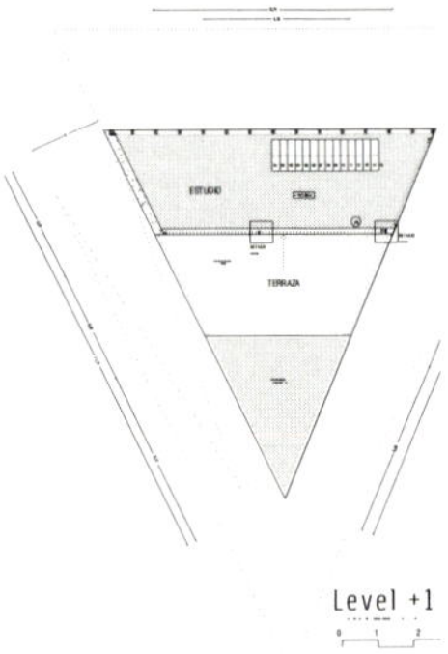

Level +1

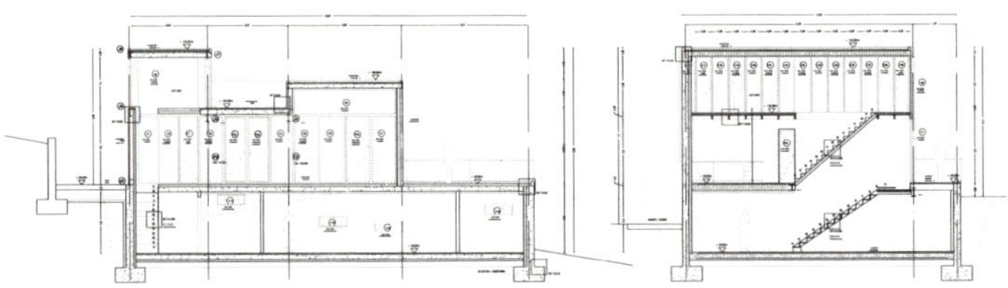

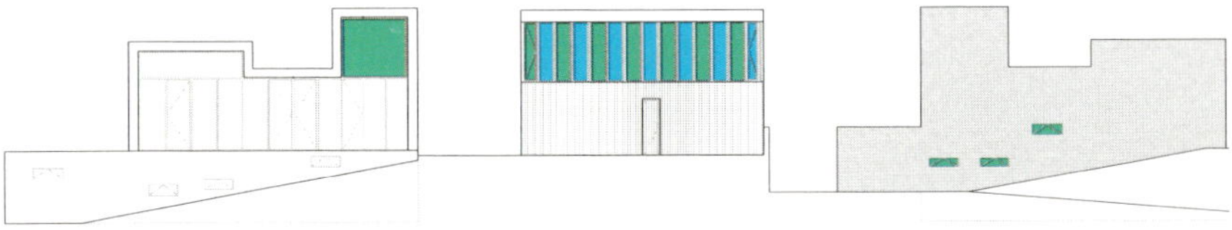

We situated the house on the right plot of land, we had a three-dimensional triangular object that we were exploring since the Barakaldo Europan, in which we proposed an urbanization model based on these triangular structures. We were exploring the form of combination, but the sections that could be produced also surprised us.
We designed a house in which the section would come first, so as to make use of all the volume the law allows us to. We ensure that a 125 m^2 house can become an almost 200 m^2 one which has interior heights of 5.70 meters and many more meters of terraces, including on the roof. We locate the bedroom level on the ground floor and a living space on the first floor, from whence to observe the whole landscape. The triangle dictated our decisions: the facades are each in one material, depending on their orientation. Stonework, metal paneling, glass and aluminum window frames and industrial flooring: simple materials and easy fitting so as not to push up the price of the building. Adjusted to everything that fitted, the house is self-explanatory.

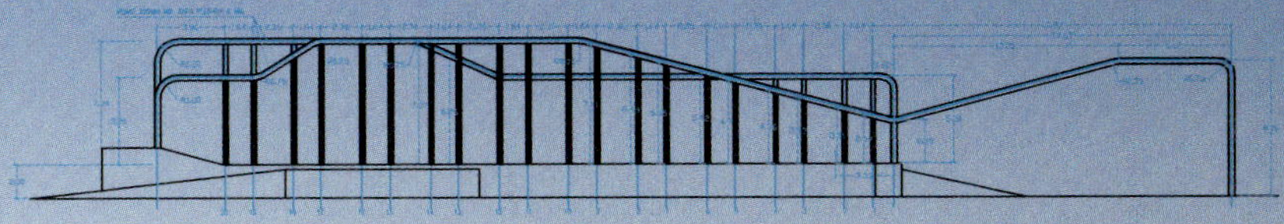

WMA Willy Müller Arquitectos

7

Punt Verd - Recycling waste plant

ARCHITECTS WMA Willy Müller Arquitectos, Frédéric Guillaud (associate architect) SITE Mercabarna - Zona Franca, Barcelona PROJECT 2001 EXECUTION 2002 ENGINEERING Greccat S.A. CONSULTANCY Ingeniería Reventós (structures) CONSTRUCTION Zeta 3 PROMOTOR Mercabarna SURFACE AREA 6,200 m² COST 1,700,000 € PHOTOGRAPHS WMA / Oriol Rigat

The Mercabarna Punt Verd installations occupy 6,675 m^2 and consist of a waste-management plant divided into two large areas, wholesale and retail. The most important installations in the complex as a whole have to do with selection and consist of the conveyor belts of materials going to the selection cabin, where they're separated into four categories, wood, cardboard, plastic and disposable material, and the chutes for organic matter, which are situated in the same unloading bay.
The entire architectural structure of this industrial complex has been thought out as a reflex movement of the circuit the materials perform from concentration to classified dispersion. For the first time in a recycling plant model the two main types of waste, organic and inorganic, are combined and in such a way that vehicle movement is rationalized throughout the plant. The forms of the undulations, in two great sections, emulate or suggest the activity within in a syncopated rise and fall, opening up spaces or becoming a single piece, rounded, gentle, gliding, *spilling over.* The structure is, however, less obvious: the great portico of the loading bay conceals the real shell in the center of the building, by making as if to distribute the two types of waste in solids and voids which are in fact the pillars of the complex as a whole developing into cantilevers of six meters on one side and four on the other. The skeleton is covered with metal sheets on the outside and Pladur and polycarbonate panels on the inside, with the declared intention of converting the building into a graphic statement of greens and silver plus white lettering.

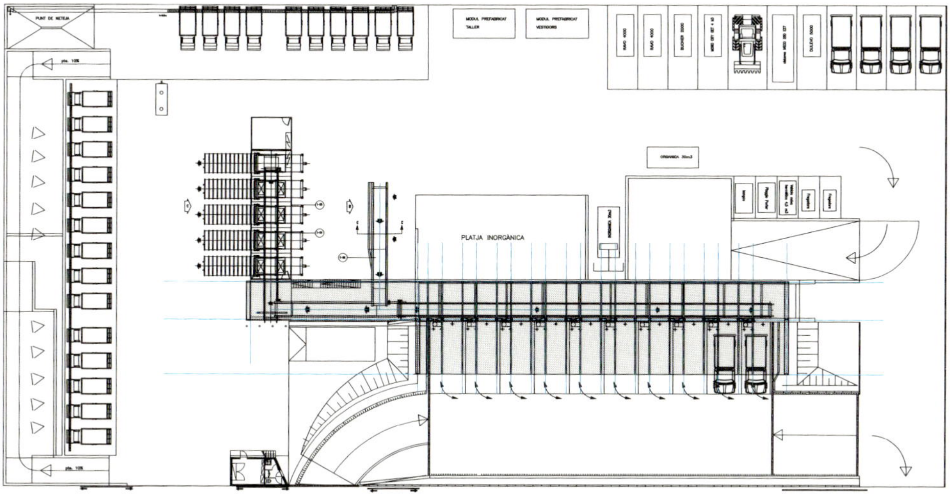
PUNT DE NETEJA
MODUL PREFABRICAT TALLER
MODUL PREFABRICAT VESTIDORS
PLATJA INORGÀNICA

T
V
E
R
D

8 Ábalos & Herreros

Valdemingómez Plant Green House

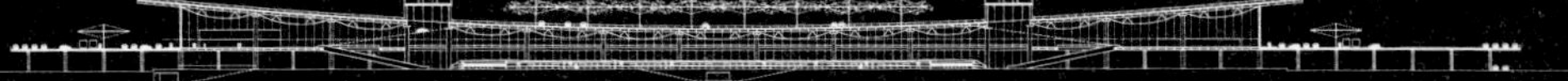

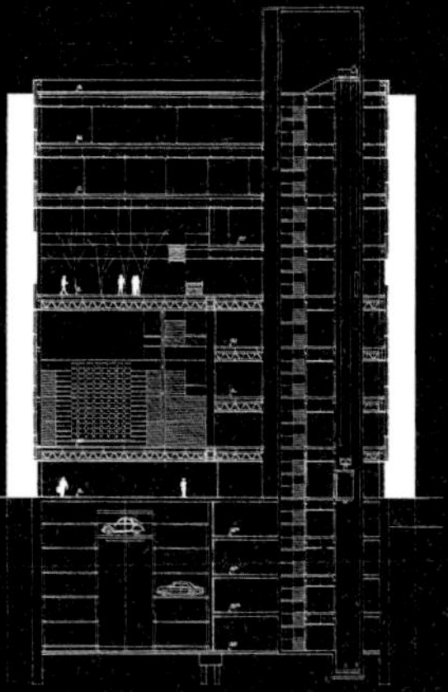

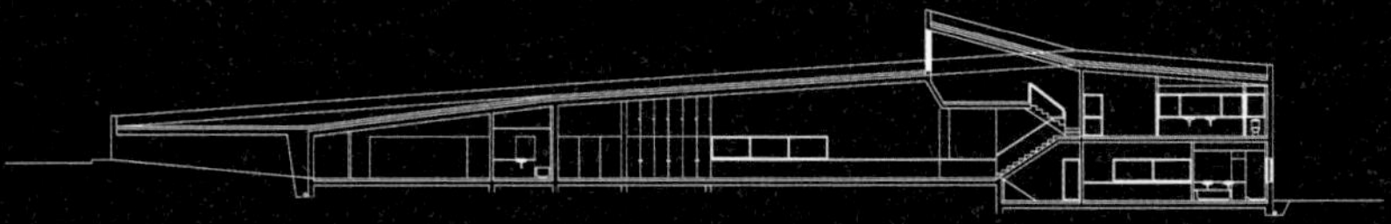

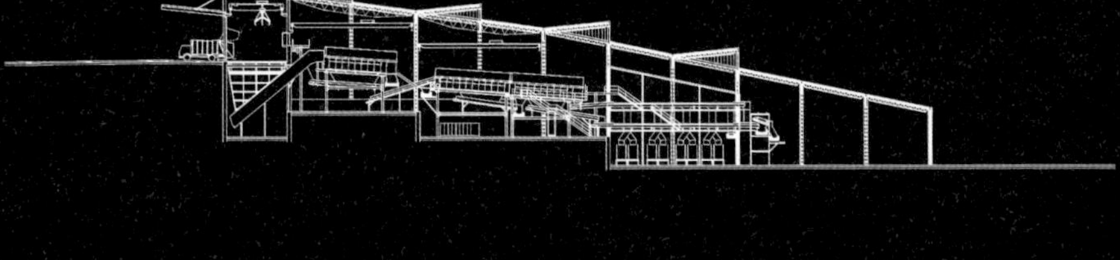

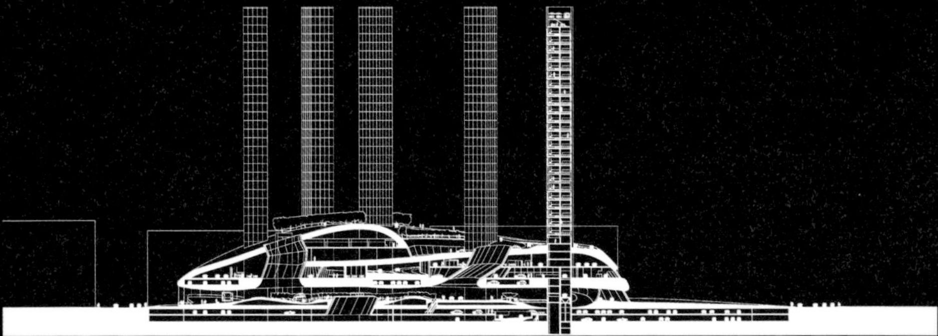

A New Naturalness and Micromanifestos

'Ecomonumentality'. We have been accustomed to conceive of architecture according to place, on the understanding that this is where we would find the keys with which to address the project. But in the last few years we have witnessed a significant transfer; a place is now seen as a landscape, whether natural or artificial, and this landscape has ceased to be a neutral backdrop that highlights artificial architectural objects with varying degrees of sculptural vocation to become an object of primary interest, the focus of the architect's attention. With this change in viewpoint, the landscape loses its inertia and becomes the object of possible transformations; it is the landscape that is now open to design, that becomes artificial. At the same time, architecture embarks on as yet vague processes of loss of traditional definition marked by a growing interest in incorporating a naturalist condition into both geometric and compositional and into constructive aspects, in search of environmental sensibility and a formal complexity that respond precisely to our society's new values. Hybrid technology, crossbred aesthetics. An increased awareness of nature policies have influenced technical paradigms, shifting interest from high-tech experiments (no doubt a residue of the modern spirit) to hybrid models, with the accent relocated on the interaction between natural materials (massive and energetically inert) and highly sophisticated artificial materials (light-weight and energetically active), with behaviour that is sensitive to variations in the context, giving way to compound systems in which the former would have the role of accumulating and reducing interchange and the latter act as generators, harnessing energy resources. This new technological model represents a shift from aspects of material organization (mass production, simplification of assembly, optimization of time and cost, etc.) to the rational organization of the energies consumed both in the production and the maintenance of built work, a shift that leads to the conception today of 'systems' based not on the coherence and unity of materials, but on their environmental coherence, thereby opening the field to forms of experimentation in which the coherent mixture of heterogeneous materials becomes a new, characteristic visual feature. A hybrid materiality that involves a far-reaching transformation of aesthetic ideals in keeping with the hybridization of our human landscapes.

Ábalos & Herreros

8 *New Recycling Plant for Urban waste*

ARCHITECTS Iñaki Ábalos, Juan Herreros and Ángel Jaramillo LOCATION Madrid 1996-1999 COLLABORATORS Aurelie Beriot, Ángel Borrego, Cristina Díaz Moreno, David Franco, Mª Auxiliadora Gálvez, Efrén García-Grinda and Pablo Martínez Capdevila CLIENT Vertresa-RWE Process and Town of Madrid MODELS Escala 9, David Franco and Pablo Martínez Capdevila LANDSCAPE ARCHITECT Fernando Valero STRUCTURES Obiol y Moya ENGINEERING Servicios Técnicos de Vertresa. Team leader: Fernando Valledor SERVICES José María Cruz and Pedro José Blanco ENVIRONMENTAL IMPACT STUDIES Javier Ceballos

The project is part of a group of projects that were to create a rational system for the treatment and recycling of the waste, as well as the transformation and the incorporation of its land into the future Southeast Regional Park, which was one of the city's most attractive projects that were intended to even-out the social and environmental differences that existed between the north and the south.

The recycling plant concentrates a heterogeneous group of buildings for the selection and processing of the refuse, storage, workshops and offices, all brought together beneath a large, inclined green roof that echoes, as much, the gravitational character of the process as it does the original hillside upon which it sits, «restored», taking advantage of the compost that is produced. The building is wrapped with recycled polycarbonate that unifies the various programmes and incorporates a museum area that has a route for visitors, aimed at making the public more environmentally aware.

The green roof, the polycarbonate, the light riveted structure and the interior finishes show this spirit, as they demonstrate the best environmental compromise that is currently possible with available techniques. This building is composed of two complementary constructions: one is dedicated to the production of compost from organic waste, and the second is dedicated to the control and the weighing of the lorries that enter the enclosure. Both have been treated as though they were industrial objects that set up a dialogue with the scale and the singularity of the landscape, built using systems that are analogous to those used in the first building. The centre has a life-span of twenty-five years, after which it will be recycled as a service building for the park or dismantled so that its components might be, themselves, recycled.

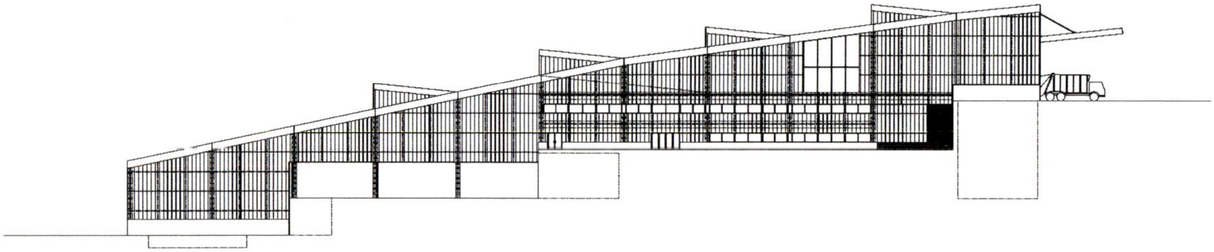

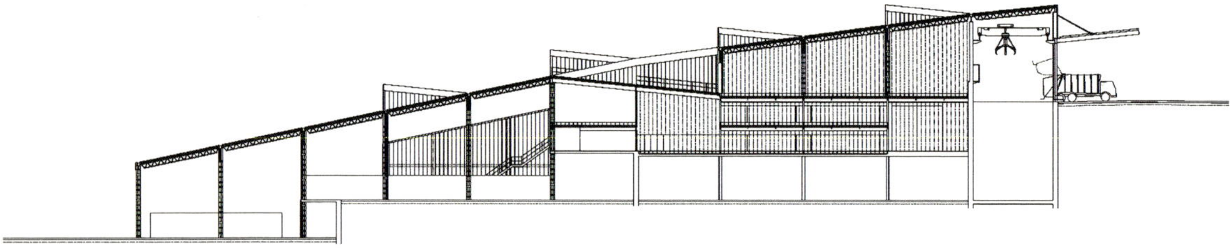

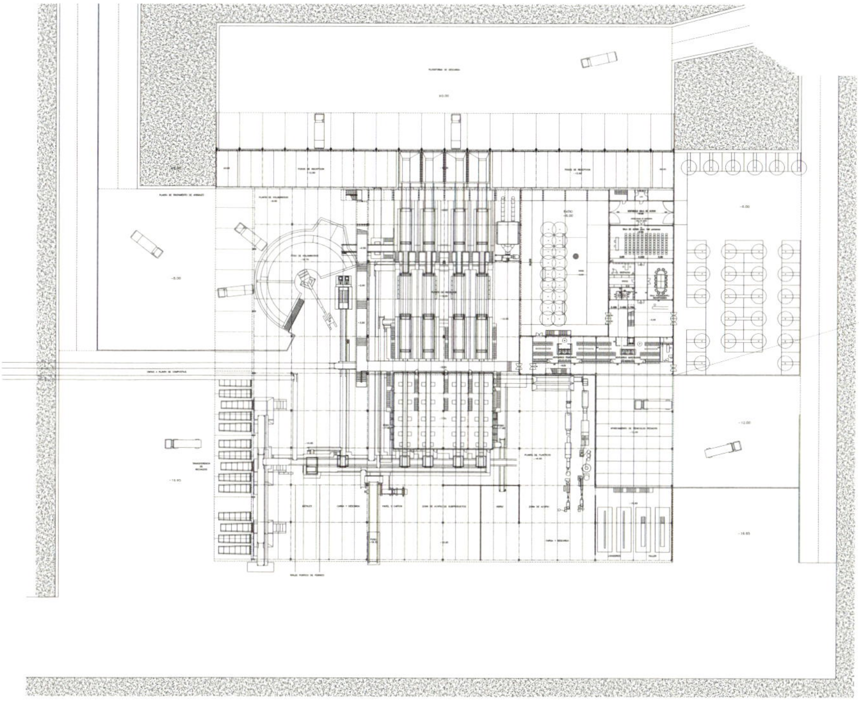

Offices -2.50

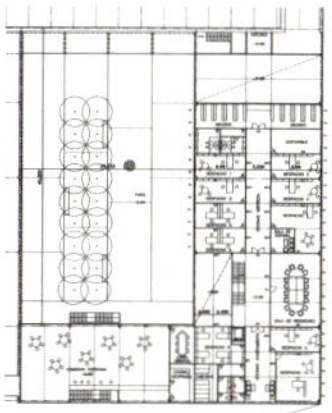

Museum +1.00

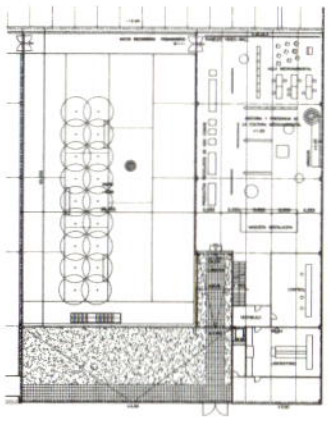

The project is located in a typical area of the middle-class suburb, in which low-density housing, voids, public facilities and small masses of pine trees intermingle giving shape to an idea of an urban life that is in contact with nature. We decided to be extremely direct and to stress this desire through the use of gardening techniques. Thus the whole house can be understood as an example of a giant ars-topiaria. This is an idea that is not alien to the fact that it will be a home for a landscape architect. The sloping topography is taken advantage of to build a house that has a continuity with the natural land, avoiding the differentiation between the house and the garden: the whole house is garden and the whole garden is house. The project is a topological mechanism for the arranging and modelling of the land to increase and to gain the maximum enjoyment from those weak stimuli of the landscape: the pine trees, the near-by stream, the setting of the sun over the skyline of Madrid from the house's highest point... Natural views and artificial views: green machine.

Ábalos & Herreros

8 *Green House*

ARCHITECTS Iñaki Ábalos, Juan Herreros and Ángel Jaramillo LOCATION Pozuelo, Madrid 1997 COLLABORATORS Mª Auxiliadora Gálvez, Carolina González Vives and Carmen Izquierdo MODEL Aurelie Beriot and Andrea Buchner STRUCTURAL ENGINEERS Juan Gómez COMPUTER GRAPHICS Gestalt QUANTITY SURVEYOR Miguel Ángel Rica

9 *Lacaton & Vassal*

House in Coutras
Houses in Mulhouse
House at Cap Ferret

AFRICA

What's striking is, once again, the common sense with which the Africans act. There's a certain context and a problem you solve without giving too much importance to how it's done. You solve it for the moment and if possible for longer, but always inventively. And in fact there's always a little, unexpected note that depends on each person's knowledge. They have an enormous capacity for organization, and a corresponding lack of bias. Everything's possible as long as it works.

LIGHTNESS

This also has to do with a certain lightness in architecture that goes against what's left of the idea of the monument, of the durable building which is there, not for a use and a given epoch, but to affirm something that's along the lines of something political or of power. We think in more lightweight terms, which doesn't mean more fragile or less solid, more in connection with the way one manufactures industrial products. When one manufactures a car, one predicts that it will have a life span of then years, let's say. The cost/usage factor is completely under control. You could reason the same way about buildings! This would make them lighter, more transformable, maybe dismountable, or even involve their disappearance. It's very interesting to work with the idea in mind that you don't build for eternity, or even for fifty years. In this way, architecture would lose its heaviness.

INNOVATION

The innovation isn't so much in the materials. The materials seen as being innovative, such as composite materials, usually come from costly and uncommon technologies. Therefore it's more the use angle we wouldn't have tought of that we look towards. The best thing is to profit from the situation.

The way how the conservatories function has nothing to do with the heating systems used by the dwelling. The main principle is, in effect, to take advantage of the outside conditions, to tame them, marshal them, transform them. It's the opposite, then, of what you do for the dwelling that's insulated and protected against the outside.

ECONOMY

Cost-effectiveness isn't the principle of less, of reduction, but that of hierarchy and the minimum. Its interest lies in the fact that it obliges you to ask yourself questions well in advance; among others, about the appropriatness of what we're being asked to do. Cost-effectiveness is above all being able to treat yourself to whatever it is you want. This means that you manage your budget to arrive at this, you don't allow yourself be taken by surprise and that way you get what you want. The fact of building inexpensively doesn't determine, and never limits, the ambitions we have as to certain essential qualities. The spaces, the sensations, the uses or the comfort. Working on cost-effectiveness helps you get there in spite of everything.

Lacaton & Vassal

9

House in Coutras

ARCHITECTS Anne Lacaton & Jean Philippe Vassal COLLABORATORS Emmanuelle Delage, Sylvain Menaud, Christophe Hutin CLIENTS Arlette Schwartz and Pierre Guinchard SURFACE 290 m² COST € 64 790 (tax excl.) BUILDING SYSTEM FILCLAIR 6,40 greenhouses: steel structure, transparent ONEX glazing PHOTOGRAPHS David Pradel

The plot of land is situated in the countryside, on the outskirts of Coutras, 50 km to the west of Bordeaux. This is an extremely long plot, having a frontage of 33 m along a local road. Part of the plot is classified as non-buildable agricultural land. The surroundings are made up of scattered dwellings, cultivated farmland with occasional thickets of trees and bushes, and conglomerations of crop-growing greenhouses. The low density of vegetation and buildings and the flatness of the land encourage a wide-angle perception of the landscape in which the sky largely dominates. In order to keep its distance from other houses and from the road, the house is set back some 30 m from the latter and on the very edge of the buildable area.

The house has only one floor, and it is made up of two juxtaposed and identical greenhouses. These are standard horticultural greenhouses, consisting of a metal framework and transparent rigid sheeting. They have the automatic features necessary for regulating their temperature, notably ventilation panels in the roof of each greenhouse, the opening of which is automated in relation to the indoor temperature. Approximately half the length of the facades can open by means of sliding doors. The rectangular plan, which runs north-south along the longer side of the plot, has two parts: the living areas – dining and family room, kitchen, bedrooms – are arranged on the west side in one of the greenhouses, and an open plan space – the winter garden – takes up the other greenhouse, on the east side. The living areas open onto both the outside and the winter garden. Outside, the house will be supplemented by the planting of different fruit trees, forming an orchard.

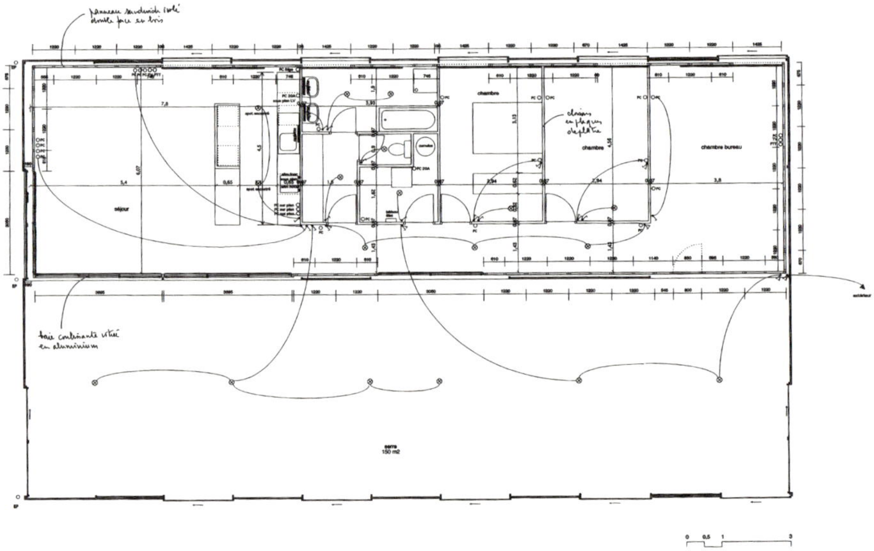

panneau sandwich isolé double face en bois
chambre
cloisons en plaques de plâtre
chambre
chambre bureau
séjour
baie coulissante vitrée en aluminium
serre
150 m2
0 0,5 1 3

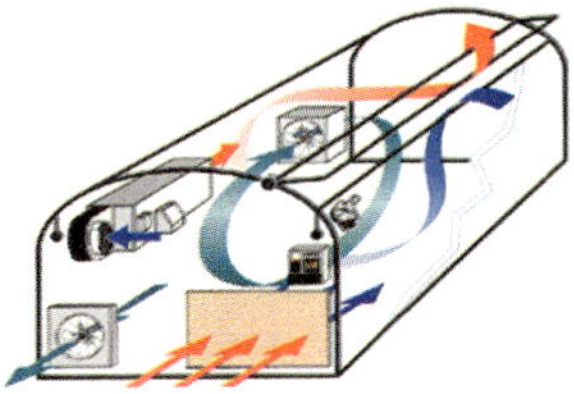

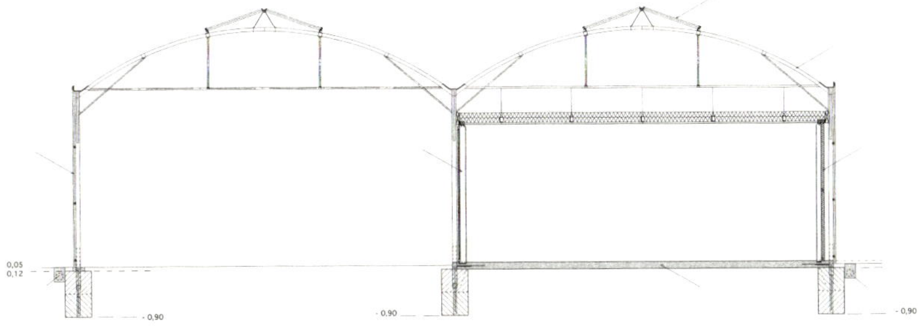
0,05
0,12
- 0,90
- 0,90
- 0,90

Lacaton & Vassal

9 Houses in Mulhouse

ARCHITECTS Anne Lacaton & Jean Philippe Vassal, con David Pradel LOCATION Ilôt Schoettle, Mulhouse PROJECT 2002 EXECUTION 2003 CLIENT SOMCO, Mulhouse ENGINEERING Loeb Ingénierie SA (cimentación, estructura), Inotec (servicios, electricidad, calefacción), Espace Economie (economía construcción)

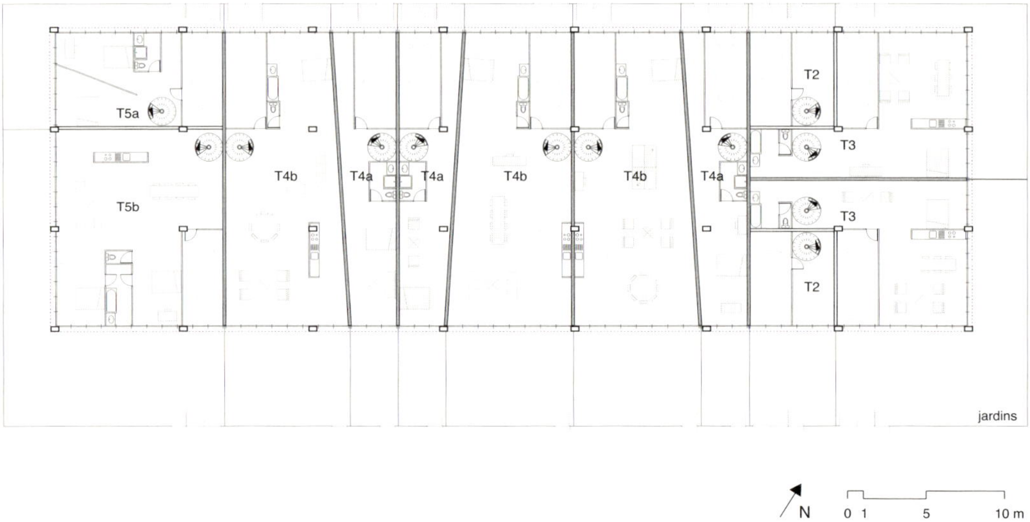

This project for twelve individual houses is part of an operation for 60 dwellings planned within the prolongation of the Cité Ouvrière in Mulhouse on the site of the former spinning-mills.
Public housing projects usually have to do with an imbrication constrained by a rigid framework of minimum surfaces and comfort, and they perpetuate a classic and traditional housing model. Our objective, within the framework of this operation, is to produce quality houses that are, for the same price, significantly larger than the usual dwellings.
The experience of the private houses we've done, the observation of such performative buildings as agricultural, industrial and commercial structures, and the way lofts work all convince us that it's possible to build bigger, more open, freer, more light-filled, more comfortable, cheaper.
The ground floor consists of a structure in reinforced concrete: posts-beams-flooring. The ceiling height is important: more than 3 meters. The facades are largely glazed and opening. On this base a greenhouse is set up of the professional, horticultural kind. The framework is in galvanized steel, the walls are of transparent polycarbonate. Part of the greenhouse is insulated and heated. The other part, left as it is, forms a winter garden. The intermediary interior facades open onto the winter garden through large glazed bays. The greenhouse is ventilated by the large roof openings and by sliding facade panels that have a 50% opening capacity.
A horizontal sunshade is arranged inside the greenhouse. The dwellings are set crosswise. Each dwelling is on two levels with a surface area that is unequal, be this mainly on the ground floor or mainly on the first. The living rooms have a linear surface area of at least 8 meters on a well-oriented facade.

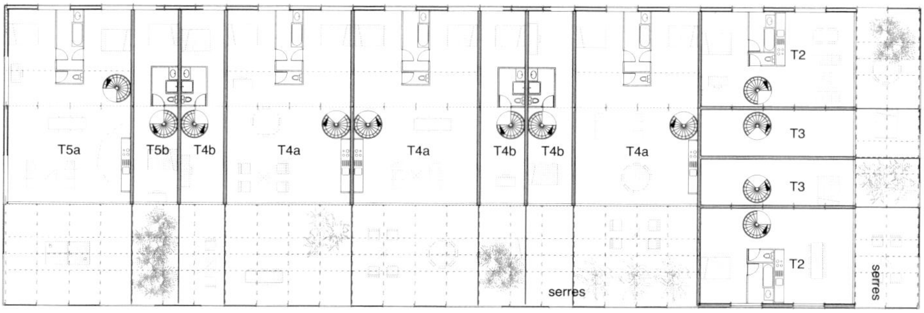

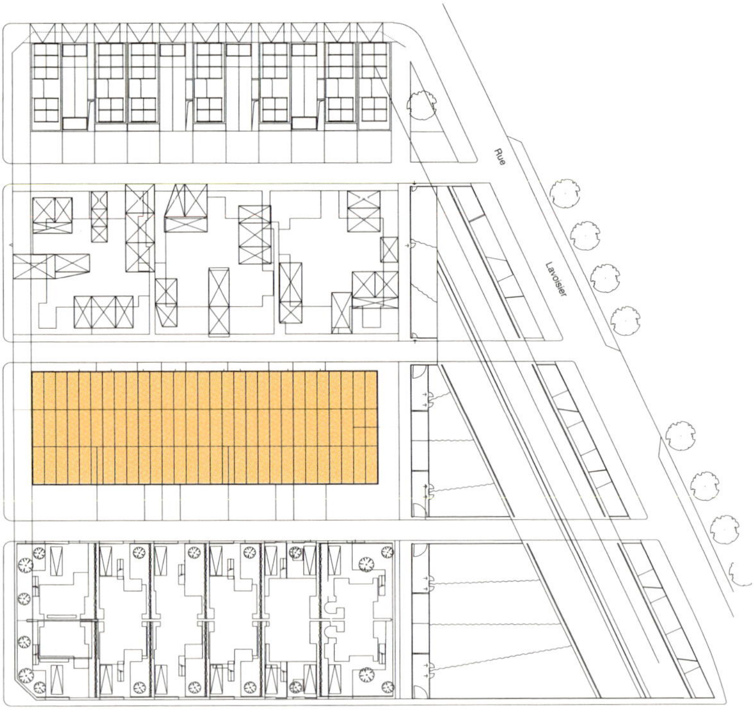

Section

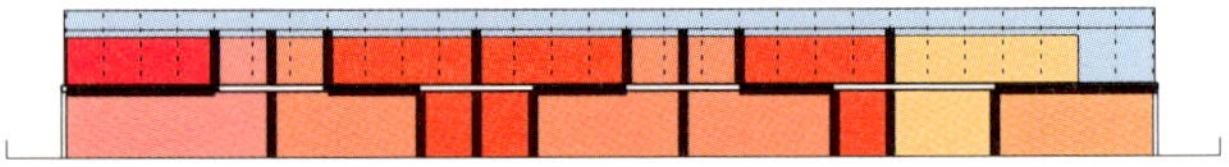

1st floor

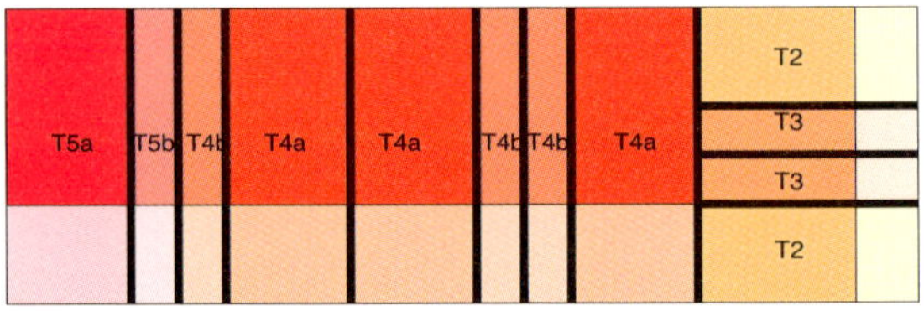

Ground

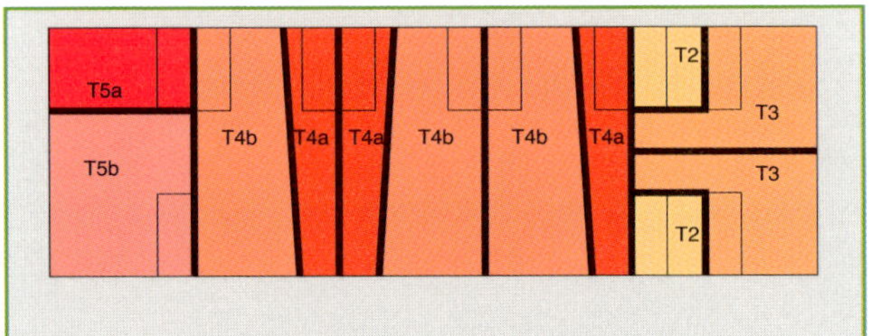

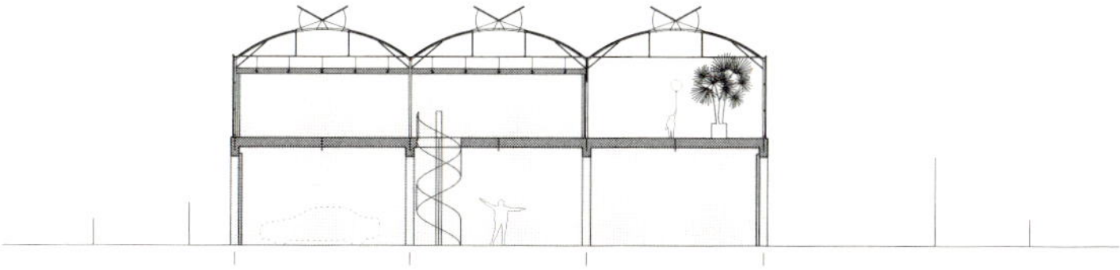

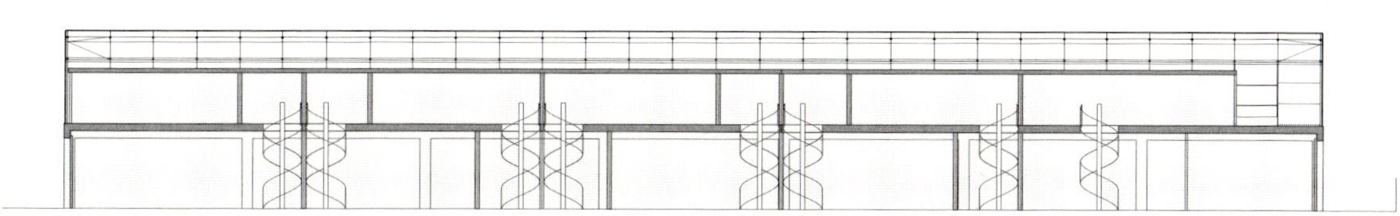

The house is located on a paradisiacal site, Bassin d'Arcachon close to Atlantic Ocean, west from Bordeaux. The area has a magnificent view on the Bassin d'Arcachon. It was never built. Fifty pine trees (30 m high) has grown on the ground, a sand dune which crest is 15 m higher than the water.
According to the wish of the clients, the problem was to build a house on this place without damaging the site and its qualities. The project keeps the density of the forest –no tree was cut– and doesn't change the undulating shape of the ground. The house is a 210 m² platform on a single level, built on piles between 2 m and 4 m high –depending on the slope of the ground–, which allows to pass under the house and to have the best view of the landscape from inside the house. The frame is in steel. Façades are in corrugated aluminium with some opening panels in transparent corrugated plastic sheets. The under face of the floor is in the same corrugated aluminium. It reflects the light coming from the reflection on the water down the dune. The front façade towards the Bassin d'Arcachon is completely transparent, in glass sliding doors. Six trees go through the house. On the roof, transparent plane plastic sheets are tightened to the trunks with flexible rubber. They can glide on the edges of holes in the roof when the trees are moving with the wind.

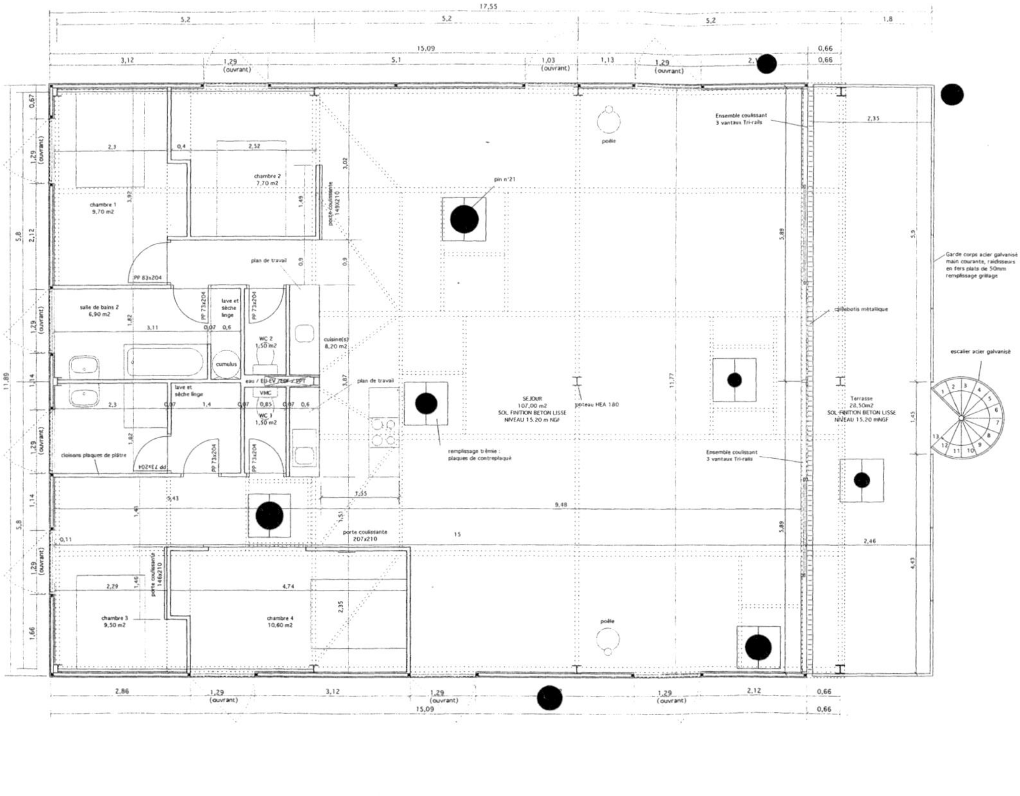

Lacaton & Vassal

9

House at Cap Ferret

ARCHITECTS Anne Lacaton, Jean-Philippe Vassal SITE Lege Cap Ferret, Bordeaux (France) PROJECT 1997 EXECUTION 1998 COLLABORATORS Sylvain Menaud, Laurie Baggett, Pierre Yves Portier, Christophe Hutin; CESMA (Structure), INGEROP SUD-OUEST (Foundations) INRA, CAUE 33 (Consultants) CONSTRUCTION Entreprise DEGAS PHOTOGRAPHS Ramon Prat

Productive logic would work with composite construction materials and techniques; that is to say, with catalogues of prefabricated components.

Interactive Logic

Duncan Lewis

10

Ouest School, Obernai
Sant Quirze Safaja Civic Centre
Kvernhuset Ungdomsskole School

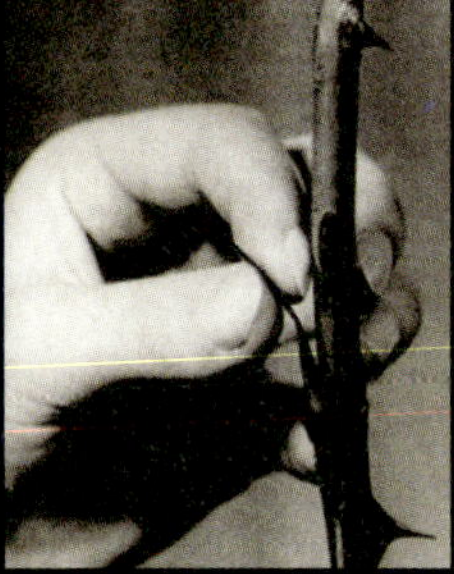
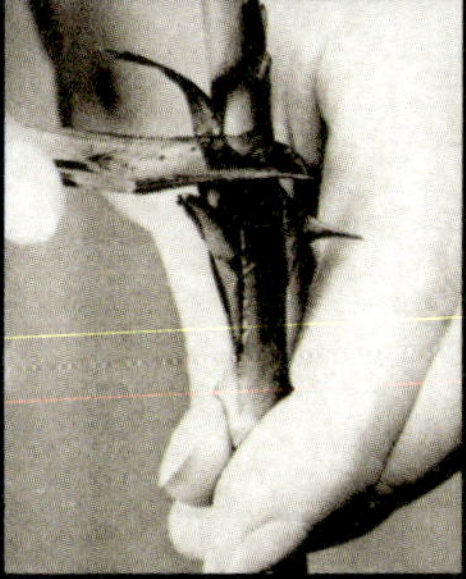
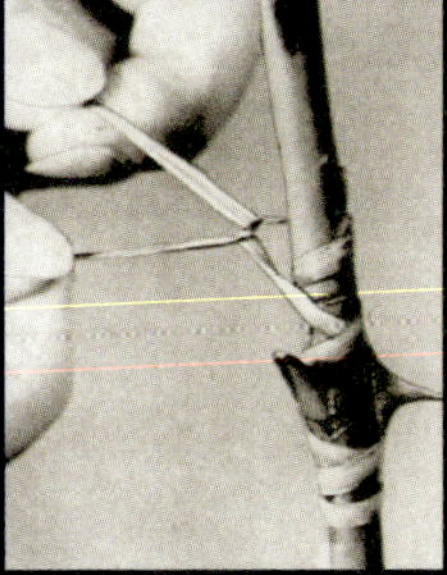
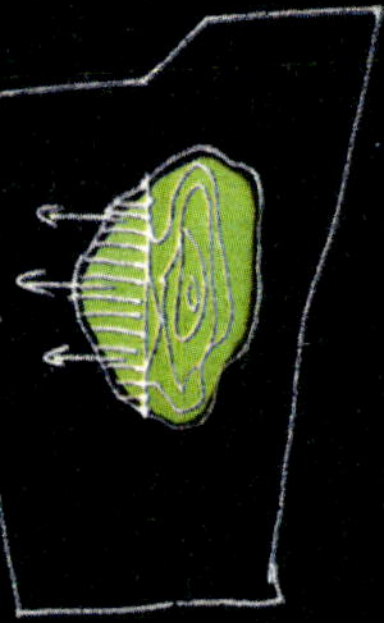
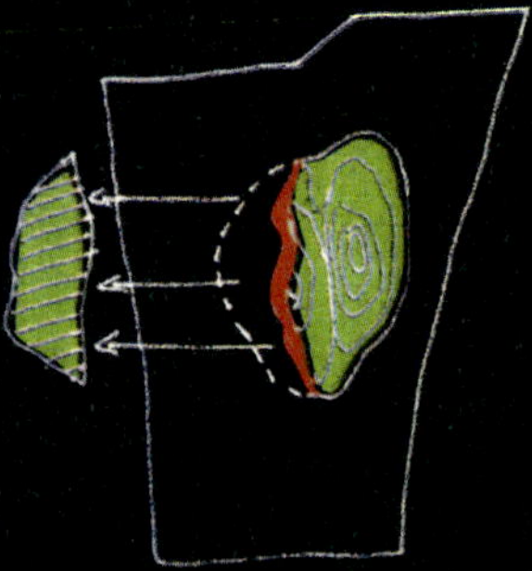
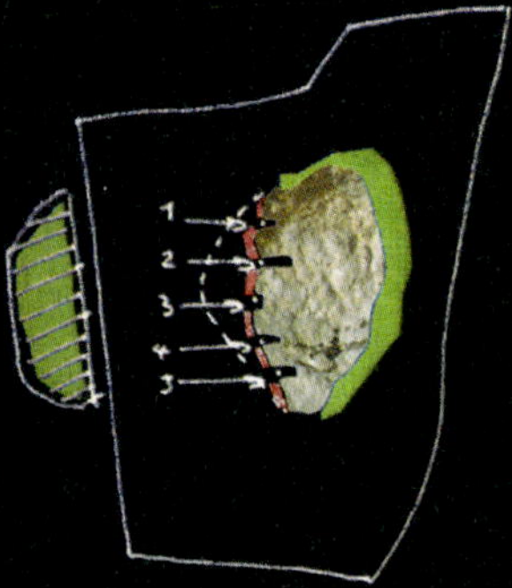
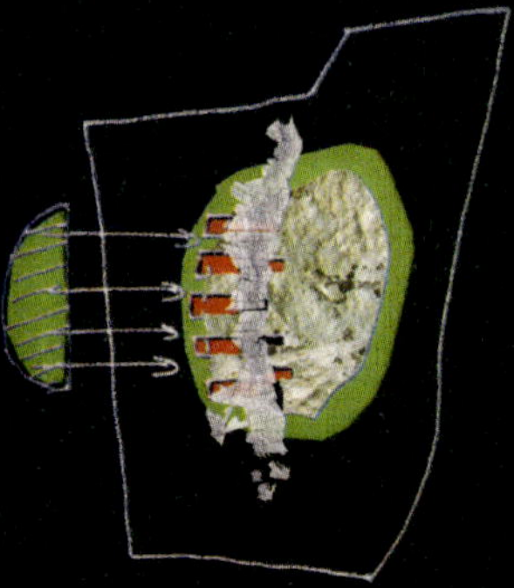
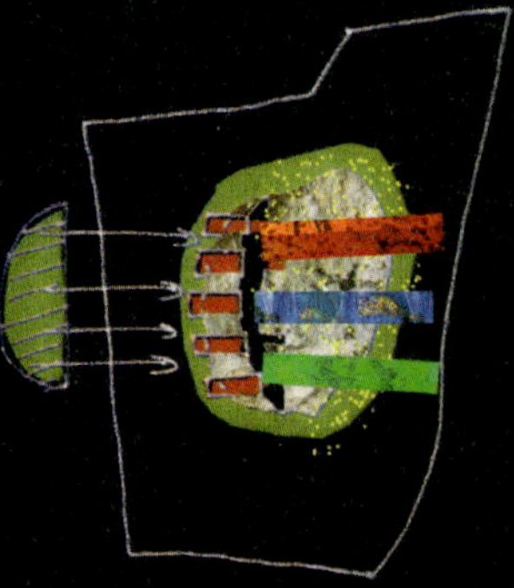
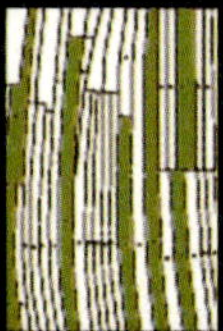
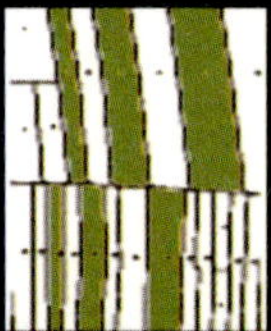
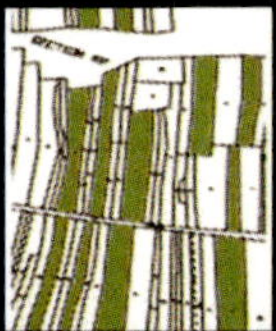

Man and his context

Like landscape, architecture consists of layers, strata, skins, to which memory must be welded. Finding this memory again and the geological faults that feed it, lead the architect to conceive of each building within an unfolding movement of fluidity, interrupted between its attachment to a specific place and its constructive reality. The projects deal with the oscillation between what is natural and what is constructed, through a permanent exchange of matter and form; neither of them is ever above the other. One cannot talk about a camouflage of architecture by nature or landscape, nor of an instrumentalisation of nature by architecture. One of our privileged tools is the aerial photograph. This enlarges very precise, intimate elements moulded on the terrain. Aerial photos allow one to define the context of the project, the existing strata, the predominant urban or landscape forms. The approximation to the place is that of a scientist and magician. The project is developed like in alchemy, with the raw materials that arrive at the office. This always relates to a way to and from nature and architecture, the context is recovered like a raw material which will be transformed later, mixed with something else (concrete, mesh, air, glass, etc.). The mimicry is not direct, it is not integration for integration's sake, it is a play on the difference between what is true and what is false; it is artifice.

The foliage gives rhythm to the project not only in the elevation drawing but also in how the project is experienced. When we go camping, under the fine skin of our tent, we can hear the rain and the wind. It is the "natural" world's way that we are interested in recreating in our projects.

Modernity has taken man out of his environmental culture. Therefore, it is necessary, especially through architecture, to re-establish a relationship between man and his context. This bond is a way of thinking, a state of mind.

Duncan Lewis

10 Ouest School, Obernai

ARCHITECTS Duncan LEWIS, Scape architecture in association with Klein & Baumann TEAM Duncan Lewis, Benjamin Jacquemet, Hervé Potin, Marc Sittig, Tanguy Vermet, Manal Rachdi Arthur Couprie, Annonciade Perron and Stéphanie Laurent (landscape architect) COMPETITION 2001 (winning entry) CLIENT Commune d'Obernai CONTRACTORS BET STRUCTURE ICAT/ BET BUILT SURFACE 2944 m² COST 4.3 M € (including development of surroundings)

The idea is to produce a project in harmony with its characteristic landscape, setting it into the wood to form part of the context and make the project 'porous' to the landscape. Our aim is to integrate the site into the strip system, emblematic of the Alsace landscape, and harmonize the latter with the project for the school. We therefore lay landscaped strips over the site; the existing stands of trees delimit the implantation of the project within the succession of planted and built strips. The strips break down into different types: exterior plots of different coloured landscaped patches; low thick topiaries; fences of trees to pick up the existing conditions of the site; creeping plants on the building façades; mineral paving strips.
The topography of the site is used to arrange the volumes in the north-south direction of the landscaped strips. Each element in the school acts as a fragment of the context: the single-storey built volumes (extracurricular and nursery spaces) alternate façades covered by plants with mineral façades of AGP formliners. The motifs imitate rock and aid absorption and anchorage of the soil. The upper volume (primary school spaces) accompanies the rhythm of the surrounding foliage in order to merge into the landscape. Its façades materialize the landscaped strips, with panels of creeping plants. This type of façade plays a natural climatic role in the buildings, marking the changing seasons: the deciduous foliage of the topiaries, fences and creepers filters the sunlight in summer and its absence during winter months allows daylight to flood in.
This interplay of light is matched by the play of colours: the leaves of certain plants (deep red vine leaves, peach trees, etc.) will bathe the school spaces with dappled colours, giving the spaces an emotive charge and offering teachers and pupils pedagogical material.

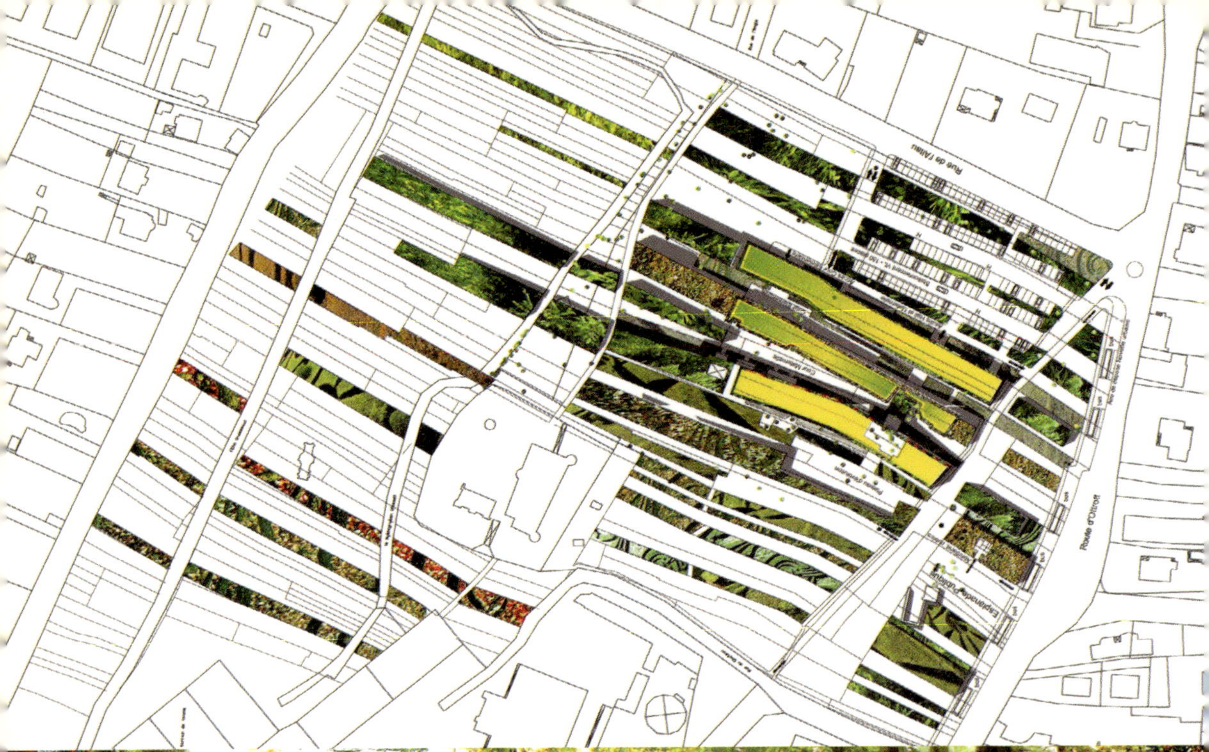
Rue de l'Altau
Route d'Ottrott
Esplanade publique

Duncan Lewis

10 **_Sant Quirze Safaja Civic Centre_**

ARCHITECTS Lewis & Potin (Duncan Lewis & Hervé Potin) PROJECT TEAM A. F. Guinée, R. Boulay, B. Aubry LOCATION Sant Quirze Safaja PROJECT 1999 INTERNATIONAL COMPETITION Second prize

The programme consists of converting the Sant Quirze Safaja sports hall into a multipurpose sports centre with assembly hall for the Mayor's offices, library and gymnasium. The existing building is an agricultural pavilion containing a sports court. It is located in the valley of Sant Quirze, a medieval village forty kilometres from Barcelona.

The project consists of wrapping the building in a green skin, using the palisade wall technique. A number of trays secured to the internal wall of sports hall are the supports of a number of plants the main stem of which will go through the wall and coil round the building. This epidermis possesses, therefore, a dual function, spatial and technique, which allows an increase in the thermal inertia of the building, cooling it in summer. A metal mesh, like the one used in construction will spread the earth over the building and guide the vegetation. The metal cladding on the sliding doors is modified with a tree-like structure that is applied to and engraved on these doors.

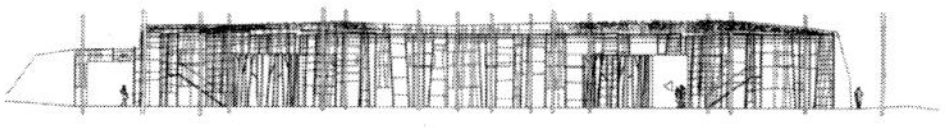

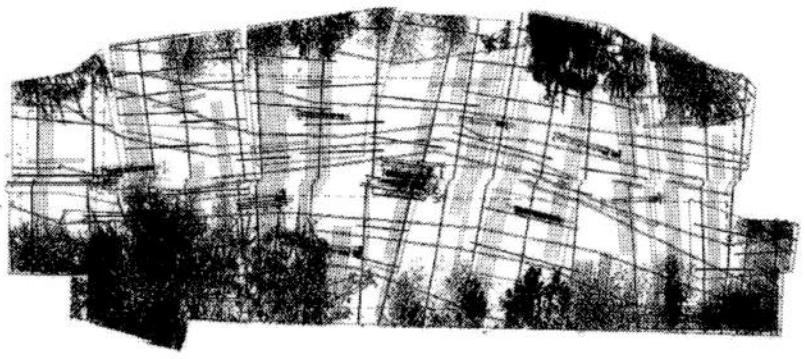

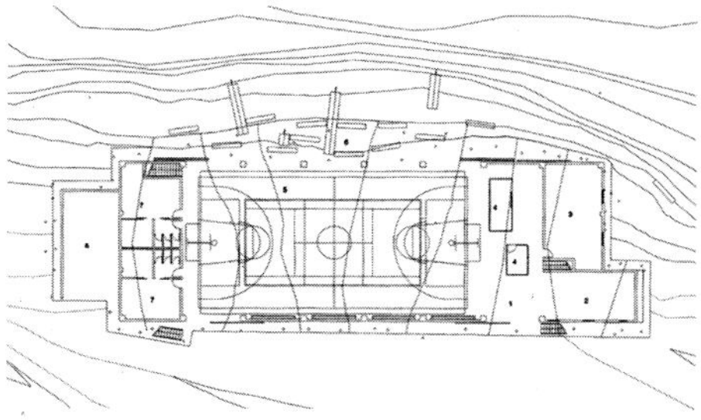

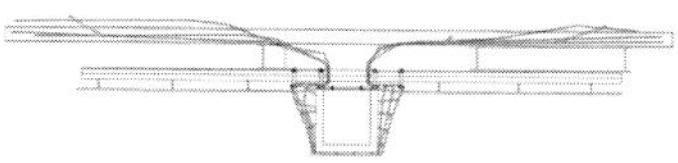

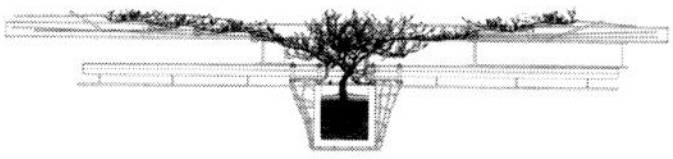

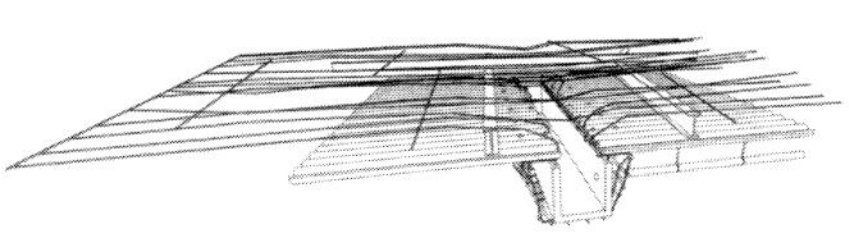

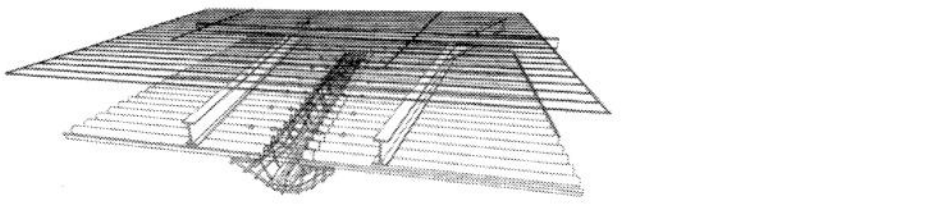

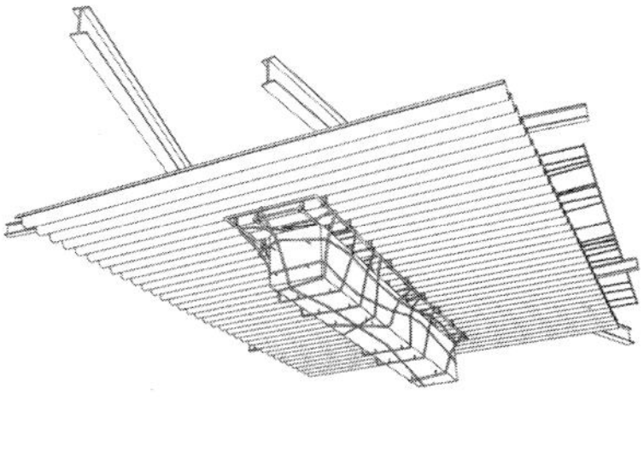

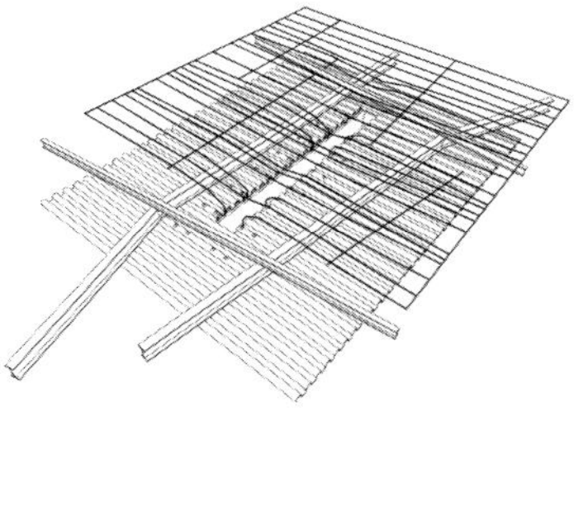

Duncan Lewis

10 Kvernhuset Ungdomsskole School

ARCHITECTURAL OFFICE Association Duncan Lewis & Pirll Arkitektkontor AS (Trondheim, Norway) PROJECT Duncan Lewis, Mette Melandso, Ogmund Sorli PROJECT TEAM Y. Bohuon, D. Brillet, A.F Guinée, S. Jorum, M. Kilinc, O. Kristoffersen, S. Lagré, C. Lancelin, H. Potin COLLABORATORS B. Aubry, R. Boulay, E. Egeland, J. Meyrault, G.Ustad LOCATION Trondheim, Norway DEVELOPMENT OF THE FAÇADES, THERMO-MOLDED TREE Dominique Lamandé, artist LANDSCAPE ARCHITECTURE Per André Hansen (1st stage), Ostengen & Bergo AS (2nd stage) 8500 m^2 - 140 MF (included landscape planning) MODEL Thierry Maitre COMPETITION 1998 (winning entry) STUDY 1999 EXECUTION 2000-2002 CLIENT Fredrikstad Kommune (Municipality of Fredrikstad) STRUCTURE Reinertsen engineering VENTILATION Dagfinn H. Jorgensen A.S. ELECTRICITY Sivilingenior BV. Olkesjo PHOTOGRAPHS Philippe Ruault

The preparation of the site to accommodate the ground level of the college will produce a semi-artificial landscape that will, however, link up closely to its natural environment. We want to reflect here on the question of overcoming the accepted conceptions which may have characterised action on the landscape, based on the hierarchical tradition of the figure/ground opposition, and of substituting this with new interpretations which are open to a fusion of outlines, a dissolution of border-lines. It's possible for the architectural project to blur its outlines into new geographies of transition. Artificial topographies on host landscapes.
Under the forest canopy three simple volumes are placed between the trees.
These three "home bases," identifiable by their colour green, red or blue, are where the classes of the three most important subjects taught at the college are to be found: science, technics and the environment. The "home bases" act as a fragment of the site which absorbs the rhythm of the tree trunks in the forest. Their coloured facades materialise the shadows of the trees, which fall onto the facades, blurring the limits between what is real and what is imaginary.
The inner limits of the building, considered not as a corridor space but as a real working area, combine with the classrooms. Breaking down the barriers and relationships between interior and exterior is to be considered the main aim of the architectural project. Kvernhuset Ungdomsskole College propounds a new teaching method and the building is looked upon as a real, living support to the students' life.

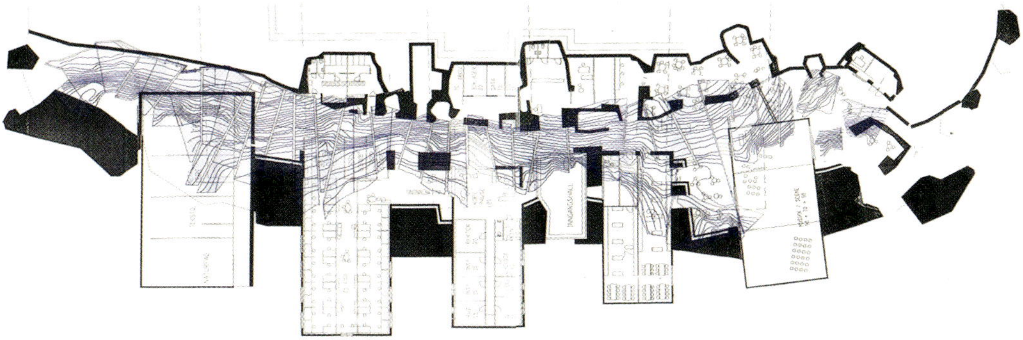

2

R&Sie François Roche

11

IUAV
Barak House
Office Building

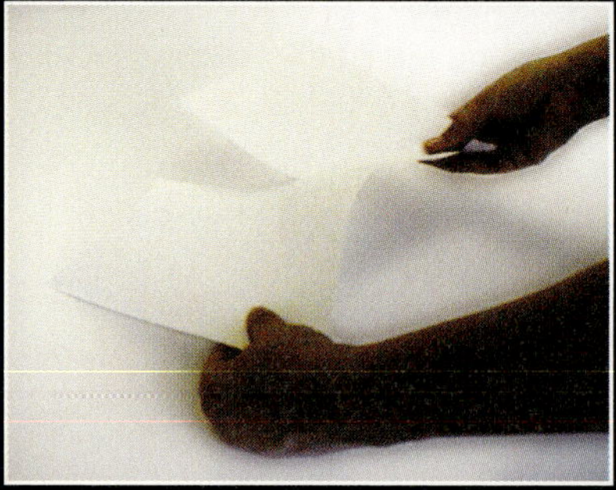

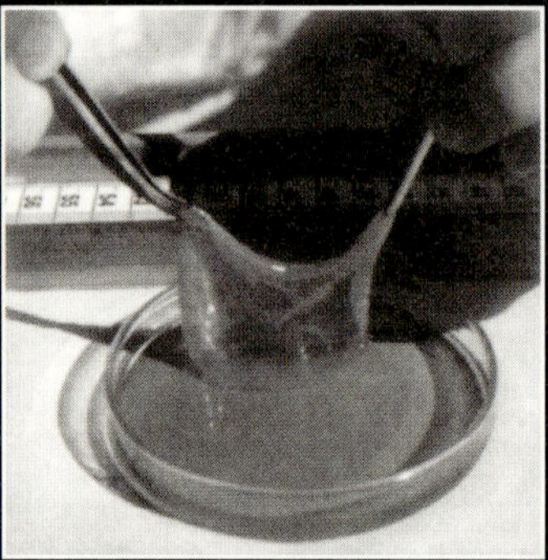

Making do with less

The processes of distortion, originating from morphing and presented here by serial tapes (or elsewhere on videotapes), stem from this dearth and open up a field of new possibilities. Over and above a fascination with the technological instrument and with the contrived metamorphosis it creates, we are exercised by its revelatory operational function. The more deceptive the morphed movement appears, the more inert its transformation, the more the urban and architectural project seems to be dominated by the prior situation. The more the morphing can be read in its artifice, the more the projection seems, this time around, to be deterritorialised.

Unlike an instrument of representation, morphing thus reveals the degree to which the hypotheses are decontextualised, and in an ongoing flux between deduction and induction, a re-reading of the successive phases will validate or invalidate the relevance of the choices, in a making do with less strategy. Like a chemist having to reproduce the experiment to read it again and understand it, this empirical and random process is built on reaction and folding on the support. The skin of the photographic, cartographic image is transformed and metamorphosed in one and the same shell. In one and the same matter, it undergoes manipulations akin to folding, extrusion and scarification. –

The pixels, fractal fragments of the real, are put back together again in a series of genetic mutations. These grafted manipulations, like images of subcutaneous piercing, operate on several registers, several identifications. It is a process of degeneration, a topological cyst, a code of tribal recognition, an exacerbation of hyperlocalism where the city is assimilated to an organism–the context, here, is not idealised or conceptualised, but a substrate of its own mutation. Paradoxically, the virtual instrument thus becomes a principle of reality, and architecture escapes from abstracted projections to be assimilated in a distortion of reality in situ.

GLAUCOUS, adj. (lat. glaucus, gr. glaukos)

1 Of a bluish green color: a glaucous sea.

2 Fam. Lusterless, murky, livid, that which gives a feeling of sadness: glaucous water, light (syn. Lugubrious, sinister).

This project is about processes of de-sedimentation, hybridization: at once cloned on the envelope of former industrial buildings (refrigeration and warehousing) but also full of corporeality, of this city's raw materials, of water and algae. Their omnipresence (even though here they're linked to pollution), their undulating movement, their matter and color, from chlorophyll green to their greenish-brown decomposition, are therefore both the referential as well as the generic support. The functions unfold, then, in many intersecting threads, like the trailing tentacles of a jellyfish in PVC, with a murky, thick transparence.

SUCTION

The visible movement in the topography of the project is the outcome of a numerical process of suction. This modification of the surface of the water has been simulated (on Silicon Graphic and Soft Image) in the preexisting volumetric envelope of the Concrete Building. Islots of resistance in these undulating movements have created the volumes needed for the public places (amphitheater, restaurant, reception) in a topological contradiction at once elastic and liquid, yet incapable of spreading.

SCENARIO

1 Destruction of the concrete warehouses

2 Projection in plan of the building's functional strata (Bookshop, Restaurant, Teaching, Amphitheaters, Auditorium)

3 Numerical suction of the water according to these strata

4 Re-readings of these acts of suction by integrating aleatory parameters therein

5 Creation of areas of resistance to the suction (public places)

6 Immobilization of the suction on the preexisting envelope of the warehouses

7 Constituting of the outer skin, a PVC membrane

8 Water vapor and plant growth.

R&Sie... François Roche

11 *Università IUAV di Venezia*

ARCHITECT R&Sie... Paris (name of the agency at that time: Roche, DSV & Sie) CREATIVE TEAM AND ASSOCIATES PARTNER François Roche, Stephanie Lavaux, François Perrin, Ammar Eloueini LOCATION Venice, Italy PROJECT 1998 CLIENT International Competition, City of Venice COLLABORATORS Martial Vieille, David Topanni SURFACE AREA 4100 m²

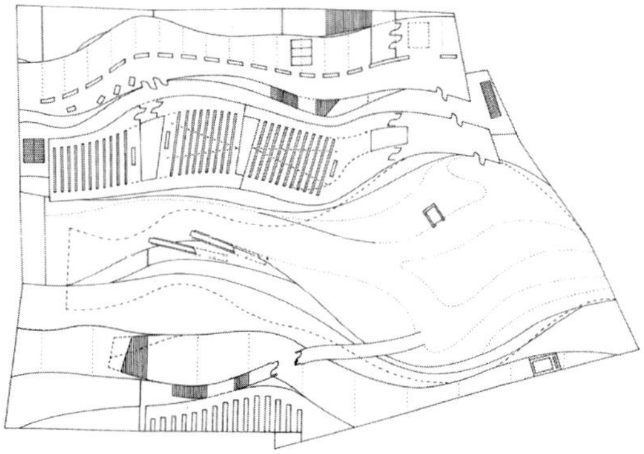

Level 1

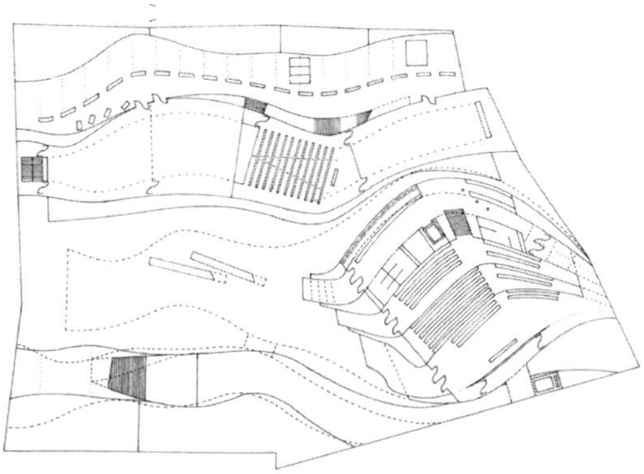

Level 2

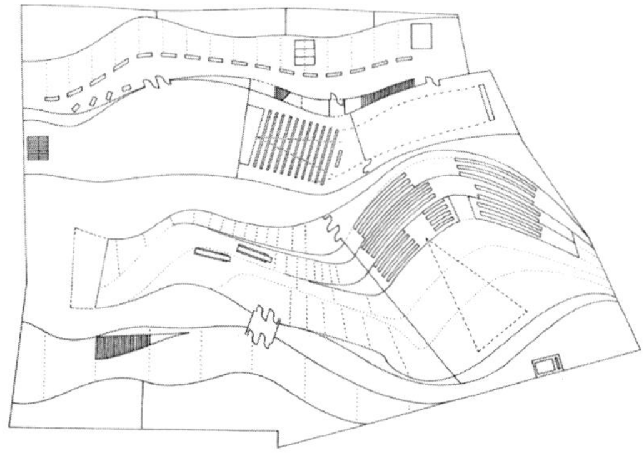

Level 3

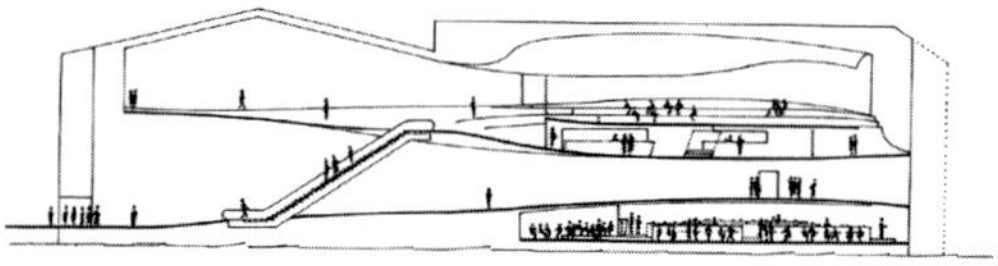

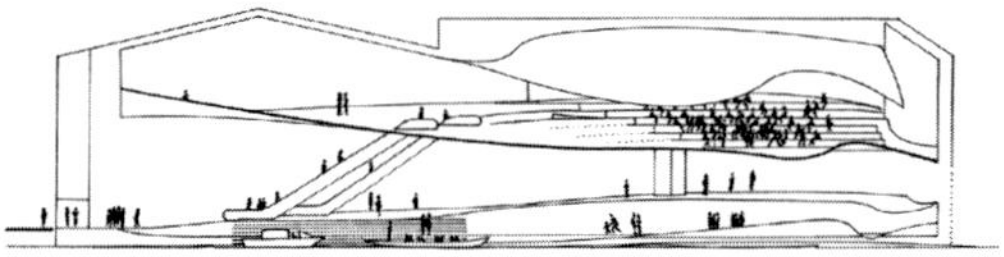

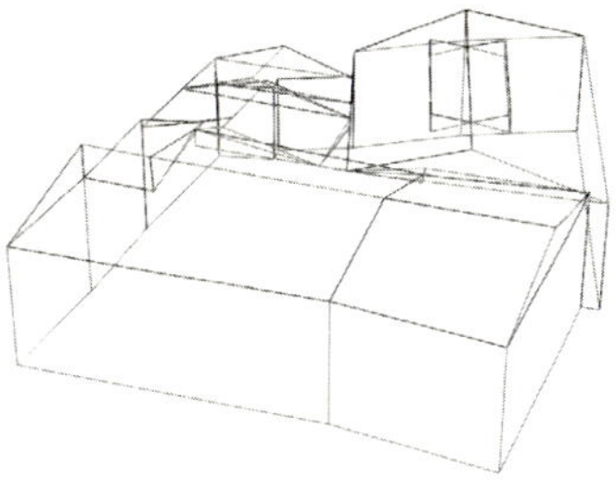

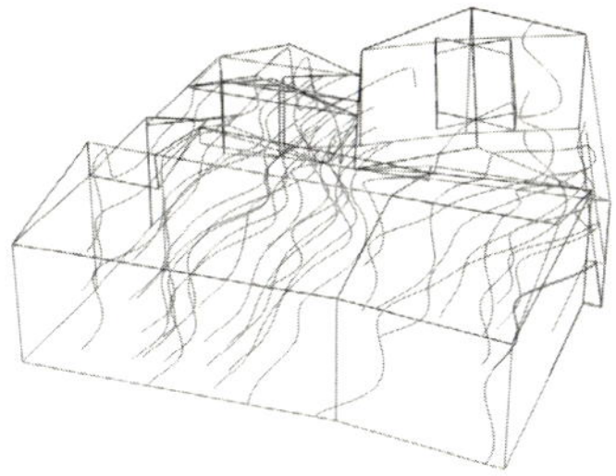

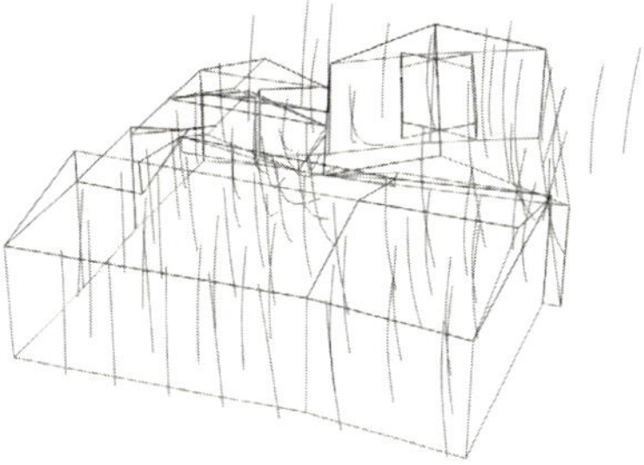

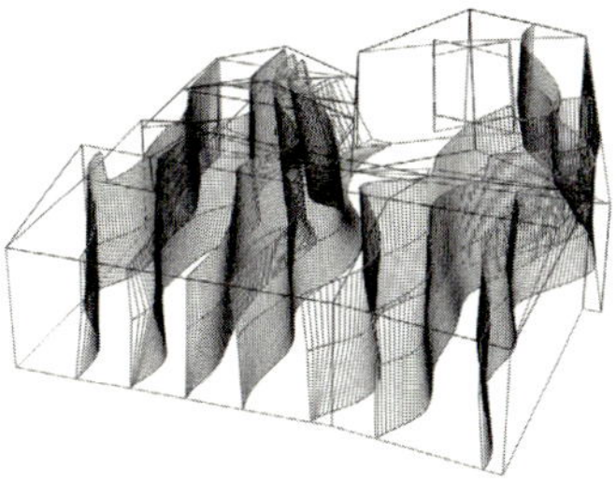

R&Sie... François Roche

11 **Barak House**

ARCHITECT R&Sie... Paris CREATIVE TEAM AND ASSOCIATES PARTNER François Roche, Stephanie Lavaux, Alexandre Boulin, Olivier Legrand LOCATION Sommières, France PROJECT 2001 ENGINEERING Abaca Ingenierie CONTRACTOR Christian Hubert de Lisle SURFACE AREA 160 m² CLIENT Ami & Judith Barak

CONSTRAINTS

- Terrain under architectural and urban heritage protection (medieval chateau nearby)
- Terrain of 1500 m^2 with obligation to build in its center (distance to boundaries of the property) on slope with height difference of 4.5m (drystone wall of olive-tree cultivation)
- Climate control (countryside near Nîmes, particularly hot in summer)
- Difficult accessibility of the terrain

BUILDING SYSTEM

- Traditional construction (breeze blocks and hollow brickwork) for the interior skeleton with small local businesses.
- Specific construction for the plastic envelope made with a specialist in the production of works of art (expense and ingenuity). This sheeting is made of Emis plastic netting (meant for agricultural greenhouses in hot countries) on braced metal frames with the mass of the superstructures in PVC.
- Heating by surface geothermics (buried pipework) as the objective exploitation of the terrain.

SCENARIO

- a geography that unfolds and is broken up by the topographic fracturing of the terrain
- a climatic tent that alternates closed space and areas beneath netting
- a principle of furtiveness vis-à-vis the Château de Sommières
- a house for a family of four
- a ground-cover vegetation continuous with the sheeting

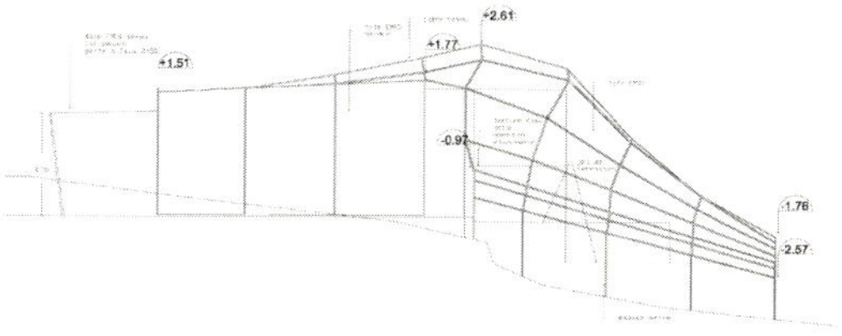
+1.51
+2.61
+1.77
-0.97
-1.76
-2.57

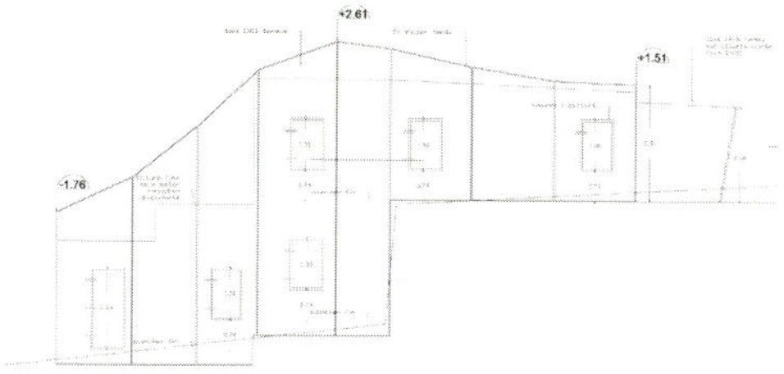
+2.61
+1.51
-1.76

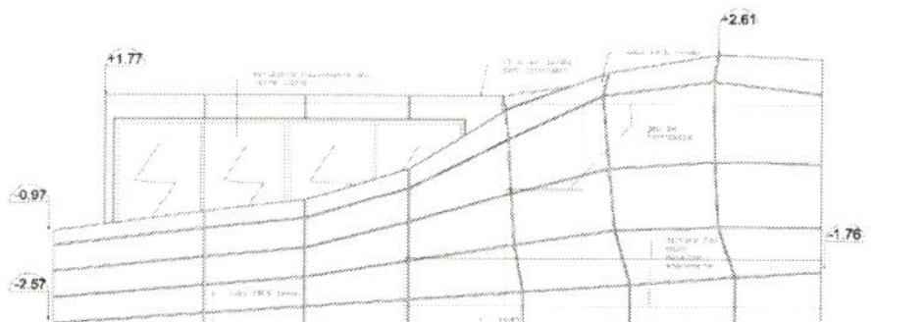
+1.77
+2.61
-0.97
-2.57
-1.76

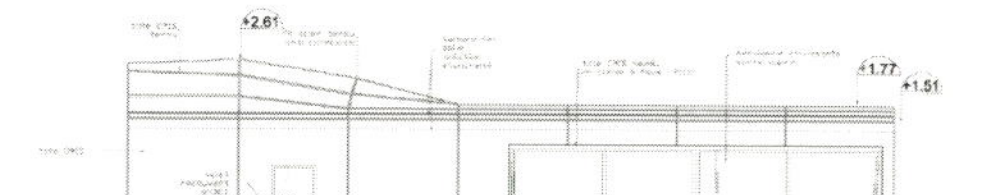
+2.61
+1.77
+1.51

This project proposes a "concept building", similar to the "concept car" designed by the auto industry, with a reactive facade able to respond to contact with renewable energy. The hairiness (thermal sensor) and swollenness (photoelectric cells) of the facade-curtains are productive membranes. The architecture becomes both a consumer and a producer of energy that can be re-injected back into the network.
This project proceeds from mutation, i.e. the transformation of a generic office building with new energy parameters (vacuum-sealed-tube solar panels and photovoltaic cells). The facade is thus reactive to this new energy input.

SCENARIO

1) Construction of a standard office building.
2) Deformation of the reactive facade to gather renewable energies:
   - "hairy" facade for thermal sensors (5 km)
   - swollen glass skin for photoelectric cells (2000 m^2).
3) Disconnection ("unplugging") of the building from the city power grid.

R&Sie... François Roche

11 *Edificio de oficinas en La Défense*

ARCHITECTS R&Sie... Paris (name of the agency at that time: R&Sie. D/B:L) CREATIVE TEAM François Roche, Stéphanie Lavaux, Alexandre Boulin, Olivier Legrand, Gilles Desevedavy; assisted by Benoît Durandin, Étienne Feher, David Topanni LOCATION Paris PROJECT 2001 CLIENT EDF SURFACE AREA 10,000 m^2

Euskalduna Conference Center and Concert Hall, Bilbao, 2000

Federico Soriano (S&Aa) 12

Six chimneys
Fleta Theatre
Museum in Bolzano

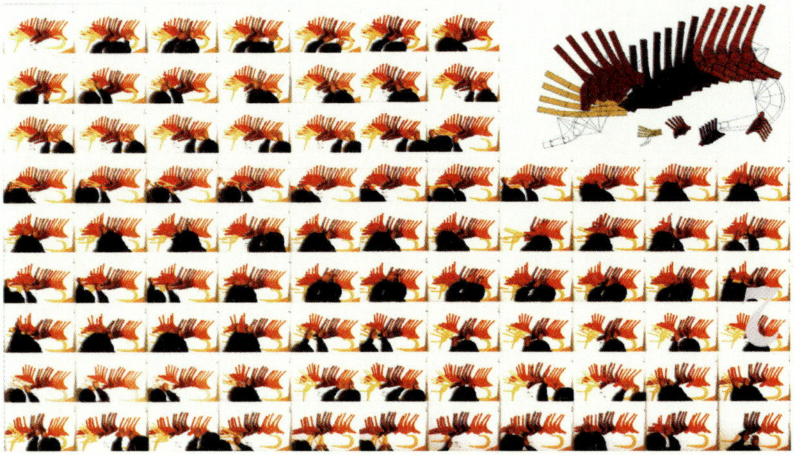

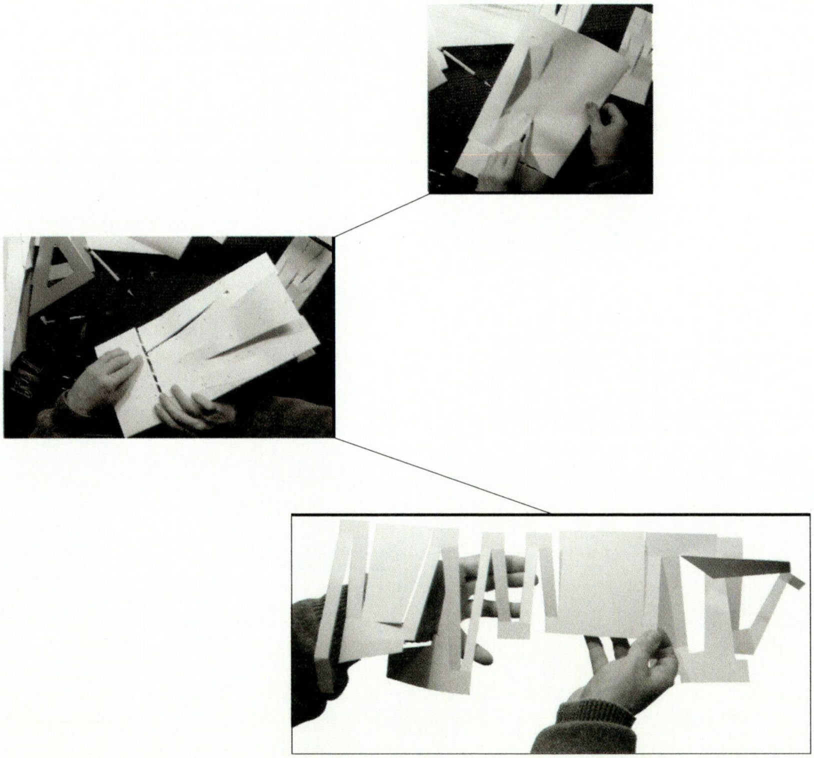

La bonita pelirroja

AQUI estoy ante todos como un hombre en todo su juicio
Que conoce la vida y de la muerte cuanto un vivo puede conocer
Experimentado en los dolores y las alegrías del amor
Que ha sabido a veces imponer sus ideas
Conocedor de varias lenguas
Que ha viajado no poco
Y ha visto la guerra en Artillería y en Infantería
Herido en la cabeza trepanado bajo cloroformo
Que ha perdido a sus mejores amigos en la pavorosa lucha
Yo sé sobre lo antiguo y lo nuevo cuanto un único hombre podría de ambos saber
Y sin que esta guerra me inquiete hoy
Entre nosotros y para nosotros amigos míos
Yo juzgo esta antigua querella entre tradición e invención
Entre el Orden y la Aventura
Vosotros cuya boca está hecha a imagen de la de Dios
Boca que es propiamente el orden
Sed indulgentes al compararnos
Con quienes fueron la perfección del orden
Nosotros que por doquier la aventura buscamos

No somos nosotros enemigos vuestros
Queremos ofreceros amplios y extraños parajes
En los que el misterios en flor se entrega a quien quiere cogerlo
Hay en ellos fuegos nuevos colores nunca vistos
Mil quimeras imponderables
Que es preciso realizar
Queremos explorar la bondad región enorme en la que todo enmudece
También está el tiempo que se puede disipar o restaurar
Apiadaos de nosotros que combatimos siempre en las fronteras
De lo ilimitado y de lo venidero
Piedad para nuestros errores piedad para nuestros pecados

Aquí está llegando el verano la violenta estación
Y mi juventud ha muerto como la primavera
Oh Sol es la hora de la ardiente Razón
Y yo espero
Para enseguida siempre la forma noble y dulce
Que para que a ella sola ame reviste
Llega y me atrae como a un hierro el imán
Tiene el aspecto encantador
De una adorable pelirroja

Diríase que sus cabellos de oro son
Un bello y duradero relámpago
O el pavoneo de esas llamas
En las rosas de té que se marchitan

Pero reid reid de mí
Hombres de todas partes sobre todo gentes de aquí
Pues hay tantas cosas que no me atrevo a deciros
Tantas cosas que no me dejaríais decir
[...]

Poema

Reúno estas palabras para cuatro personas,
alguien más puede cazarlas al vuelo,
oh mundo, lo siento por ti,
no conoces a esas cuatro personas

¡Adelante!

Si no supiéramos lo que es
y lo que no es; si sólo
atendiéramos a ciertos motivos
y ciertos colores; si las raíces del existir
se encontraran en
otra vida; si la esperanza fuera
poca y mal dibujada y si
la palabra no fuera un acto,
tampoco estas líneas
serían un poema.

Encontré sólo telarañas

Encontré sólo telarañas. Viejos valses caídos en los rincones. Encontré sonrisas: de debutante, de condesas arruinadas, de cazadores de dotes. También la sonrisa del Rey, feliz por el regreso de su hijo. Las Damas de la Caridad se dedicaban a enjaular ruiseñores, para que dejaran de cantar, y una muerte lenta, y así hacerse collares con sus pequeños huesos brillantes.

Si me dejas solo

Si me dejas solo
Y te encierras en la vieja ilusión
Entonando la misma canción
Que cantaban los dueños de todo

Si me dejas solo
Y te vas por la senda marcada
Con palabras que ya no dicen nada
Sonriendo a quien tiene el poder

Que el demonio te lleve
Al infierno que tú has elegido
Porque tú me condenas a tu olvido
Te condeno yo a mi soledad

Cuando miro tus ojos
Voy buscando la luz de tu mirada
Y sólo encuentro la imagen reflejada
Del espanto que siento yo

Ya no estás a mi lado
En la lucha diaria por la vida
Y ahora somos dos balas perdidas
En la misma estupefacción

Que el demonio te lleve
Al infierno que tú has elegido
Porque tú me condenas a tu olvido
Te condeno yo a mi soledad

Dices que tu vida es sólo para ti
Pero te llevas mi alma contigo
Dices que no tienes nada que perder
Entonces, di por qué te dejas hacer

Muestrame tu cara pálida y azul
Tu sabes bien lo que te cierra el camino
Vuélvete a por ellos y empieza a luchar
Da lo que tienes que dar

Si no apuestas conmigo
Y abandonas el juego en otras manos
Si escondes las cartas a tu hermano
Dime en quién podrás confiar
Si me dejas fuera
Y le das a tu llave otra vuelta
Yo me quedo plantado a tu puerta
Porque no sé silbar con los dedos

Que el demonio te lleve
Al infierno que tú has elegido
Porque tú me condenas a tu olvido
Te condeno yo a mi soledad

Si me dejas solo

Santiago Auserón.- "Si me dejas solo" en "Canciones de Radio Futura". Pre-textos. Valencia 1999. (1990)
Joan Brossa.- "¡Adelante!" en Joan Brossa- "El Tentetieso". Plaza y Janés. Barcelona. 1998. (1969)
Ezra Pound.- "Cause" en "Personae". (1929)
Guillaume Apollinaire.- "La bonita pelirroja" en Guillaume Apollinaire.- "Caligramas". Catedra. Madrid. 1997. (1918)

Federico Soriano (S&Aa)

12 *Six Chimneys*

LOCATION Barakaldo, Bizkaia PROJECT 1999 PRINCIPALS S&Aa (Federico Soriano, Dolores Palacios) COLLABORATORS Alessandra Abbruzzese, Carlos Arroyo

We want to resolve the Galindo area with a metaphor and not by means of a plan. The industrial elements, the warehouses and above all the chimneys are the visible face of the estuary. It's good that the city, that housing avails itself of the margins that were hitherto the purlieu of heavy industry, but can't our new buildings preserve that formal structure? We propose six slim and slender towers, six chimney-towers. You have to defend an image.
In order to resolve the residential building capacity six towers have been developed with occupation on the bottom floor at 120 m^2 or 90 m^2 when built. Each tower has a bottom floor of parking and 25 floors with an individual apartment per floor. The apartments program for each tower consists of one, two and three bedrooms plus a three-bedroomed duplex.
The economic activities program has been foreseen as dividing the planned surface into two areas and two distinct types. Spaces intended for office activities on six plots of land and a type of edification on two elongated floors. Each building has direct access from the main road system, a green zone and a small harbor that isolates it from the other volumes. On the other hand, the spaces intended for light-industrial activity on three plots of land for a type of edification of greater size. It keeps to the same orientation and access criterion as the above yet with a different image. The sports-usage program is distributed throughout the rest of the proposed area by applying the idea of a wood trapped in the city, in the interior of which are laid out the sports facilities, the sports center tower and the football pitch, the latter, given its great volumetry, in the part closest to the city. In this way the sports fields are open.

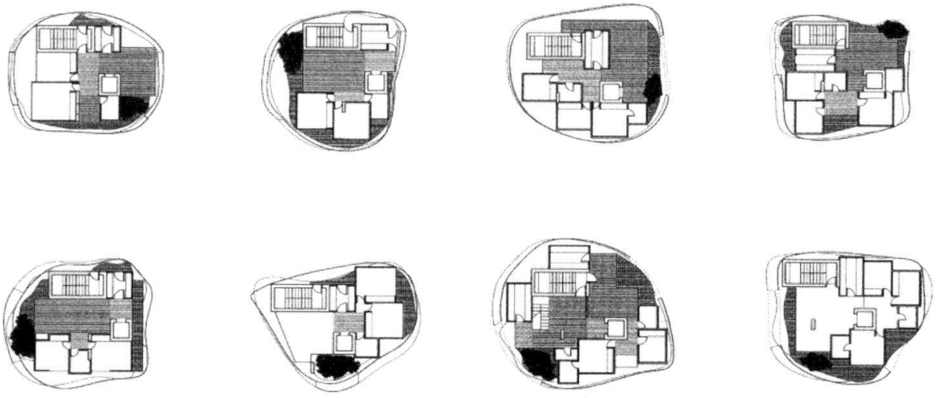

Federico Soriano (S&Aa)

12 **Fleta Theater**

ARCHITECTS Federico Soriano, Dolores Palacios LOCATION Zaragoza PROJECT 2000
COLLABORATORS Amanda Schachter, Luis Valdivieso and Ana Valenzuela

1 We must find a free plot within our piece of ground. A plot has to be invented where none exists.

2 We propose a constructed cloud floating over the existing building.
A weightless island.

3 A readjusted program exists and a clear and differentiated organization of flows and different people: management, public, actors and technicians don't mix, they'll have their workplaces and isolated and independent access routes to them.

4 These are the plans already elaborated.

5 In order for the existing auditorium to be able to function acoustically for opera, we must work with a reverberation time of around 1.2 to 1.4 seconds. For that reason the volume of the auditorium has to be increased to 8,000 cubic meters.

6 We propose to keep to the outline of the existing roof by substituting the original truss structure with very thick new curved metal profiles in such a way that the interior bubble of the empty space of the auditorium may be increased in size.

7 The final seating capacity will depend on the balance between the maximum possible volume, the sightlines and the acoustic envelope which enable one to act on the audience as a whole.

8 This is the resulting section.

9 The new rehearsal hall, which also functions as an extra auditorium for 250 people, is connected to the original lobby, although it also has its own entrance. It is an acoustic bubble whose roof is a continuous transparent skylight.

10 The space of the lobby and the staircases is preserved by opening more apertures between the walls so as to give it more transparency and unity.

11 The cloud will be constructed by a spatial structure of bars, like a self-sufficient box supported on the access cores (stairways and elevators) alone. Its skin will be light and immaterial, of glass and metal fabric that will cause it to lose its shape and heaviness.

12 From the city it will appear that the original Fleta Theater has not been extended, is untouched.

13 We recommend being valiant and daring, professionals but dreamers, investors and conservatives.

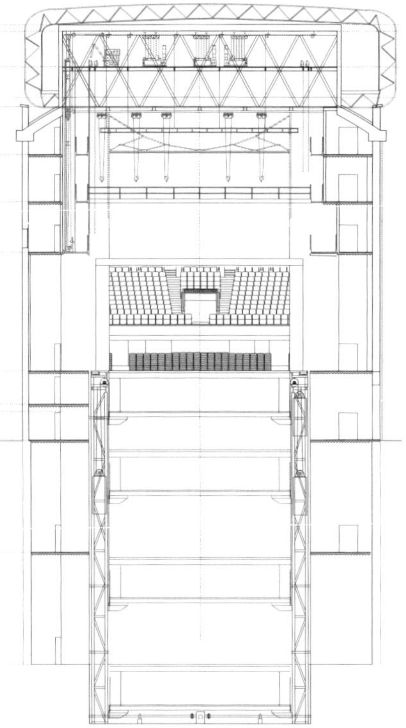

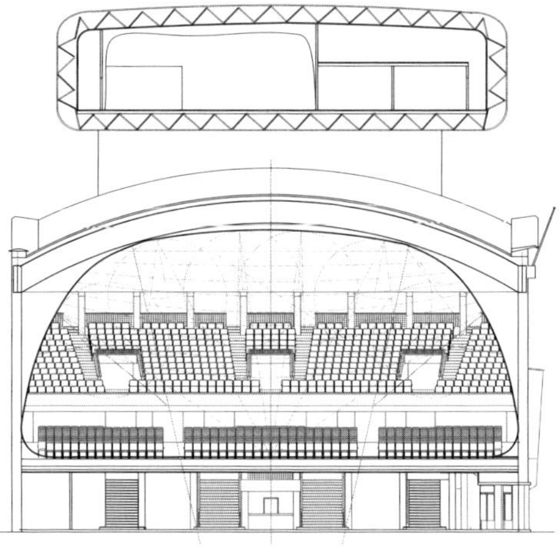

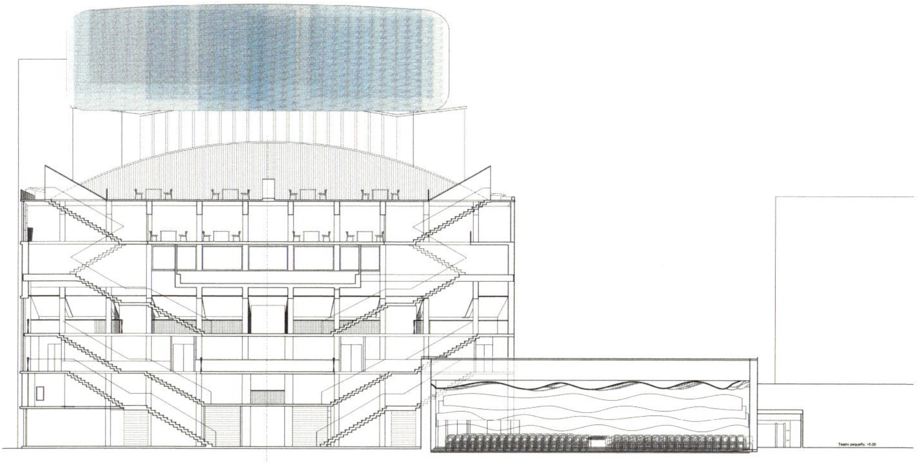
Teatro pequeño. +0.00

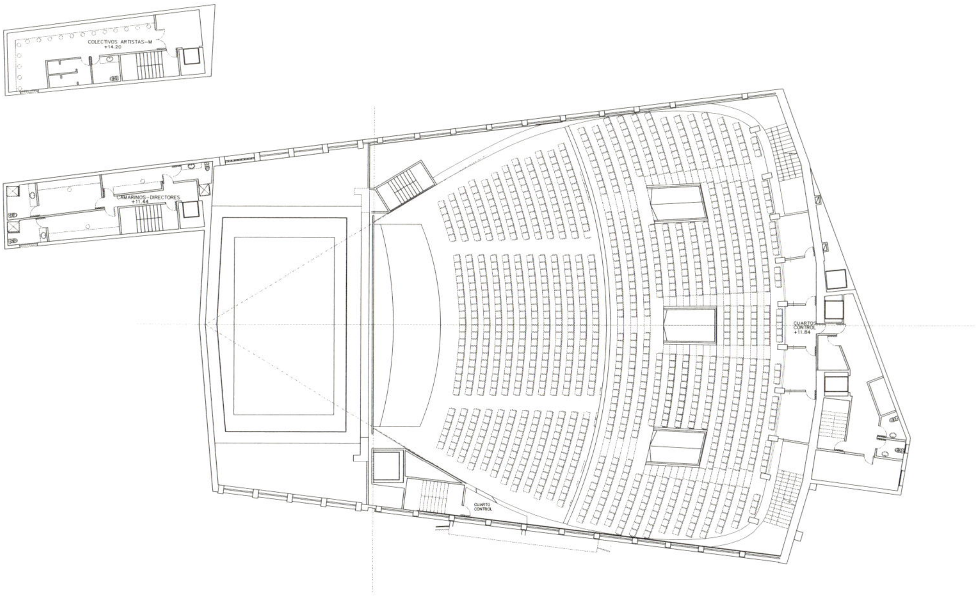
COLECTIVOS ARTISTAS-M
+14.20
CAMARINOS-DIRECTORES
+11.44
CUARTO CONTROL
+11.84
CUARTO CONTROL

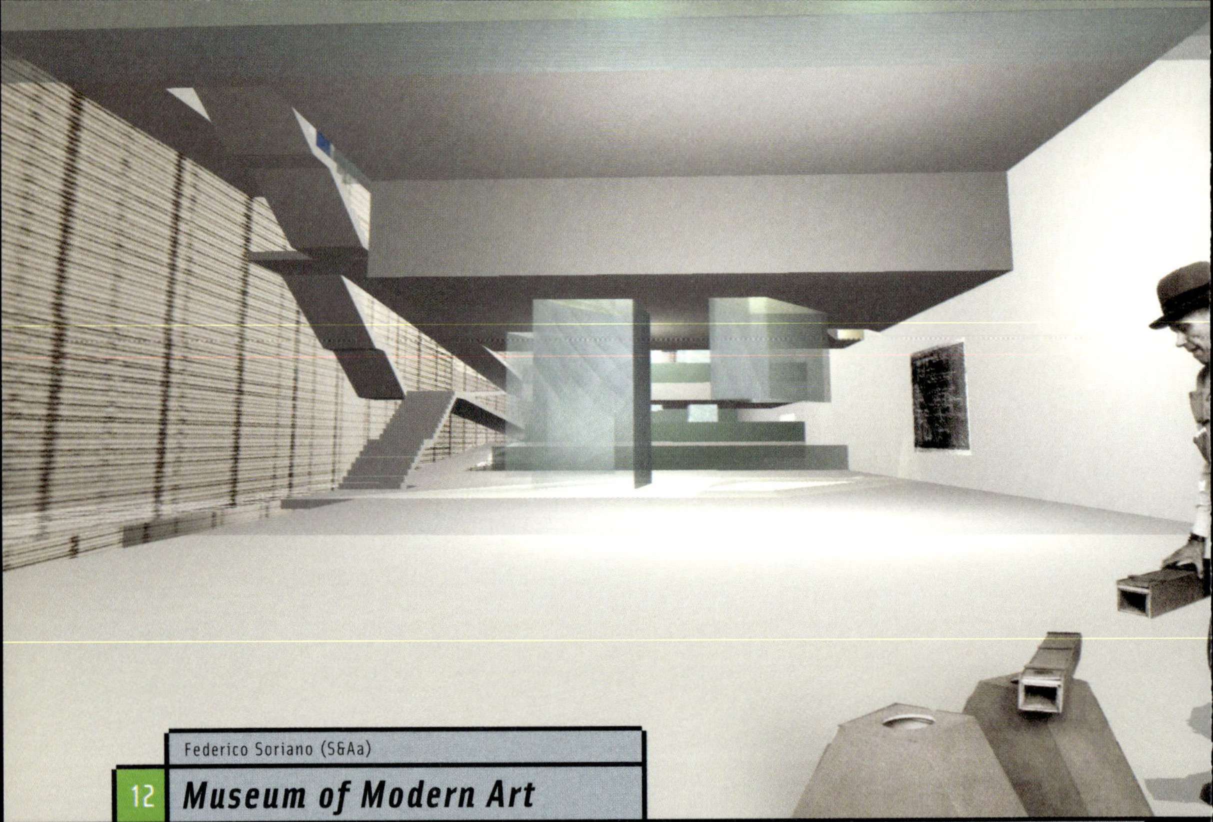

Federico Soriano (S&Aa)

12

Museum of Modern Art

LOCATION Bolzano, Italy PROJECT 2001 PRINCIPALS S&Aa (Federico Soriano, Dolores Palacios) COLLABORATORS Amanda Schachter, Lieven de Grote, Luis Valdivieso, Ana Valenzuela and Jan Tröber

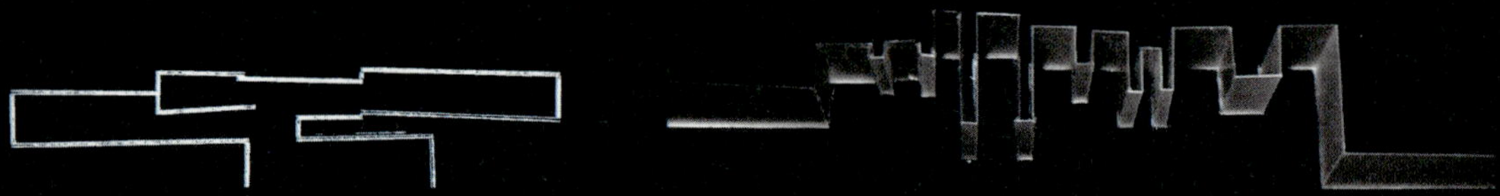

The MZMK museum fits into the urban structure. Green zones, public spaces and pedestrian paths form a united network. This urban unit is integrated with remarkable gentleness, its corners reducing its scale to adapt a low-density residential area. The building is a covered throughfare aligned with one edge of the site to free up a public garden inside the block. The museum spills visually and spatially onto this green zone, turning it into an outdoor exhibition space. Conceptually, the museum develops a continuous 2200 m² room on a site with 900 m² of free space. The mechanism we use to do this is to stack and provide continuity to the programmes, developing different exhibition rooms that can be used jointly or individually in a diagonal continuity.

To provide the rooms with the same conditions, we use the same system of skylights which traverse the building to the positions of each exhibition space, converted into patios, voids and opaque skylights. The result is a clean floor plan with a rhythm imposed by the skylights.

The museum is a skin of continuous opal glass, a curtain wall without orientation, roofing, walls or floors. The cross-section reveals a diagonal space and two lines that slice the exhibition spaces: a dotted line of light (skylights) and another line of vertical communications (service lift for art works). A system of ramps and stairs links the museum spaces; a single, dynamic, flexible system that provides access to every point without fragmenting the stairs, the foyer or the museum.

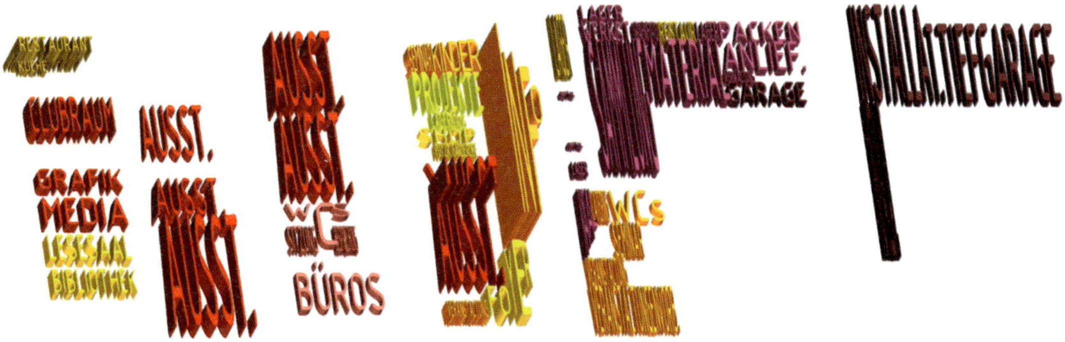

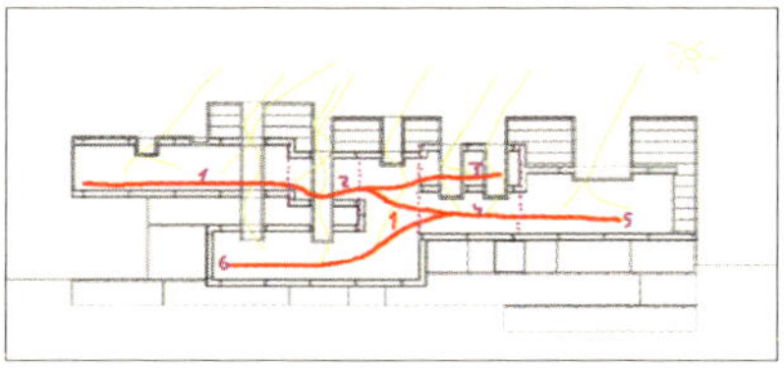
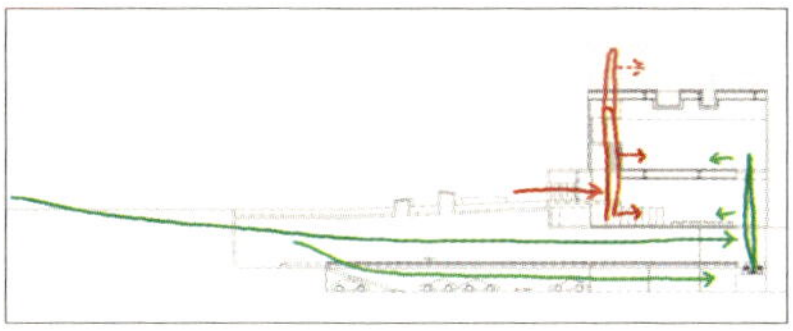
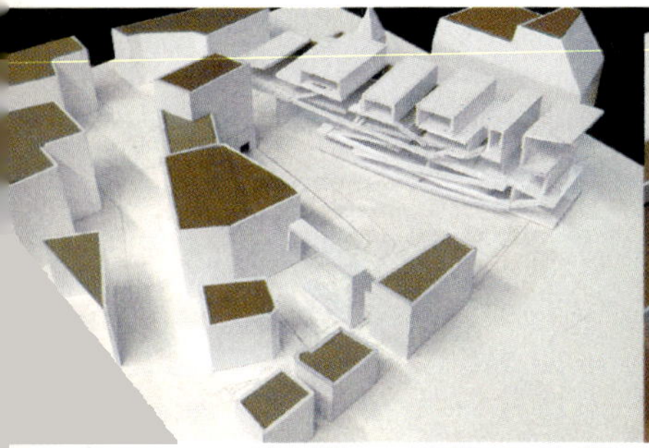
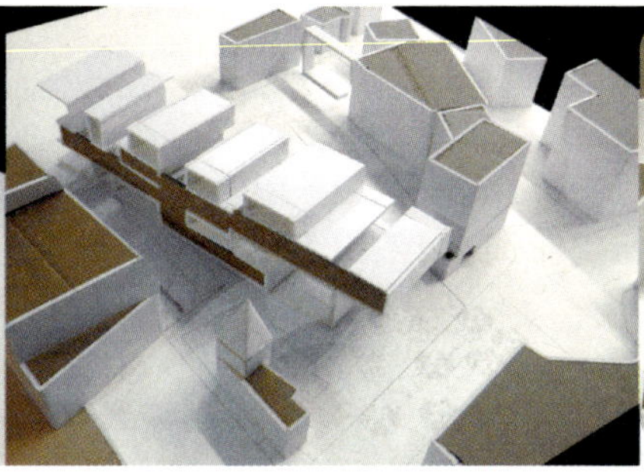
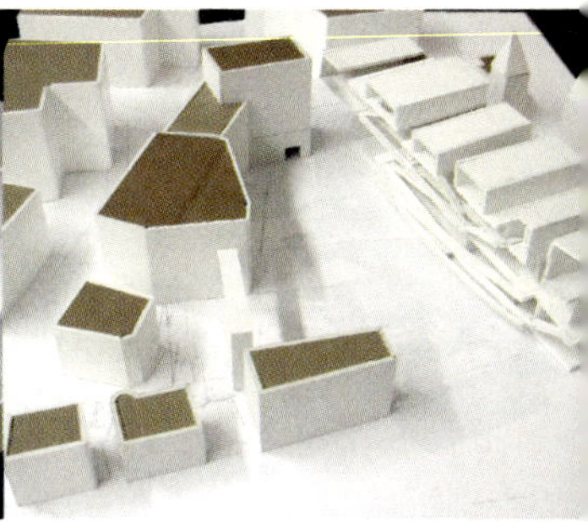
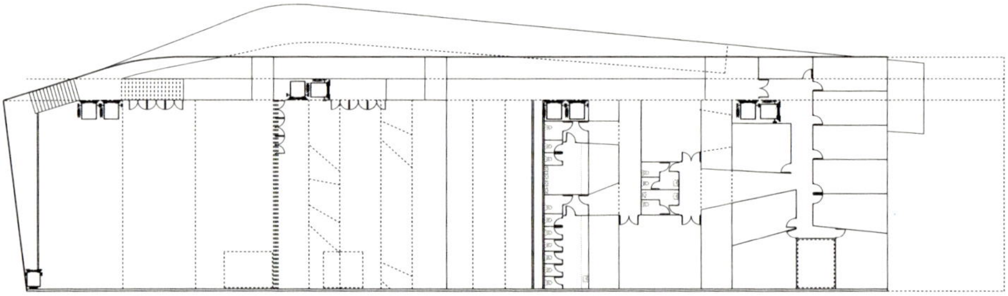
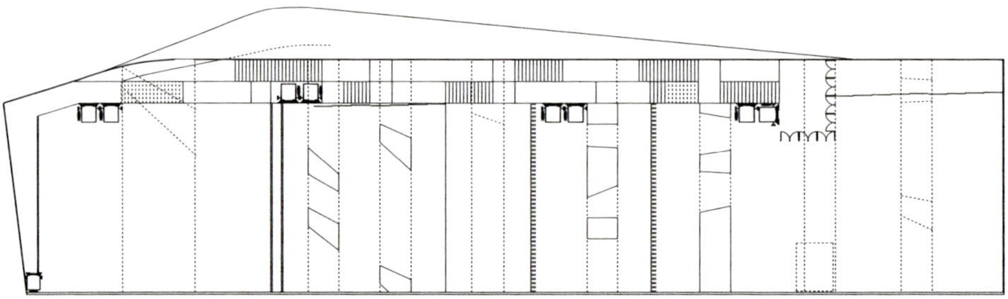

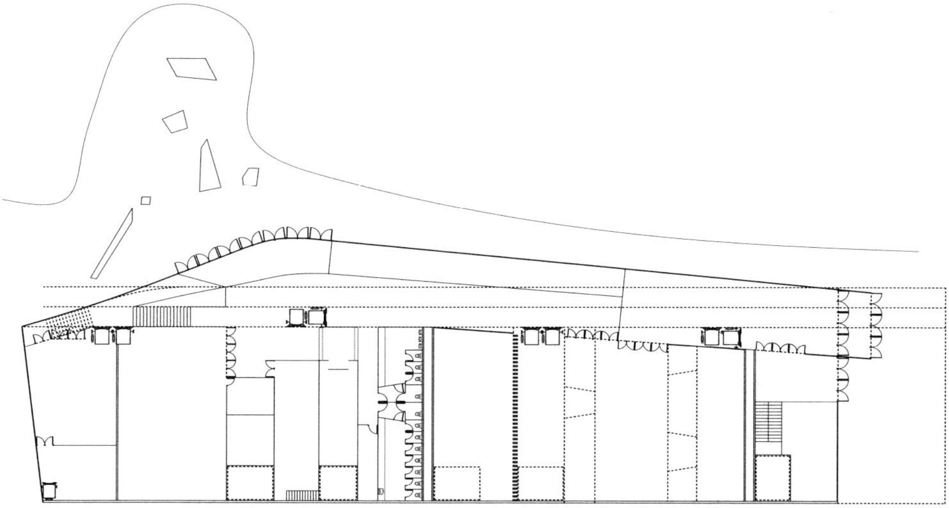

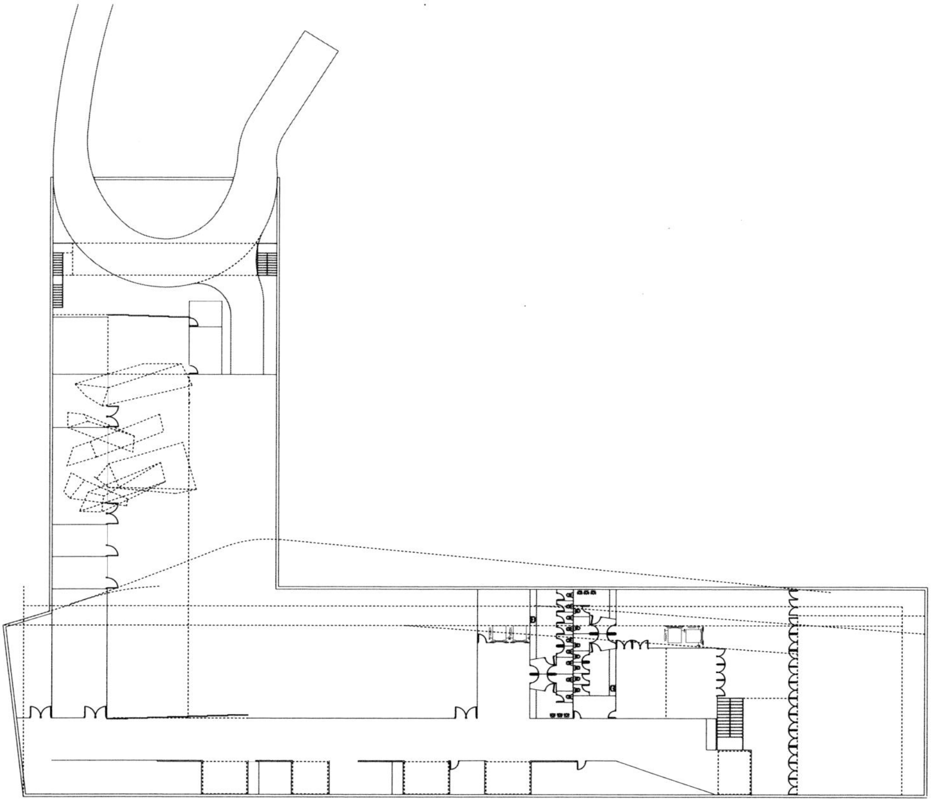

Processing logic would draw on information processes and strategies, working on the basis of data.

Processing Logic

Img: Competition for auditorium and conference centre, Pamplona, 1998

NO.MAD (Eduardo Arroyo) 13

Olympic Village, Paris 2008
University Urban Center
Desierto Square

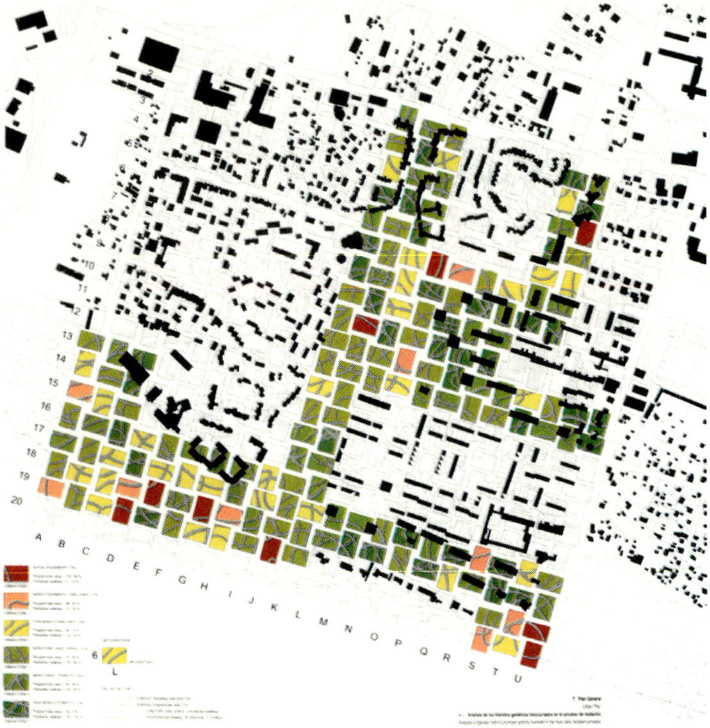

Processes

An evolutionary process, which provides a release from compositive burdens from the outset, implies the work with transformation systems, with correlative and independent stages.

The first step of the process: to create an objective percentile distribution of the usage programme to be inserted. These uses lead to individual grids that distribute each function uniformly, defining different densities of usage from the percentiles information about the total area of their point of application.

Second analysis: to determine the pre-existing factors and future actions considered to be unchangeable. The interaction between these reality vectors and the previous distributions of each function is used to produce a tabulation of attraction and repulsion between the latter. Once tha balance of mutations is reached, the construction uses and open spaces are defined and grouped, leadingto the configuration of the constructed hybrids.

Third: once the territory is hybridised by the multiplicity of programmatic functions, the process proceeds to read the constructive accumulations to create an archive of hybridisation in which the percentages of participation on each function in the composition of the constructed unit can be read.

The primigenial volume arises from a simple calculation of areas, potential constructions and the superimposition of uses on the plan. This virtual volume is transformed by the environmental conditions that are fed in as values of installing this construction in the real built-up landscape. These conditions are: accessibility of uses from the public level, heights of each use or placement of minimum communications cores to meet fire regulations. The generic section of the building appears during this transformation, which is typified using the information on functions, relationships between them and their constructed volumes.

The multiplicity of personalities and the hedonism of modern individuals, their habits and their increasingly atypical mobility and communication patterns make their dwellings extremely variable and heterogeneous places. The proposed process will thus be able to span anything from uses traditonally regarded as being functional to perversions and the most disparate lifestyles admitted by the growing tolerance of modern society.

NO.MAD (Eduardo Arroyo)

13 Olympic Village in Saint Denis

ARCHITECTS Eduardo Arroyo PROJECT 2000, Competition Olympic Village, Paris 2008 COLLABORATORS Nerea Calvillo, Malca Mizrahi, Francesco Monaco, Raúl Ortega

Time has only one reality, the instant. And to build a complex instant full of simultaneities we have to destroy the linked time in the traditional city.
A close look to the landscape provides us the illusion of relief and distance, if nothing stops our look we can get lost. We want to find obstacles, solid relations between the existing objects and to extract what is permanent and meaningful in the city.
Those objects will bring their characteristic brightness to the site shaping a fragmentary and exciting image of the city around. The mix of those changing images will provide a new urban structure related to three different horizons and symbolizing each of them the big questions about dwelling: rest, enjoyment and production.
These perceptions are brought into the site by means of reflections on the new buildings and they can qualify certain parts of the public space with programs related to the horizons they belong to.
We don´t want to trust appearence anymore, we rather believe on discourses. But we can also keep a kind of encripted key to decode the project, our way of looking into the world that we want to share with the other, and the perception of a certain geography that we know it belong to us.
The buildings are born of the objects in each horizon and they construct an urban structure full of sensations, imposible without their dancing morphology. The buildings are grouped around private open squares as complex structures to house the residential programs as well as the Olympic comittees and parking plots.
Man likes infinity, sometimes he likes leaving the earth towards the sky and his dreams. Only then he can reach the drama and happiness of life, a world close to its heart. There will be no place during the Olympic games that could be related to a memory, it will be a new space empty of references. We need time to acclimatize, to make the space ours. Our doubts will end only when we recognize the objects in wich we can reflect.
Our consciousness and the materiality around us take multiple and radically different shapes, and they are arranged more or less by each inhabitant. Architecture is a necessity but our conscience needs freedom. The post-olympic life of the neutral inhabitant will be the sharing point of his freedom and his necessity.

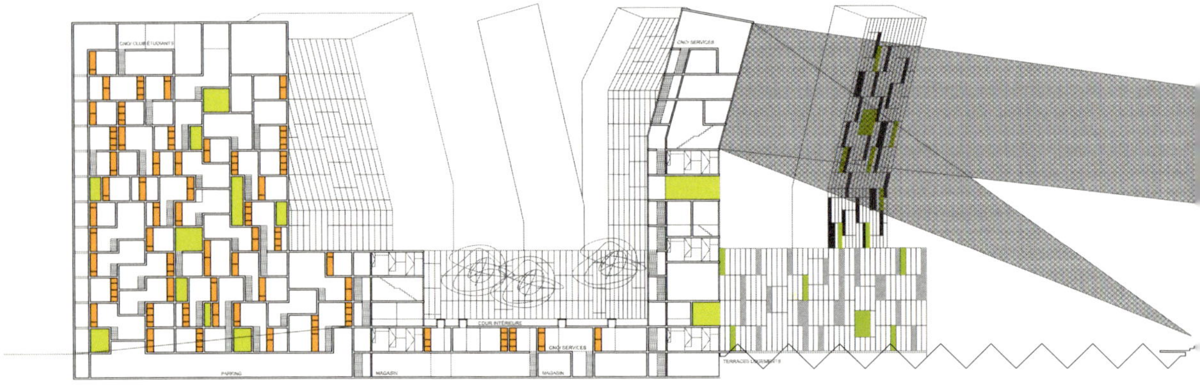
CNO/ CLUB ÉTUDIANTS
CNO/ SERVICES
COUR INTÉRIEURE
CNO/ SERVICES
PARKING
MAGASIN
MAGASIN
TERRACES LOGEMENTS

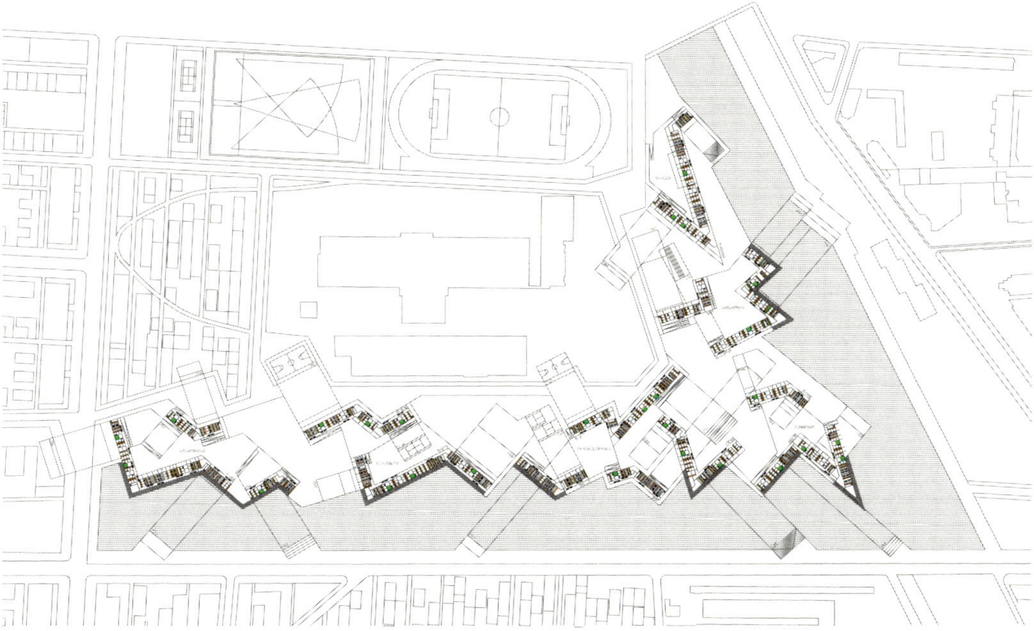

NO.MAD (Eduardo Arroyo)

13 New Urban center Marijin Dvor

ARCHITECT Eduardo Arroyo LOCATION Marijin dvor Zones C y C1, Sarajevo COLLABORATORS Nerea Calvillo (architect), Francesco Monaco (architect), Raul Ortega (architect), David Casino (student), Ignacio Toribio (student) EXECUTION 2000

DENSITY The relation between programs and the quantity of people using them will provide an intensity of use and also the mix of functions and volumes. The way people use the actual city will give the clue to the use of the new programs on an exciting way.

DYNAMICITY Rhythm is important. The city can be accelerated or slowed down gradually if we can control the continuity of its dynamics and this will provide no cuts on its flow and so a sense of fluidity.

DEVELOPMENT POTENTIAL The consumption of ground surface on every new program should be minimized, though some programs tend to consume more ground, so that they will provide public ground space, surfaces free of speculation.

TIME BAND To avoid a dead city at night, different programs should be mixed in a way that their superposition will give a richer use on the day-night period. This will provide, once again, a sense of continuity on the use of the city.

FOREIGNESS The world is becoming small, people of different races and creeds mix and interrelate. As we focus on the third millenium, our cities should get ready to absorb on their programs this arising new condition without creating racial ghettos.

PUBLIC – PRIVATE On a more social world, integration of people into the city structure means to avoid the creation of big islands of privacy, letting the public space flow along the city without any cuts or economic borders.

STAY Some programs are used on a quicker way than others. By placing them on the right position, we can create a sense of continuity with no disruption between their using times.

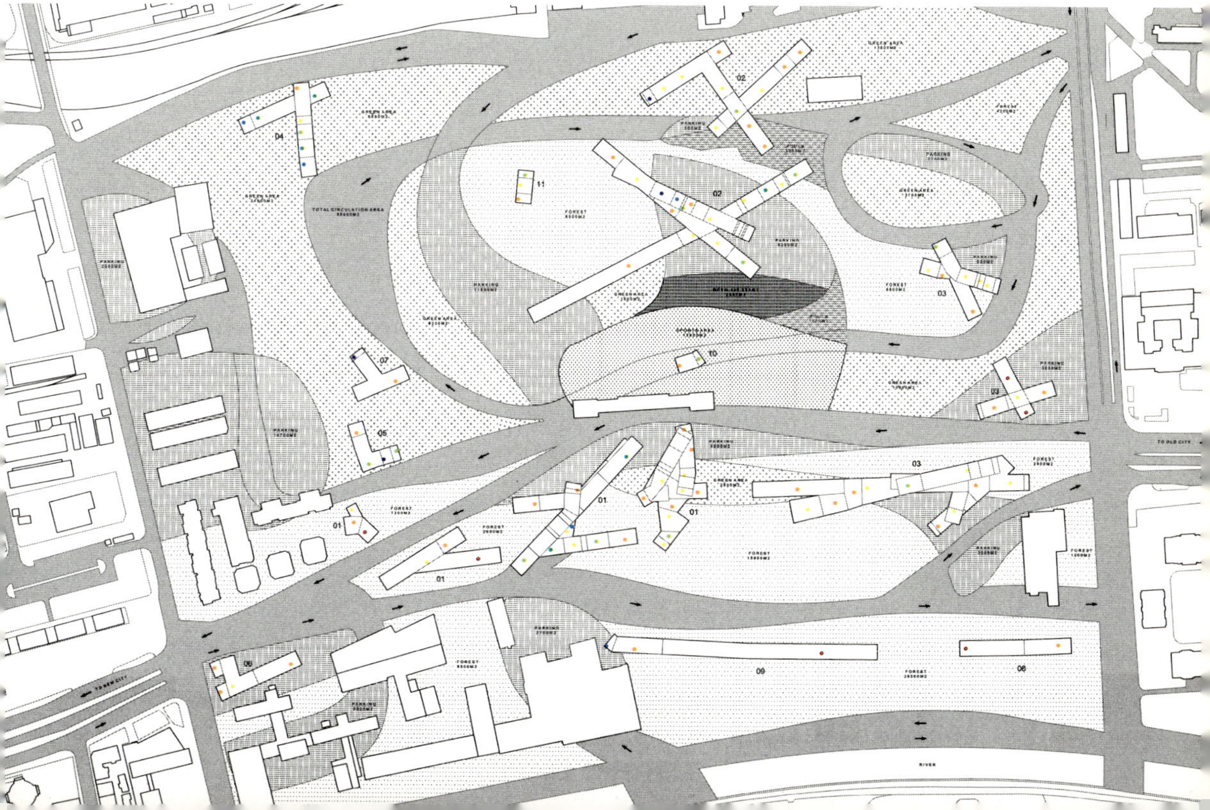

NO.MAD (Eduardo Arroyo)

13 **Desierto Square**

ARCHITECT Eduardo Arroyo COLLABORATORS (ARCHITECTS) Sergio L. Piñeiro, John Garcés, AIE GALINDO 98 LOCATION Barakaldo, Spain SITE SUPERVISION Nerea Calvillo Gonzalez (arquitecto), AIE GALINDO 98 (arquitectos), José Luis Villanueva (arquitecto técnico), Javier Inclan (arquitecto técnico) STRUCTURAL ENGINEERS Fernando Subinas LANDSCAPE ARCHITECT Teresa Galí EXECUTION 1999-2002 SURFACE AREA 1.2 Ha DEVELOPER Bilbao Ría 2000 PHOTOGRAPHS Roland Halbe, Hisao Suzuki

...something is born, something dies... but people remember...
...a primitive place, evening fires, steel in the air, sleepers and rails, black coal and dark water...
...everything flows, and the memory of that strange amalgam struggles to survive in the recollection of the landscape...
...and men build once more, mad architects, homeless nomads, exciting places for the sedentary written on the ground...
...distributing the discovered material uniformly across the new plaza...
...recognising the reality of conditions that may affect their transformation...
...and letting the definitive redistribution emerge on its own as the fruition of the process...
...in a place wherein resides the memory of the steel alquemists, the boatbuilders, the land tillers, with all the components of that crucible amalgamated for the public...
...steel and stone, wood and rich soil, all dead long ago, now revive, mixed together in small transitable spaces apt for discovery of frolic, intimate or collective in which one can just look or listen, or perhaps try to speak once more...
...with an alternative topography...
...a geography for pocketing the surrounding landscape...
...and a flat estuary that vibrates with the mountains it envies...seven hills in the plaza landscape with raised steel structures as places for contemplation and punctuation in the night, crystalline luminosity, the memory of those who knew other flames silhouetted in the darkness...

...two years later...

...a work that builds itself, with predetermined codes of materials and mixings that constructors understans and execute...
...a numeric topography where vertex are more important than lines...
...the space has self generated and we don´t know its use, but it seems to be a set of multiple possibilities, surely the population will create their own using system...
...maybe lovers will hide on the shadowy living rooms and the elder will tell their stories joined around the salix...
... kids will make paper boats on the water ponds and pick them up in the other side, the skaters cannot wait to use that funny topography, everybody will have something to do...

...but I don´t really know...

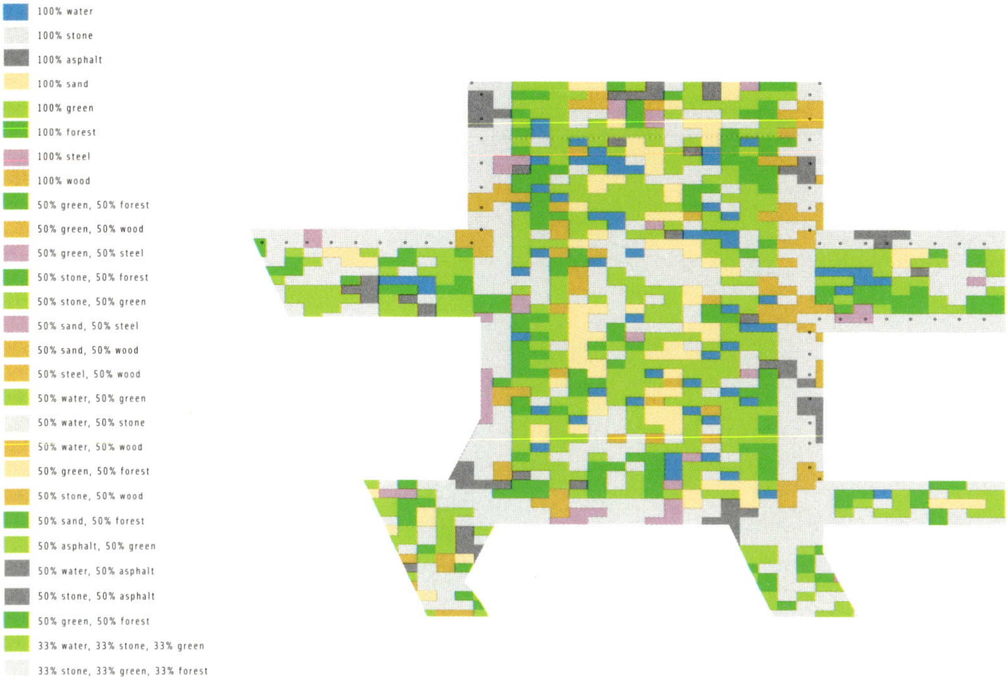

100% water
100% stone
100% asphalt
100% sand
100% green
100% forest
100% steel
100% wood
50% green, 50% forest
50% green, 50% wood
50% green, 50% steel
50% stone, 50% forest
50% stone, 50% green
50% sand, 50% steel
50% sand, 50% wood
50% steel, 50% wood
50% water, 50% green
50% water, 50% stone
50% water, 50% wood
50% green, 50% forest
50% stone, 50% wood
50% sand, 50% forest
50% asphalt, 50% green
50% water, 50% asphalt
50% stone, 50% asphalt
50% green, 50% forest
33% water, 33% stone, 33% green
33% stone, 33% green, 33% forest

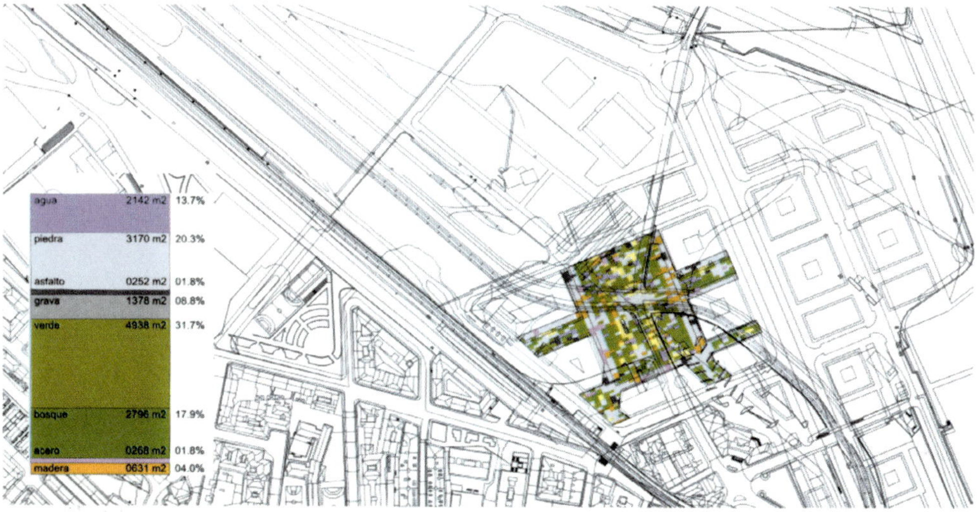

agua 2142 m2 13.7%
piedra 3170 m2 20.3%
asfalto 0252 m2 01.8%
grava 1378 m2 08.8%
verde 4938 m2 31.7%
bosque 2796 m2 17.9%
acero 0268 m2 01.8%
madera 0631 m2 04.0%

Vicente Guallart

14

Denia Mountain
Hortal House
Sharing Tower

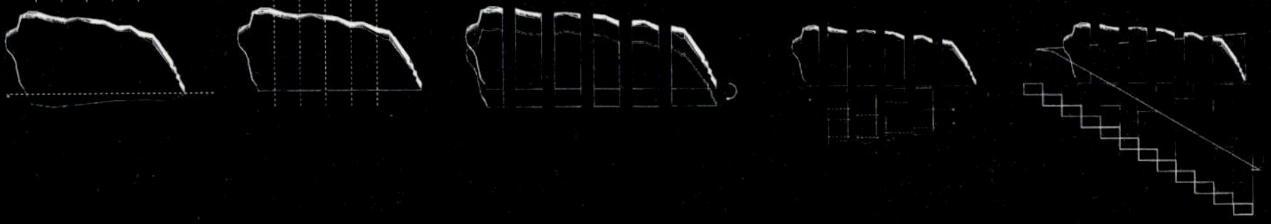

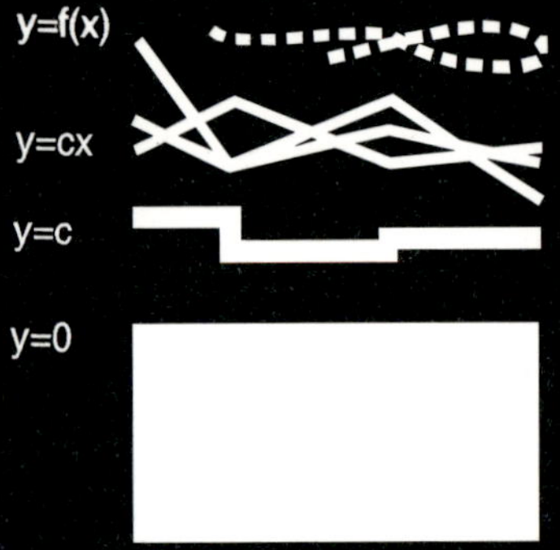
y=f(x)
y=cx
y=c
y=0

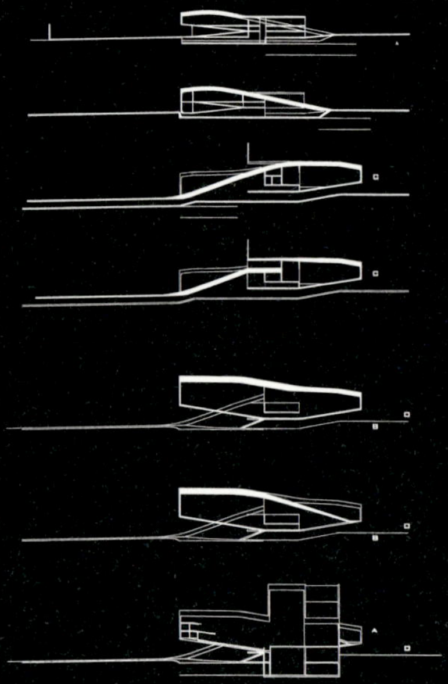

Intelligent Realities

We realise that we are now seeing the emergence of a new reality in which information technologies provide a way of inhabiting a networked world that requires a new approach to the conception of architecture and cities.
We are now seeing the development of bases for the construction of "intelligent realities" as a result of the interaction of persons, objects and spaces, in which architecture and its associated disciplines can be the integrators of processes and occurrences of this "metareality."
Faced with this new situation, architects cannot merely be passive problem-solvers; they have to accept a new active condition, like that of strategists who ask questions of their surroundings and anticipate lines of action, whose form of procedure is based not on the application of a profession that is learned and mutually consented, but on innovation in planning processes and the application of the new techniques and materials that they help to develop.
The scale of the architecture project therefore ranges "from bits to geography." From the software that interacts with places and projects them beyond their physical reality, to the flows and synergies running through the territory and organising the local action of the construction of new inhabited landscapes. An interaction between the natural, the artificial and the digital that draws up new rules for "the art of dwelling."

VICENTE GUALLART

14 ***Denia Mountain***

ARCHITECTS Vicente Guallart, María Díaz LOCATION Denia (Alicante, Spain) DESIGN TEAM Façade with Max Sanjulian / Auditorium design with Jordi Mansilla COLLABORATORS Ivan Llach, Moon Puig, Nacho Alonso, Miquel Moraques, Raquel Colacios, Barbara Oelbrant, Guillem Auge, Ana Verges, Carlo Mezzino, Ines Ribaya PROJECT 1st Prize International Competition CLIENT Town of Denia DEVELOPER Denia Town Council IMAGES Laura Cantarella MODELS Cristine Bleicher, Susanne Schulte STRUCTURAL ADVISOR Robert Brufau ACOUSTICS TECHNICIAN Higini Arau CRYSTALLOGRAPHIC ADVISOR Albert Soler PROGRAM CONSULTANT José Miguel Iribas

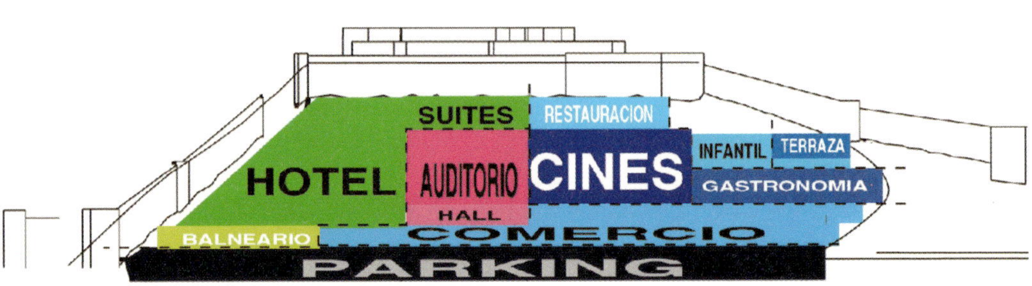

Denia is a town on the Mediterranean coast with an economy based largely on tourism. A hill rises from the centre of the town, crowned by an Arab castle. In the late 19th century, the hill was being farmed. In the early 20th century they started quarrying the north face of the hill to get stone for the enlargement of the port. During the Spanish Civil War a shelter was tunnelled out of it.
The Parque Cultural del Castillo de Denia is a city project for the redevelopment of the castle and its surroundings with cultural, civic and social facilities with the aim of making site a territorial point of reference that promotes urban recycling and compact development in the city.

The main points of the project are:
1. The conservation and protection of the castle
2. The creation of a cultural centre in Plaza del Consell
3. The enlargement of the pedestrian tunnel
4. The construction of a multifunctional centre.
5. The protection of the city's Roman ruins at the Hort de Morand.

The main new construction is the multifunctional centre (with various facilities, services and open space) sited in the quarry and designed to restore the hill to its original volume.
Since, in the end, the best way to preserve heritage is by enlarging it, this project entails the conservation of the historic ruins coupled with the creation of a new architectural landmark which will act as a cultural, tourism and economic attractor. The project is led by public initiative with participation from the private sector.

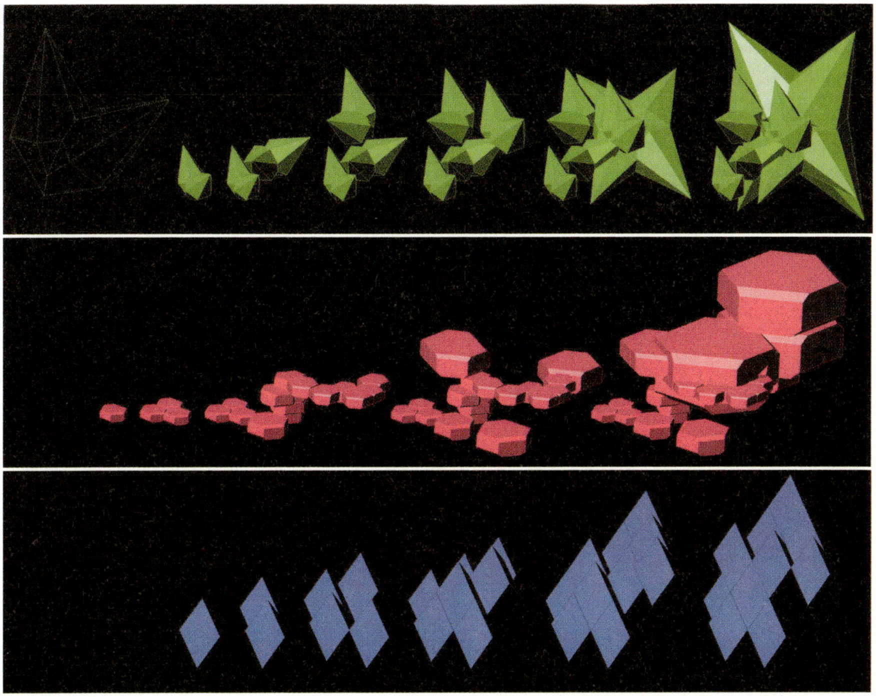

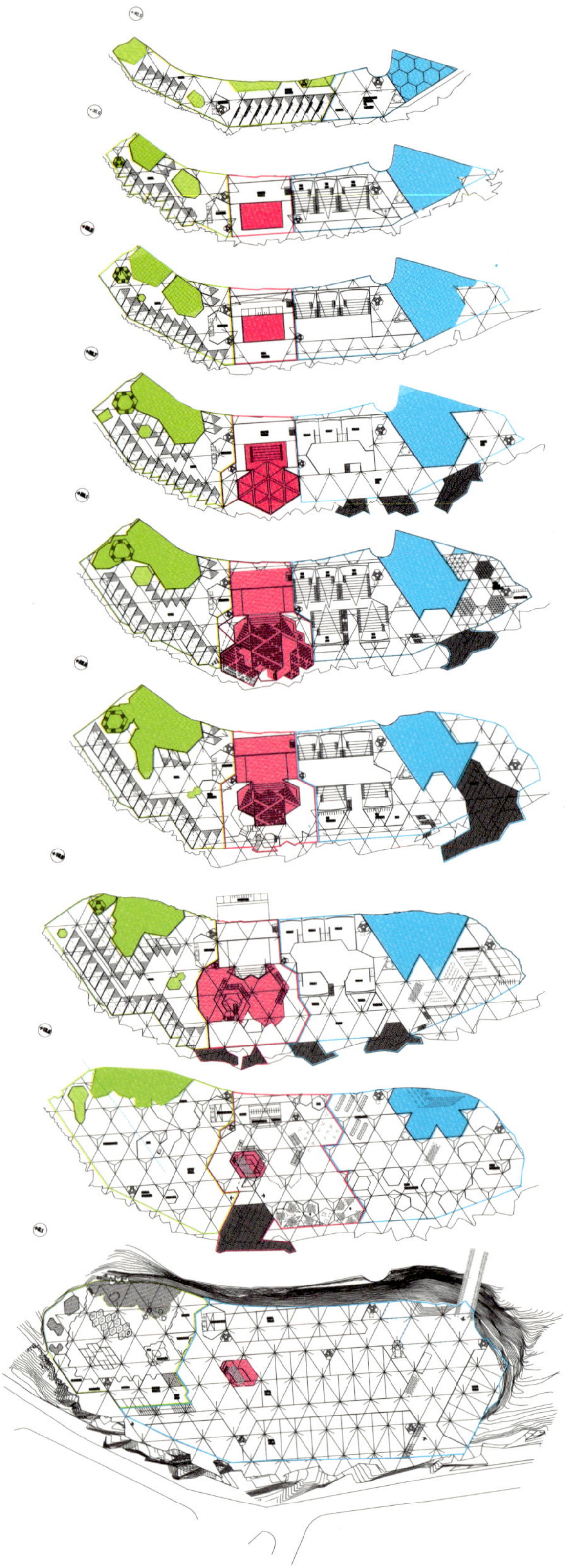

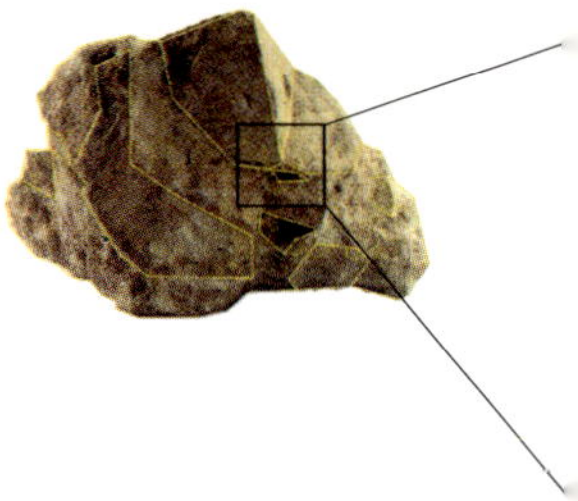

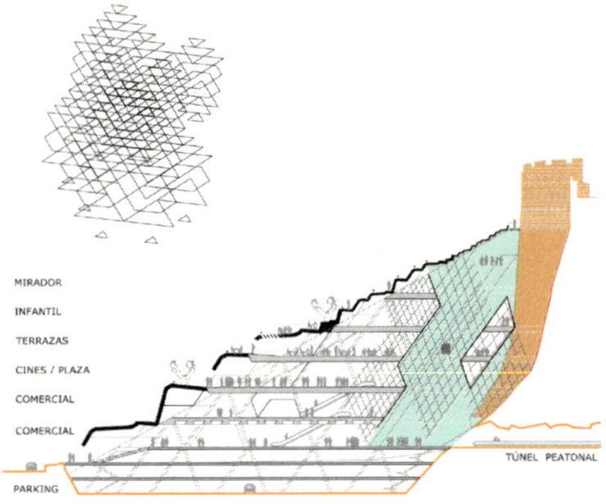
MIRADOR
INFANTIL
TERRAZAS
CINES / PLAZA
COMERCIAL
COMERCIAL
TÚNEL PEATONAL
PARKING

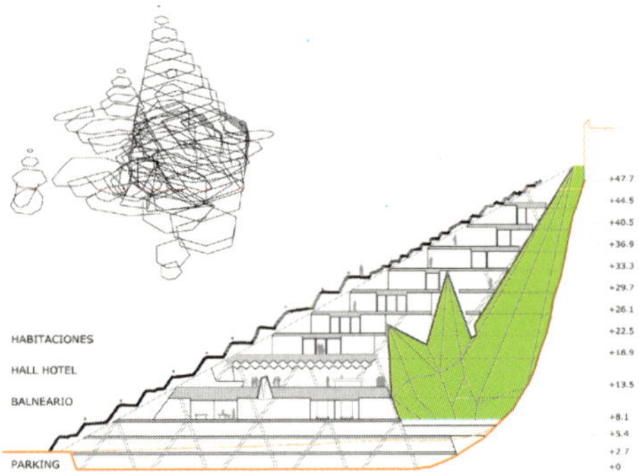
HABITACIONES
HALL HOTEL
BALNEARIO
PARKING
+47.7
+44.5
+40.5
+36.9
+33.3
+29.7
+26.1
+22.5
+18.9
+13.5
+8.1
+5.4
+2.7
+0

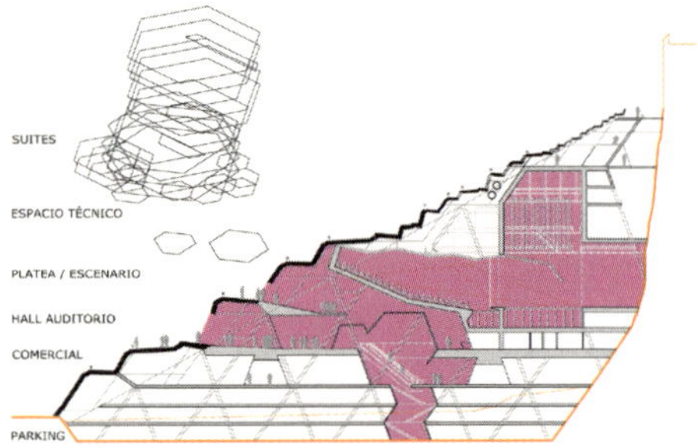
SUITES
ESPACIO TÉCNICO
PLATEA / ESCENARIO
HALL AUDITORIO
COMERCIAL
PARKING

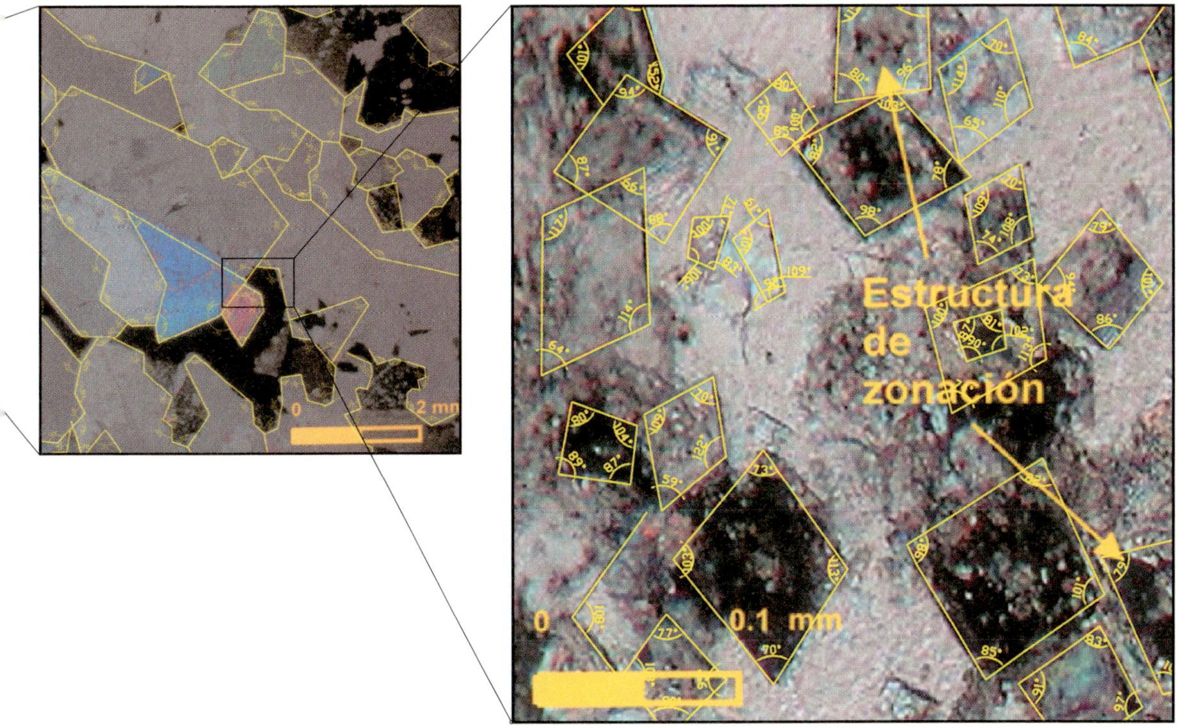
0
2 mm
Estructura
de
zonación
0
0.1 mm

JOURNEY OF MAN
AMAZING CAVES

VICENTE GUALLART

14

Hortal House

ARCHITECT Vicente Guallart LOCATION Comarruga (El Vendrell, Tarragona) PROJECT LEADER María Díaz COLLABORATORS Pilar Gasque, Bárbara Oelbrandt, Christine Bleicher STAINED GLASS Alex Sesplugues, CRICURSA SURFACE AREA 400 m² DEVELOPER Miguel Hortal STRUCTURAL ENGINEERING BIS ARQUITECTES, David Garcia CONSTRUCTION José Jiménez TECHNICAL ARCHITECT Ton Feliu

On a hill overlooking the Mediterranean some three kilometres from the beach we built this villa anchored in the terrain, projecting out towards the sea. The construction was conceived as a great concrete bracket, almost like a geographical feature that operates according to its own rules to claim a privileged position amidst its surroundings.

Given that buildings are far more expressive during construction than when they are completed, this building deliberately appears unfinished, with a rough concrete exterior and exposed metal structure and floor slabs in the interior.

The wall openings have, in contrast, been given a more delicate finish, with stained glass windows, like gems incrusted in a massive rock, creating personalized landscapes in the interior. The house interacts with its environment on four different scales: to the west, fronting the access road, it is a single-storey volume defining a domestic scale (characteristic of a small house) with a pitched roof covered with rocks. To the north the volume rises up from the garage access ramp in a flat, compact form to create a place for mobility. To the south, the pool (which can be partially enclosed) slides under the stepped bracket with a sun deck around it. To the east, facing the sea, the villa is metallic and transparent, an almost urban building of three floors, with views of the sea.

We cannot say if this villa is a beautiful building or not. We would prefer to judge it using the same criteria with which we appraise a mountain or a rock: strong, hard, amorphous....

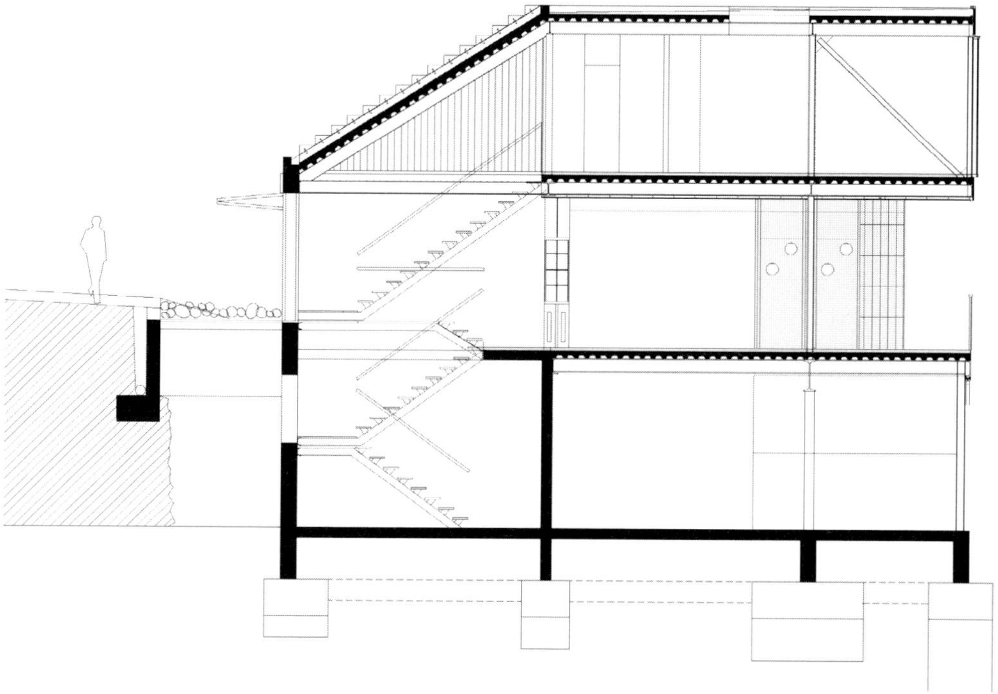

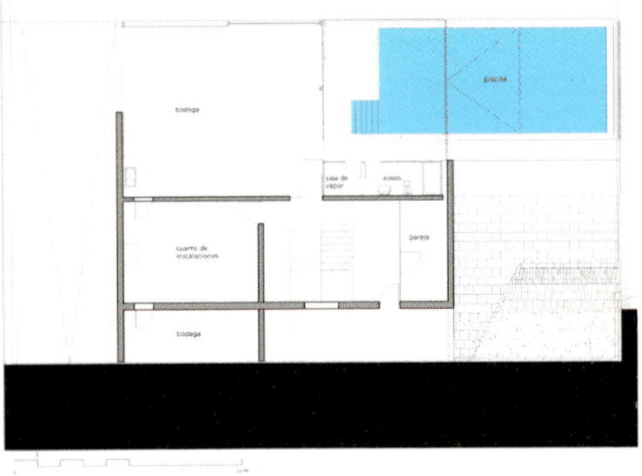

bodega
sala de vapor
aseos
cuarto de instalaciones
garaje
bodega

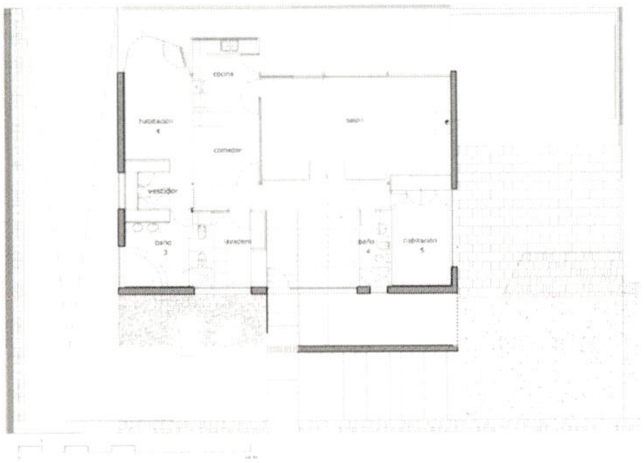

cocina
habitación 4
comedor
vestidor
baño 3
lavadero
baño 4
habitación 5

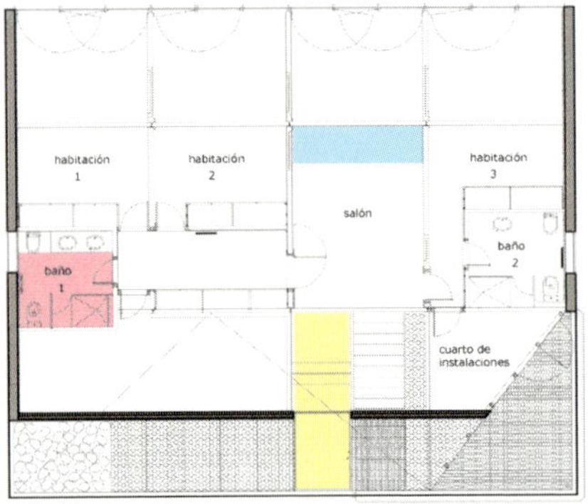

habitación 1
habitación 2
salón
habitación 3
baño 2
baño 1
cuarto de instalaciones

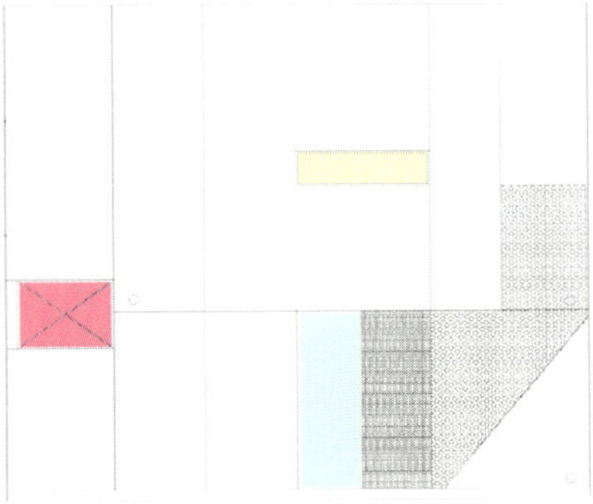

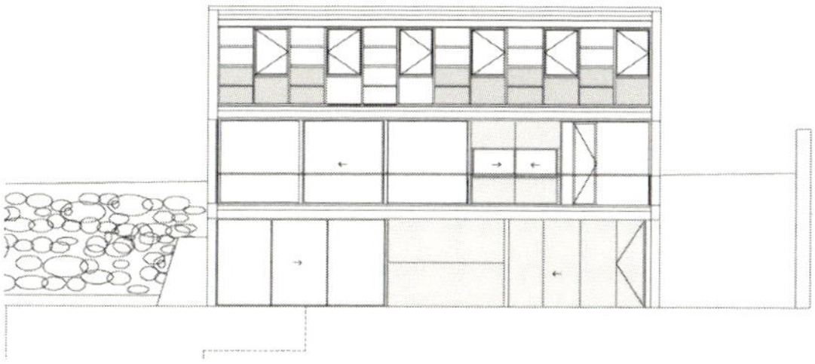

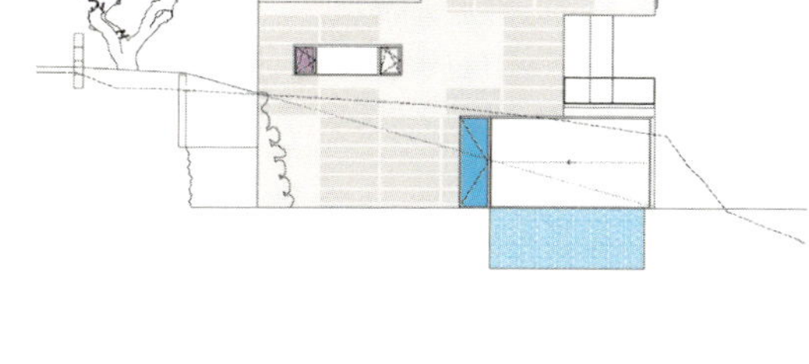

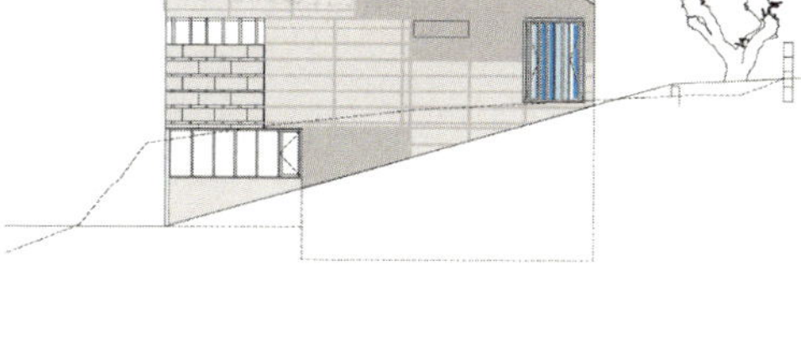

VICENTE GUALLART

14 Sociópolis. Sharing Tower

ARCHITECTS Vicente Guallart, María Díaz LOCATION Valencia, España COLLABORATORS Cristina Dorado, Leonardo Novelo, Sonia Ayala, Martín Osuna, Andreas Allen 3D Lucas Cappelli + UokU.com – net architects; Lucas Jagodnik, Mariano Castro, Horacio Suaba, Martín Escoyez, Cristine Bleicher MODELS Cristine Bleicher TOTAL SURFACE 6600 m² PHOTOGRAPHS Laura Cantarella

The sharing tower is a centre of social information, parking space and 99 student dwellings. In accordance with the 'four factor' law, we should be able to do twice as much in half the space or with half the resources in order to increase the efficacy of our environment. With this aim in mind, it is crucial to construct more efficient buildings and dwellings in which the occupants share facilities. The characteristic activities of dwellings: sleeping, eating, cooking, bathing, storing, washing clothes and resting – are organised around specific elements and appliances: bed, table, kitchen, shower, fridge, washing machine, TV and so on. It makes no sense for small dwellings to contain all the elements needed for these activities, especially when only 10% of their potential is exploited.

Accordingly, The Sharing Tower dwellings establish dynamic mutual relationships on each floor, through the use of spaces shared two-by-two, four-by-four or eight by eight. As a result, the useful space of the dwelling is increased from $25m^2$ to $75m^2$. Common use of space fosters social interaction.

The project site, which stands on the boundary between the garden and the city, contains an underground car park that acts as a speed interchange between the urban city and the garden city proposed by Sociópolis. Between an environment in which people move by car and a pedestrian city, between the fast city and the slow city.

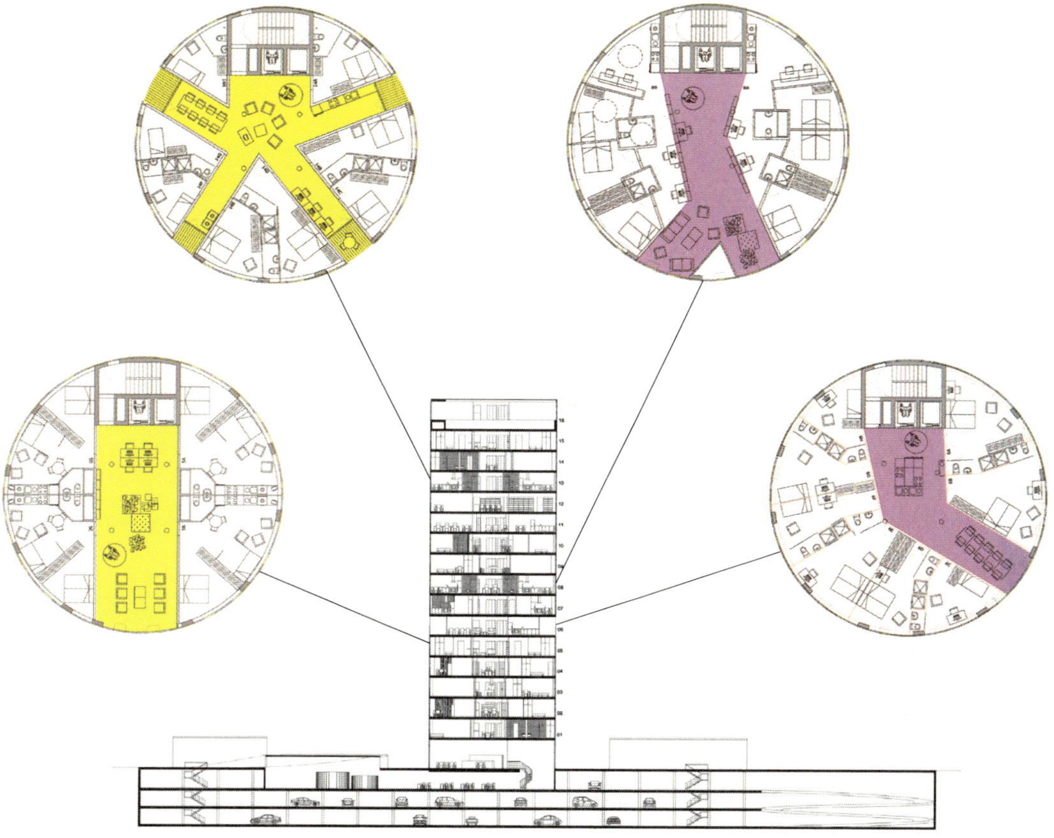

MVRDV

15

Silodam

Galaxy

Ministry of Agriculture

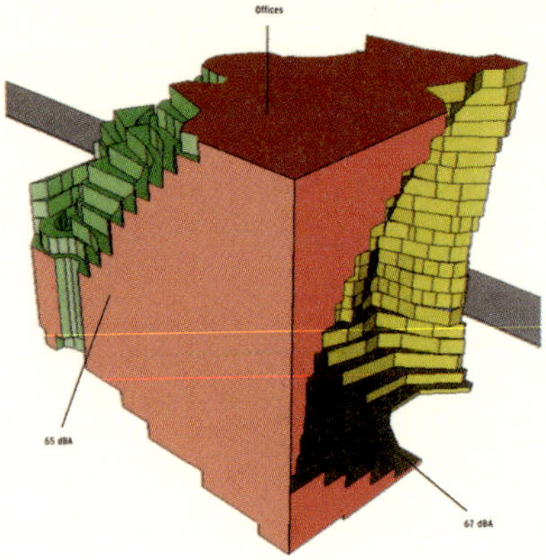

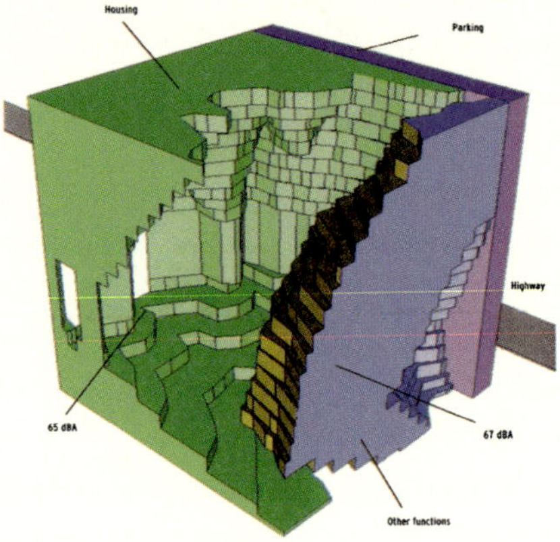

Fields of fire

Possible building zones

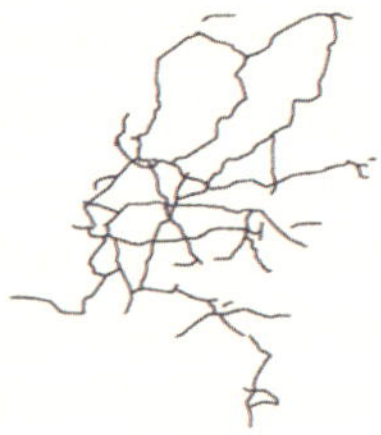
Parkways

Possible building zones

Parkscape Holland

Holland town

Parks

Possible building zones

Datascapes

Datascapes can be seen as a kind of technique or a tool that tries to unfold the chaos theories, which appear so much in the current architectural debate. By using this it tries to escape from the mythical hideaway of the existing chaos notions. 'Artistic' intuition lies in the use of the technique, in the way you can look at things. It is a kind of mirror in a way of showing these limitations. Normally it is very hard to show these limitations since they are 'hidden', swallowed by other parameters. But by pushing things to an extreme, compared to a pressure cooker, these limitations 'appear', which makes it possible to discuss them and to create a discourse around them.

LANDSCAPE

If 'landscape' can be translated as 'endlessness' then 'landscape' is a pretty serious and endless topic to be examined. If 'nature' can be equated by 'freedom' then lots of explorations can be considered. Most of our buildings seem to investigate these matters.

We tend to be extremely site-specific, without becoming critical regionalists.

You could consider it as a doubling the landscape. In our work we tend to enlarge or emphasise certain aspects of a site. Site is not an unavoidable force of nature. Sometimes you have to redefine the site, make a new site.

So, an architect should be both a creator and a technician. We combine the technique of assemblage with strong zoning envelopes, often 'discovered' through a thorough recombination of programme and site-specific elements.

PROGRESS

Architecture has overcome the state of the object as such. It has reached a state of interrelations more than ever with all its communicative possibilities. Even in architecture, the post-Einstein era has come to an end, where linear attitudes towards progress have dissolved into a more gaseous situation where the architect combines elements in order to handle relative progress.

Although we don't exactly know what progress means, it does provide space for experimenting and argument, for renovation and for new ideas. It's a very optimistic culture. There is no fear of progress, of the new.

People are starting to realise that it's worthwhile investing in architecture in general... And that's where the young architects come in.

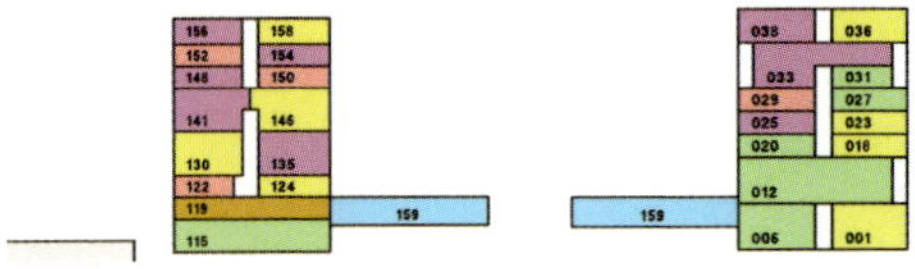

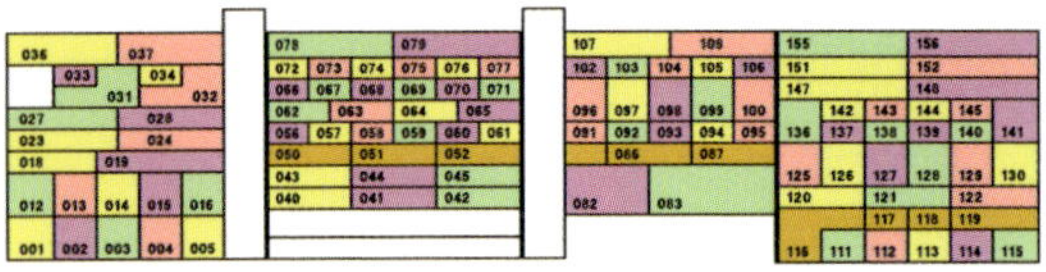

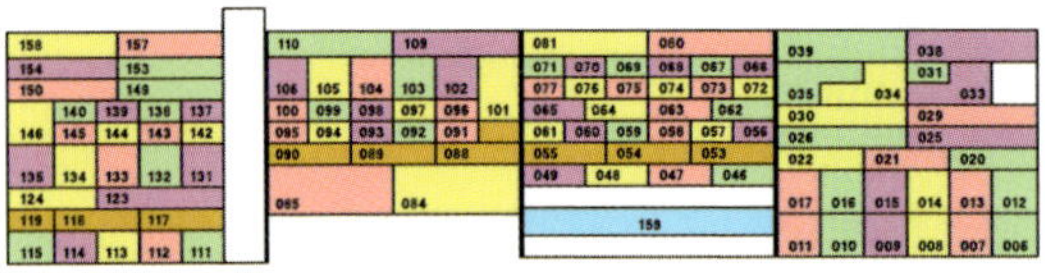

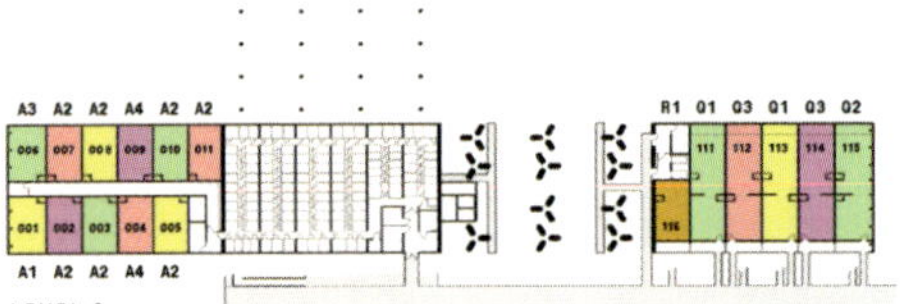

LEVEL 0

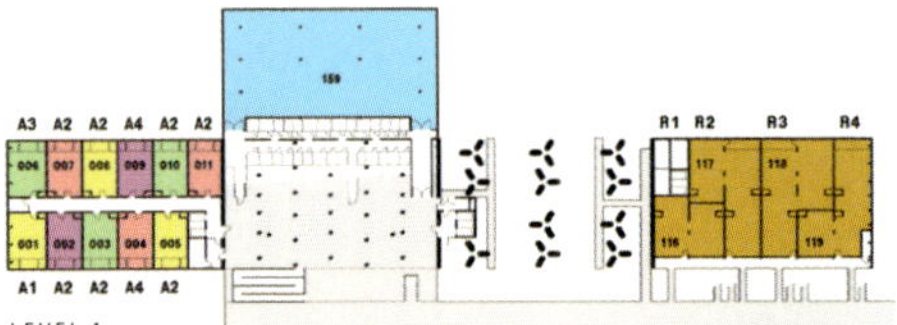

LEVEL 1

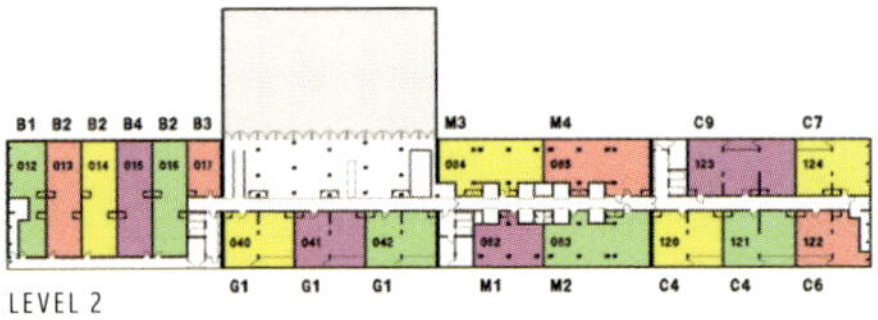

LEVEL 2

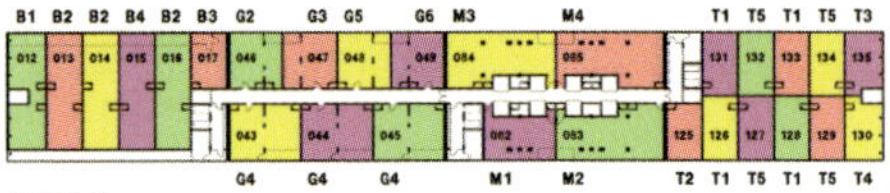

LEVEL 3

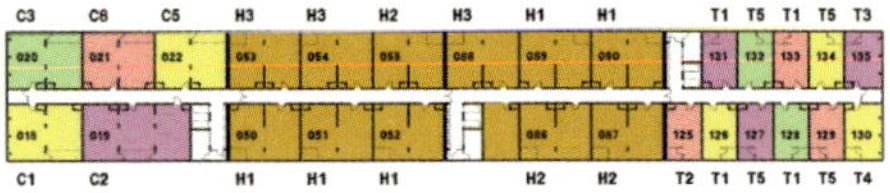

LEVEL 4

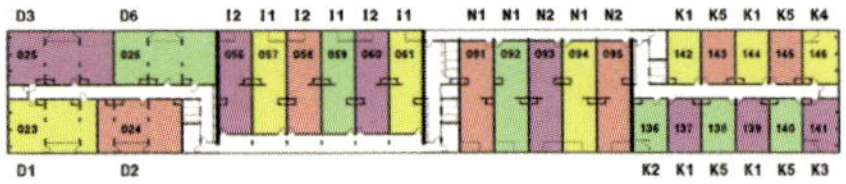

LEVEL 5

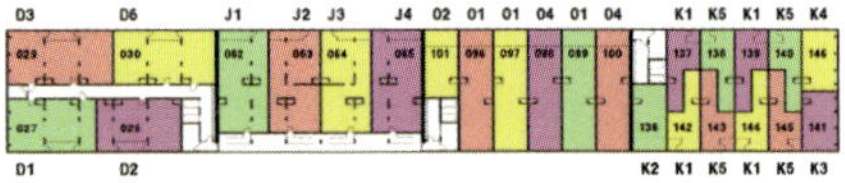

LEVEL 6

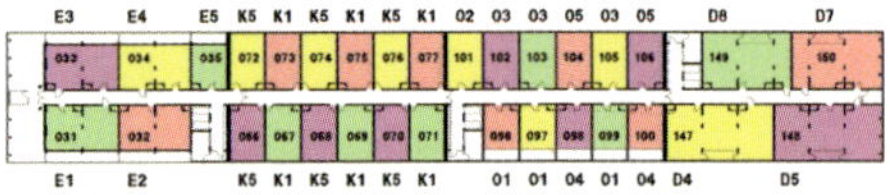

LEVEL 7

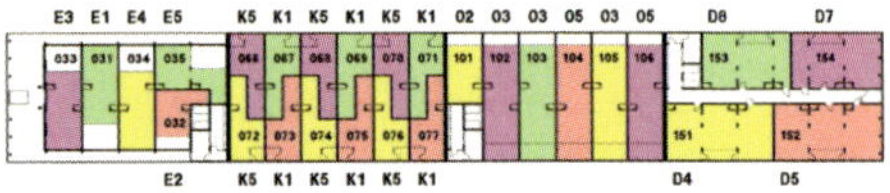

LEVEL 8

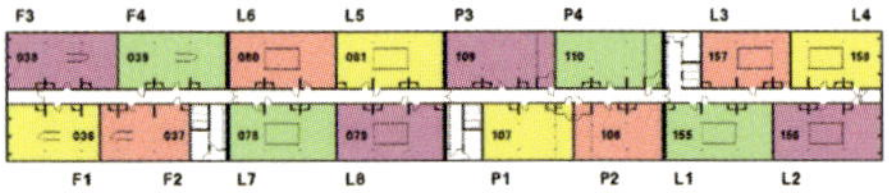

LEVEL 9

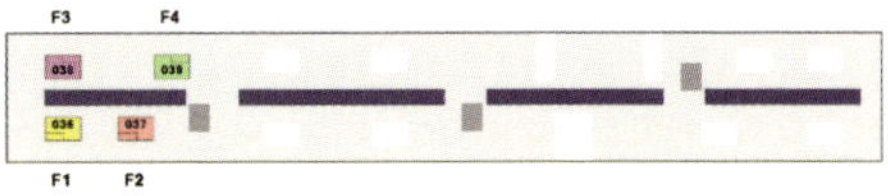

NIVEL 10

MVRDV

15 Silodam

ARCHITECTS Winy Maas, Jacob van Rijs and Nathalie de Vries with Frans de Witte, Eline Strijkers, Duzan Doepel, Bernd Felsinger. Prijsvraagontwerp with Tom Mossel, Joost Glissenaar, Alex Brouwer, Ruby van den Munckhof and Joost Kok FACILITARY OFFICE Bureau Bouwkunde B.V. Rotterdam CONSTRUCTION Pieters Bouwtechniek, Haarlem, Delft STRUCTURE Cauberg Huygen, Rotterdam CLIENT Rabo Vastgoed, De Principaal B.V. CONSTRUCTION Bouwcombinatie Graansilo’ V.O.F. (Bouwbedrijf M.J. de Nijs en Zonen B.V. en Kondor Wessels Noord)

In the Housing Silo, Amsterdam, 157 apartments (for purchase and rent), plus some business units as well as public space, are compressed within a tight, ten-storey-high and twenty-meter-deep urban envelope. The building is in line with adjacent existing silos and warehouses along the jetty that have also been converted into housing, and refers to container piles that you can find in harbours. To compensate for the loss of the windy spot at the end of the jetty, the pier has been pulled through the building, ending in the water again with a balcony accessible to the public. Under the balcony a business unit offers an equally magnificent view of the river.
The demand for a large variety of housing types has led to the design of as many spatial qualities and different housing types as possible. As a counterbalance to the increasing individuality, the housing types have been brought together in mini-neighbourhoods. These groups of four to eight houses are of the same type and can be recognised by their handling of elevation and the specific colours used in their corridors and galleries.
The houses not only differ in size and position within the building, but also through the placing of interior walls, widths (5-15 metres), depths (9-20 meters), levels (1-2-3 storeys, including diagonally), construction elements (walls, columns, beams), exterior spaces (greenhouse-style, balcony, patios, rooftops), heights (2.7-3.6 m), access (corridor, gallery, bridge, stairs), number of rooms (1 to 5), voids and different types of windows. The design enabled the removal of several walls, and furthermore the contractor has fulfilled many of the future inhabitants' individual wishes.
A large common balcony is positioned at the head of the building on the west side for all the inhabitants. Residents can also take a walk through the building that takes them past all the facades and roofs and along the marina and hall. Boats can be docked and moored in the marina under the building.
Within the bounds of the tight urban, structural and building regulations, the building represents the limits placed upon it by the desires of government, clients, city, inhabitants and designers. In the process of designing and building the Housing Silo, it was also possible to incorporate many of the participants' wishes.
The building is thus an index of the interaction between restriction and innovation.

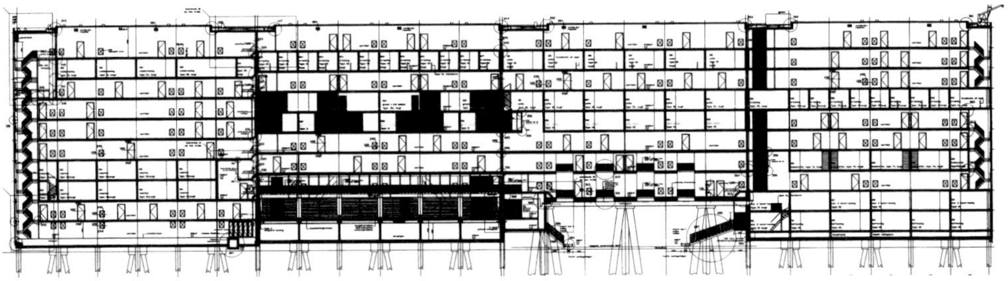

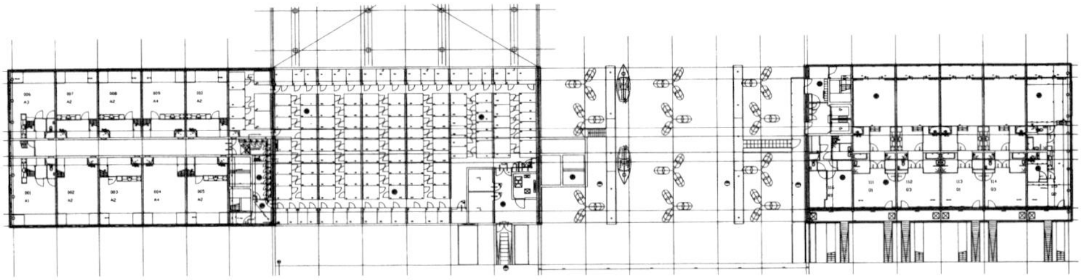

Level 0

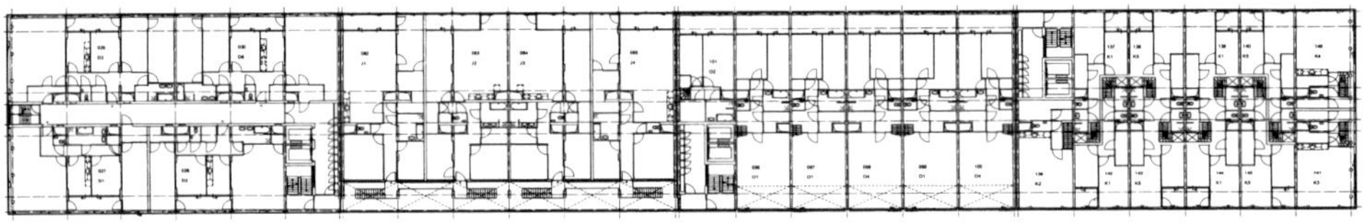

Level 5

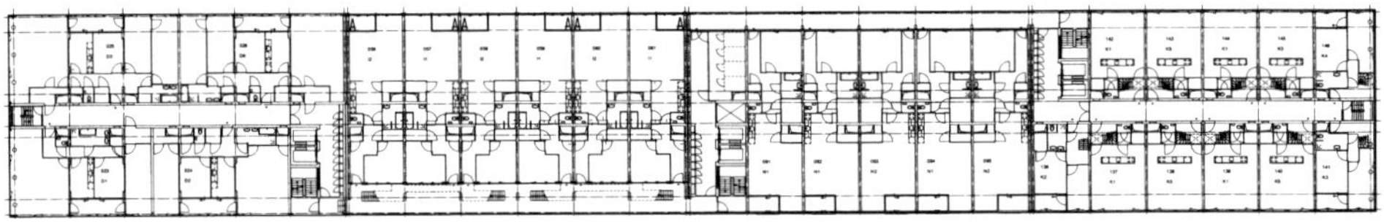

Level 6

MRVDV

15 ***Galaxy***

ARCHITECTS Winy Maas, Jacob van Rijs and Nathalie de Vries with Rene Marey, Andrew Tang, Bart Hollanders, Kersten Nabielek, Kok Kian Goh and Kristján Örn Kjartansson, Kersten Nabielek, Jeroen Zuidgeest, Sven Thorissen, Marc Joubert, Anet Schurink, Caroline Nagel, Ismael Miguel, Andreas Pedersen ASSOCIATED ARCHITECT Garrison Siegel Architects, New York, Robert Siegel LOCATION New York STRUCTURE Ove Arup and Partners, London and New York Rory Mc Gowan, Matt King, Chris Carroll GEOTECH Mueser Rutledge Consulting Engineers, New York SERVICES Ove Arup and Partners, London, Stephen Jolly FIRE Ove Arup and Partners, London and New York, Andy Passingham COST Pete & Company (New York), Peter E. Federman VIDEO Eline Wieland and Marino Gouwens, Rotterdam MODEL Vincent de Rijk, Rotterdam GRAPHIC DESIGN Graphic Language, Rotterdam

GALAXY is a design entry for an invited competition from Eyebeam Atelier for the new Museum of Art and Technology in New York City. The new EYEBEAM repositions the architecture of the museum as an ongoing investigation into the production and consumption of art. It combines education, research, development, communication, and exhibition, simultaneously thinking, doing, and showing.

To take advantage of the digital workplace, the old standard of a peripheral working zone surrounding a service core is inverted, creating maximum work space with minimum interruptions. The double perforated skin becomes not only space for circulation, but a control for lighting and acoustic levels and a massive and continuous projection screen - an experiential sieve.

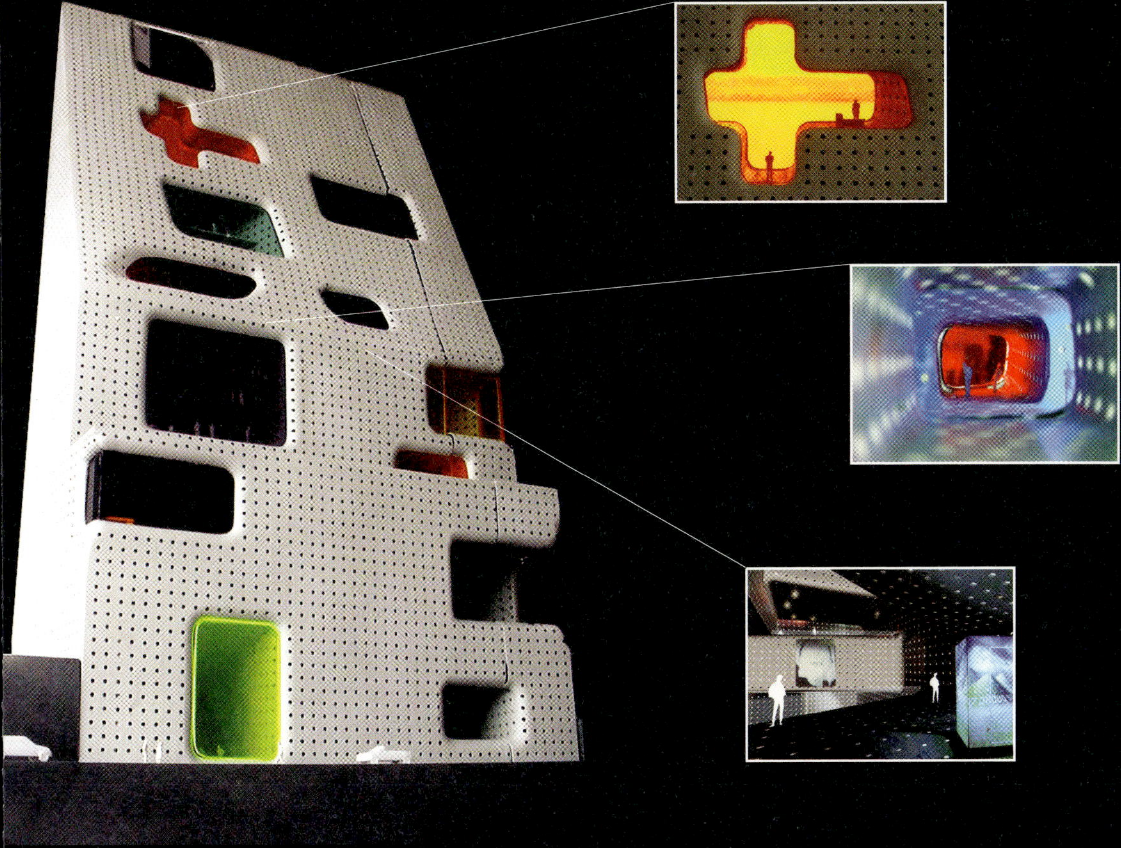

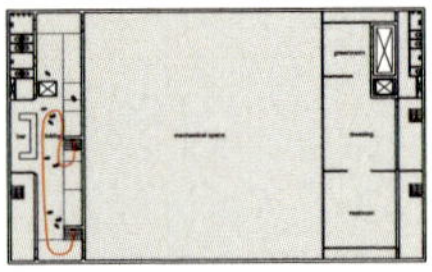

-3

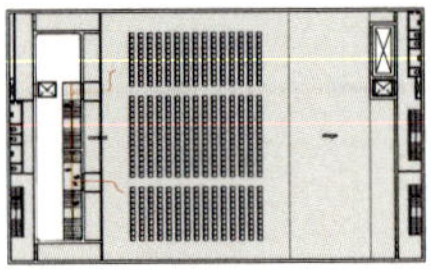

-2

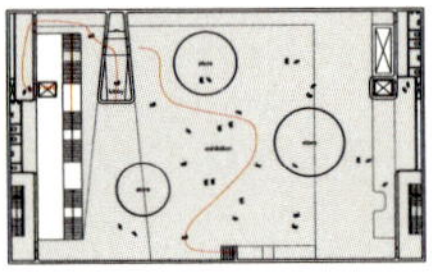

-1

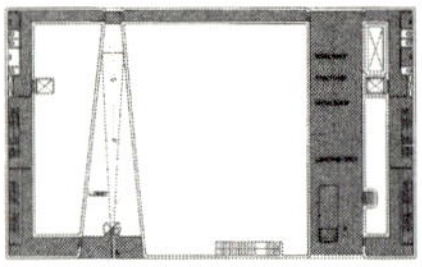

±0

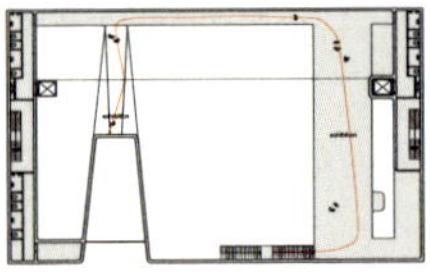

1

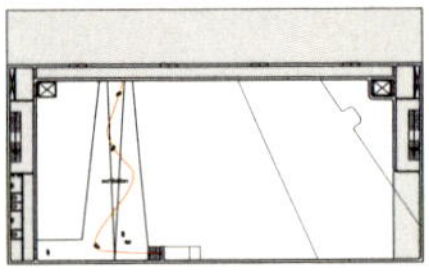

2

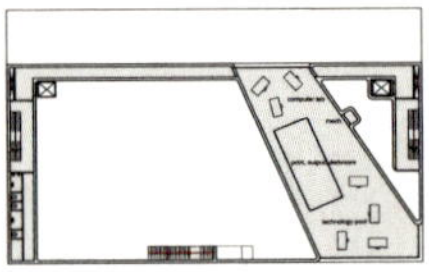

3

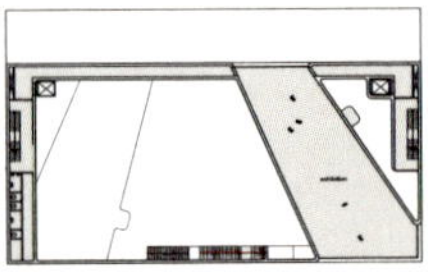

4

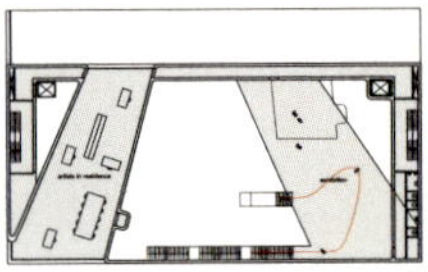

5

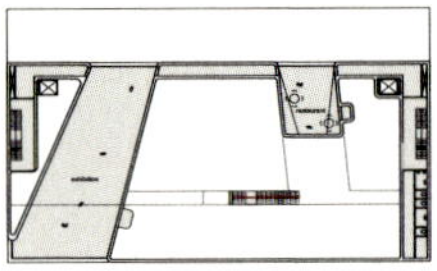

6

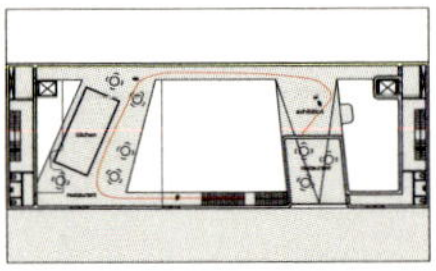

7

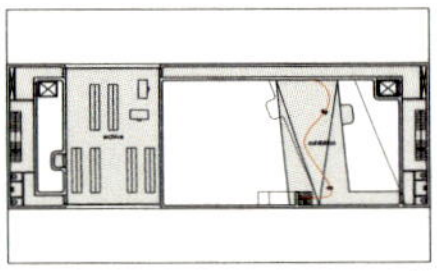

8

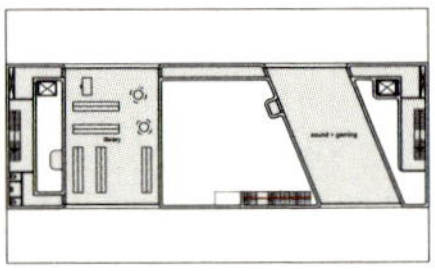

9

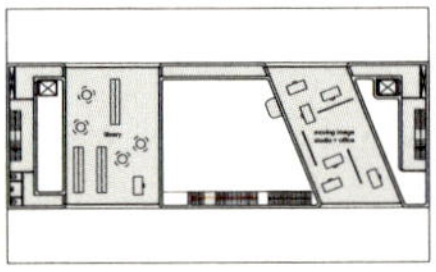

10

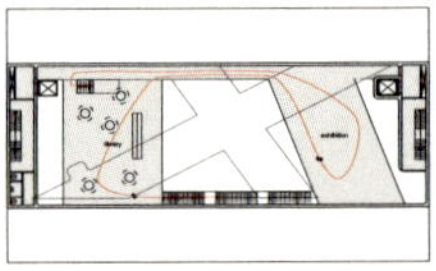

11

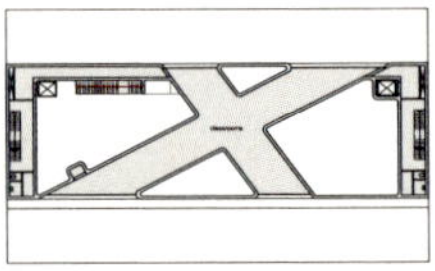

12

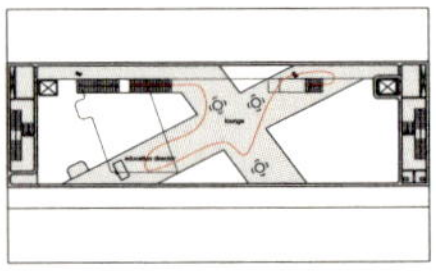

13

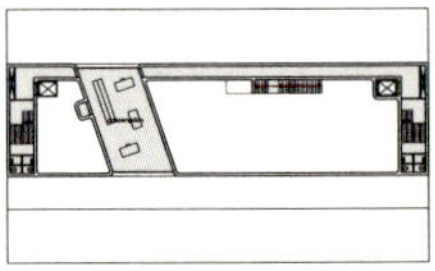

14

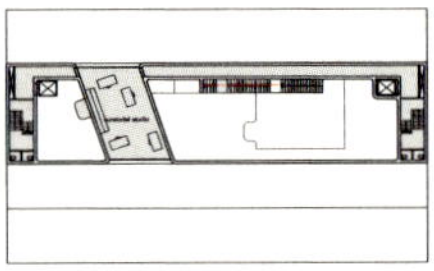

15

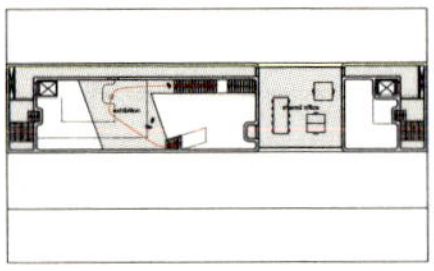

16

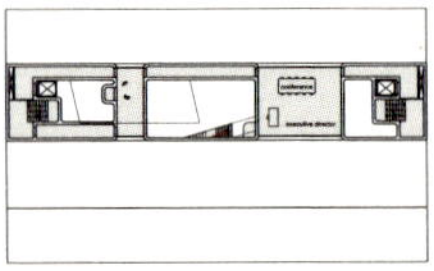

17

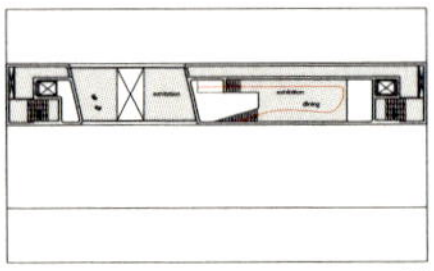

18

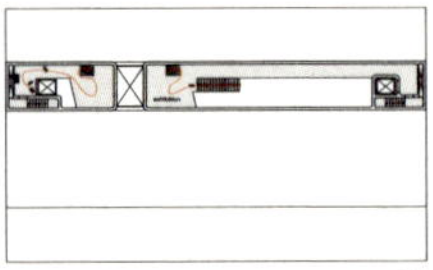

19

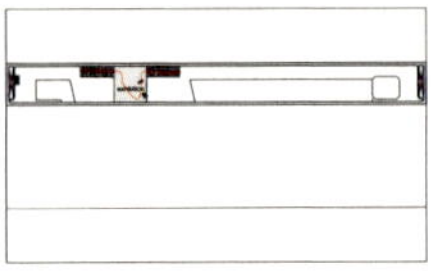

20

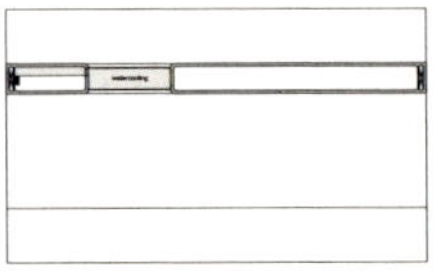

21

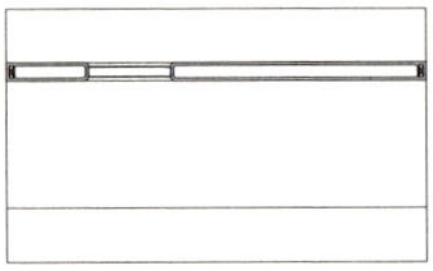

22

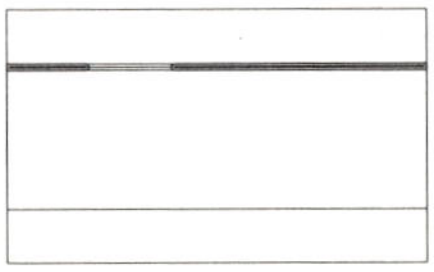

23

Just go away. You're
everyone knows w
like, so obvious.
u look at me. Just go
thetic. I mean, every
kinny eno
unny enou
young enou

15 Ministry of Agriculture

PROJECT TEAM Winy Maas, Jacob van Rijs and Nathalie de Vries with René Marey, Kersten Nabielek, Yves Malysse, Bart Hollanders, Marco de Francesco, Arthur de Roover, Andrew Tang, Sören Christian Madsen LOCATION The Hague, The Netherlands, 2001 CLIENT Rijksgebouwendienst, The Hague STRUCTURE Ove Arup & Partners, London SERVICES Ove Arup & Partners, London BUILDING PHYSICS DGMR Arnhem, Paul van Bergen CONSULTANTS Office for architectural engineering Bureau Bouwkunde Rotterdam, PKB Amsterdam (costs) Grontmij, De Bilt (ecology)

The Ministry of Agriculture has resided in a classic, almost Kafkaesque building in the heart of The Hague for the last forty years. Due to its age the building has technical faults. The building doesn't stand up to the functional demands of its users: the routing is long and boring and work spaces are placed in office cells allowing little communication between different groups of employees. The current building doesn't display any of the contemporary élan of the Ministry.
Designing a new building for the Ministry raises fundamental questions:
What should the role of a public building be in times when market mechanisms dominate? Could "ideology" again have a place in these fleeting times? Might the building emphasise invisible but very necessary basics, like food and natural resources?
Instead of replacing existing windows with double-glazing we propose to put a skin of glass around the building. The existing building will not be touched and can maintain its increased status as a monument. The skin of glass functions like a raincoat in which the climate can be controlled by means of plants. The plants provide a "buffer" between the workspaces and the outer climate. They offer shade, create oxygen and provide the right levels of humidity. A green "fortress" arises: a forest building surrounded by a petrified world. A huge greenhouse made up of four floors gives this forest "presence" and content.
A three-dimensional "arboretum" will become possible in which all the plant varieties of the Netherlands, all possible vegetation and habitats can be created. A modern Noah's Ark arises in which a series of different workspaces are made possible: from cells along a corridor, through cells around the square, open cells in the forest or around the water to open workplaces in a hall, in a forest, around the water.
It gives the different departments an identity. It creates "addresses", villages in a Kafkaesque continuum. A three-dimensional landscape arises.
The Ministry will become a public park and will contribute thereby to the existing public spaces in The Hague. The Ministry itself becomes public. It forms a manifesto on how to create new agriculture and new nature in a dense country like the Netherlands.

Genetic logic would manifest itself in systems and organisms and infrastructures through the development of evolutive trajectories.

Genetic Logic

1 2 3 4 5 6 7 8 9 10 11 12 13 14 15 16 17 18

Möbius house, Netherlands, 1998

UN STUDIO

16

NMR Facilities
Arnhem Central
Penn Station

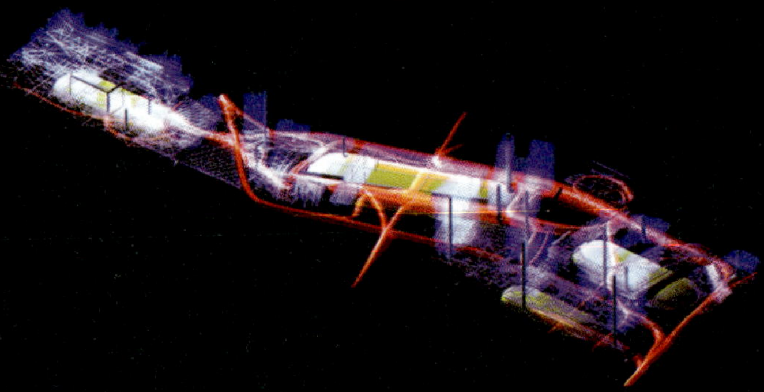

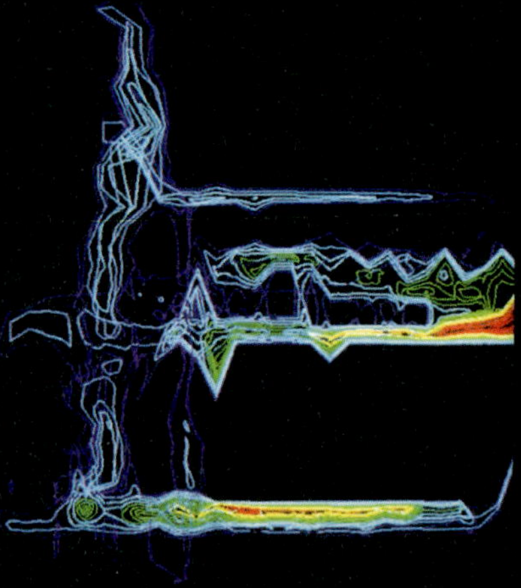

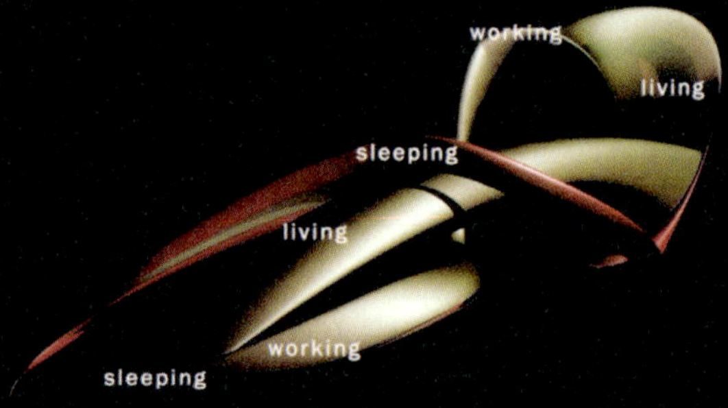
working
living
sleeping
living
working
sleeping

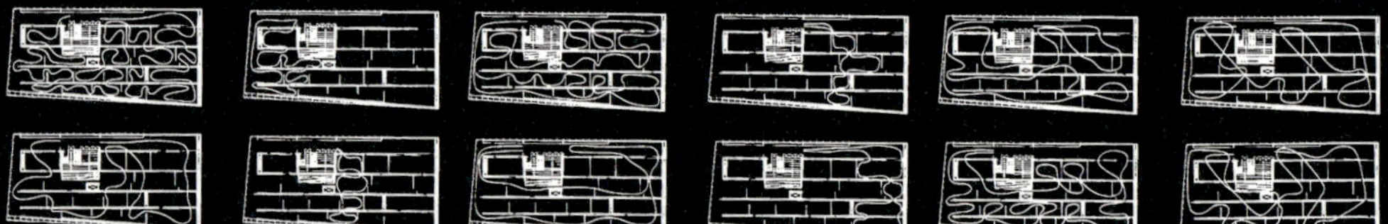

The new concept of the architect

The architect is going to be the fashion designer of the future. Learning from Calvin Klein, the architect will be concerned with dressing the future, speculating, anticipating coming events and holding up a mirror to the world. The architect's practice will be organised as a limitless virtual studio, like Andy Warhol's Factory scattered about; a network of superstars. Network practice extends existing forms of co-operation with clients, investors, users and technical consultants to include design engineers, finance people, management gurus, process specialists, designers and stylists. The new architectural network studio is a hybrid mixture of club, atelier, laboratory and car plant, encouraging plug-in professionalism. Making use of new technologies, the network architect benefits from the increased transferability of knowledge. The will to invent is fundamental, ensuring that the basic values of the discipline, ranging from geometry to materialisation, are always evolving. Because all experiments require proof of evidence, experimental practice continually oscillates between the abstract world of ideas and the physical world. New procedures and new techniques are tested out in site-specific, project-based experiments. Time is on the architect's side. The correlative approach to plan development makes use of the mapping of time to reveal relations in informational data and logistics. Developing specific visualising techniques, re-thinking virtual and material organisational structures, engaging public space, public forces and the public imagination, puts the architect once more at the centre of his own world. New concepts of control transform the untenable position of master builder into a public scientist. As an expert on everyday public information, the architect collects information that is potentially structuring, co-ordinates it, transforms it and offers ideas and images for the organisation of public life in an endless, seamless system.

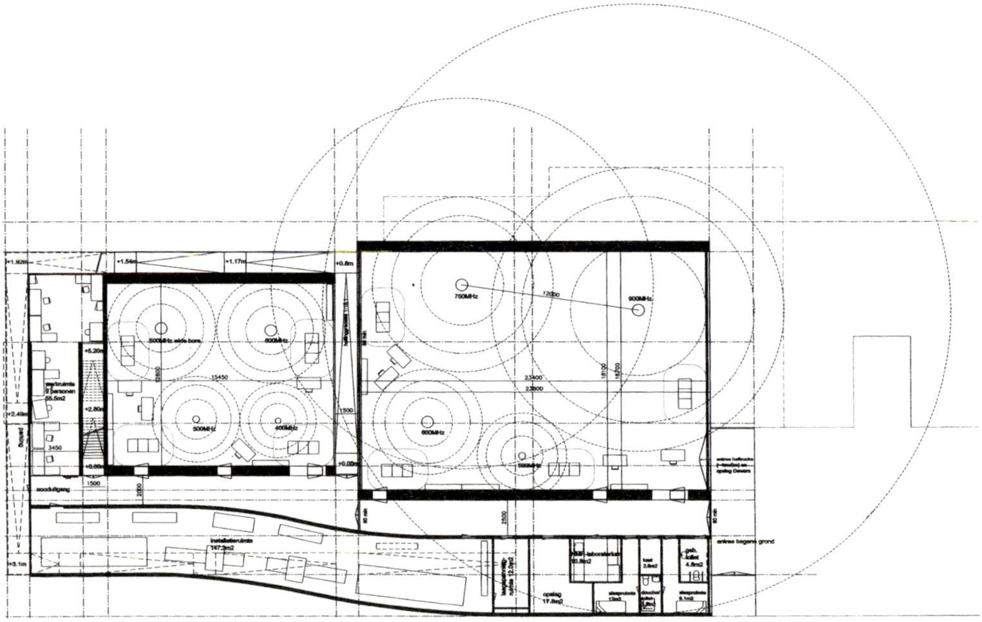

UN STUDIO

16 NMR Facilities

ARCHITECT Ben van Berkel LOCATION Leuvenlaan, De Uithof Utrecht PROJECT 1997-2001 CLIENT University of Utrecht COLLABORATORS Marion Regitko, Jacco van Wengerden, Ludo Grooteman, Laura Negrini, Paul Vriend, Mark Westerhuis, Jeroen Kreijnen, Henri Snel, Marc Prins, Aad Krom PROJECT COORDINATION Harm Wassink, Walther Kloet BUILDER ABT, Velp CONTRACTOR Nelissen van Egteren, Utrecht and Hoofddorp SURFACE 10.000 m² PHOTOGRAPHS Christian Richters

The organisation of the building is in its surfaces. Inside, experiments are conducted with sensitive research equipment emitting Gauss radiation. The clouds of radiation are essentially untouchable space, around with the planes of floor, ceiling and wall surfaces are wrapped. These thin wrappers contain the construction, installations and routing system of the laboratory. Together they form a loosely knotted assembly of smooth planes that flip over from floor to wall to ceiling.
The small pavilion-like laboratory for the NMR (Neutron Magnetic Resonance) facilities is situated on the university campus of Utrecht, "De Uithof." The unusual research technique itself and the molecular structures that it uncovers have strongly influenced the architecture of the laboratory. The two-storey laboratory contains eight spectrometers (high-frequency magnets), eight consoles and other ancillary equipment, as well as public and office spaces. The magnets all have specific behaviour patterns and requirements, creating magnetic fields of differing sizes and sensitivity. These affect the performance of other equipment present within a variable radius of the magnets. The sensitivity to movement, types of structure, installation and climate of the magnetic fields depends upon the differing frequencies of the magnets. Basically, these force files should not be disturbed.
As a result, the radiating powers of the magnets constitute the virtual core of the projects, and modify the organisation of the building. They provide permutations for the structure and surface of the building, the materials that can be used, the disposition of the program and the equipment, and the possible routing systems.
A second important structuring principle is the column-free spatial organisation, which enables efficient use of the small centre. The combination of these two central principles results in a multidirectional surface condition in which the walls flip over and meet each other to generate a situation in which all ends meet.
The building is split up in two different kinds of spaces: specific spaces and non-specific spaces. Both spaces have a maximum possible flexibility. The specific spaces are changeable because of time-bound technological progress; the flexible spaces (such as offices and public areas) can be changed in the event of an increase or decrease in the size of the department.

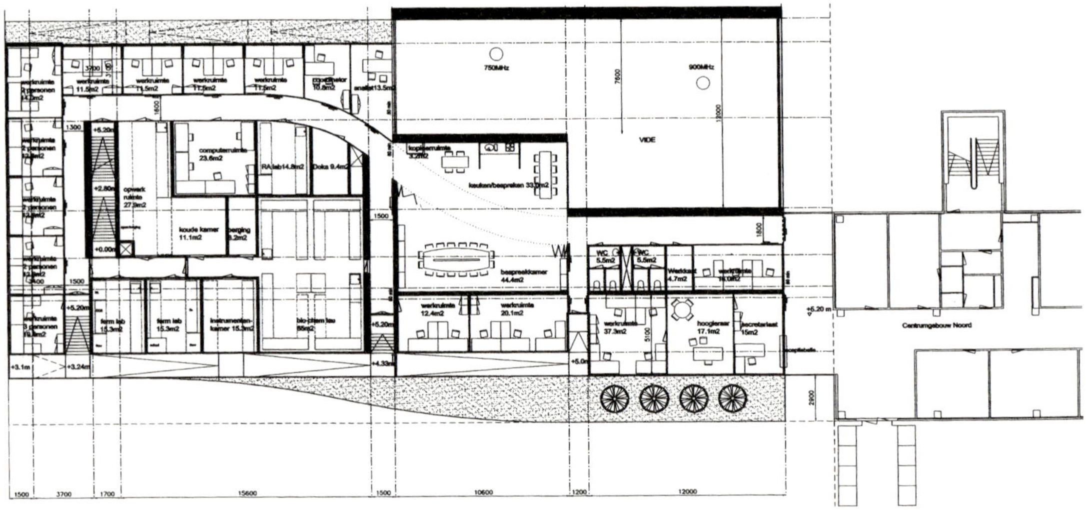

werkruimte 11.5m2
computerruimte 23.6m2
RA lab14.8m2
Doka 9.4m2
opwerk ruimte 27.3m2
koude kamer 11.1m2
ferm lab 15.3m2
ferm lab 15.3m2
750MHz
900MHz
VIDE
keuken/bespreken 33.0m2
bespreekkamer 44.4m2
werkruimte 12.4m2
werkruimte 20.1m2
WC 5.5m2
WC 5.5m2
werkruimte 37.3m2
hoogleraar 17.1m2
secretariaat 15m2
Centrumgebouw Noord
+6.20m
+2.80m
+0.00m
+5.20m
+3.1m
+3.24m
+4.33m
+5.0m
+5.20 m
1300
1500
1600
1800
2900
5100
7600
12000
1500
3700
1700
15600
1500
10600
1200
12000

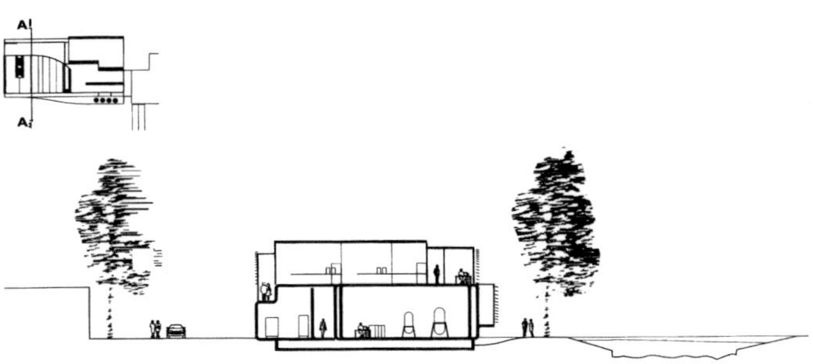

Coupe transversale AA

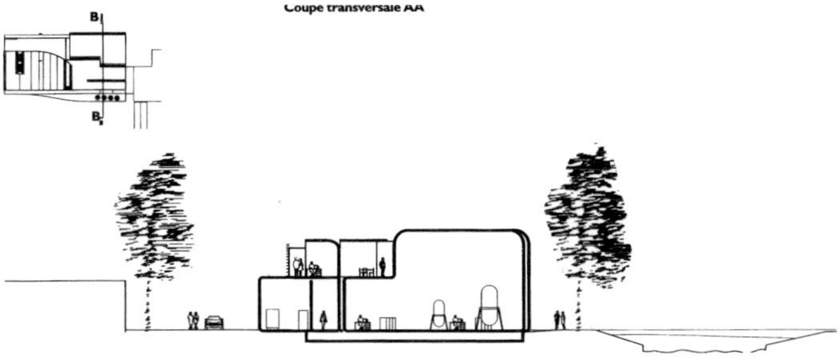

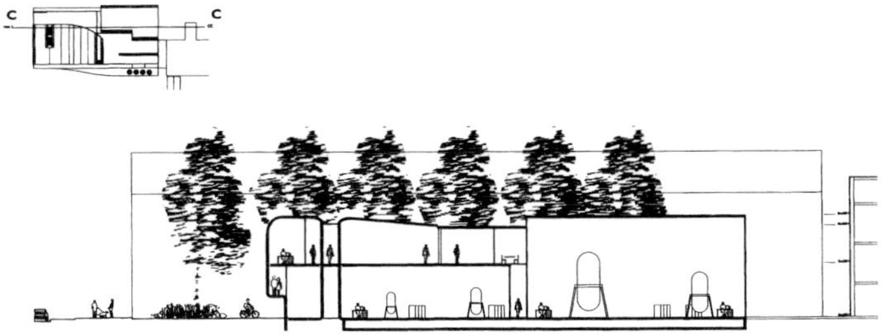

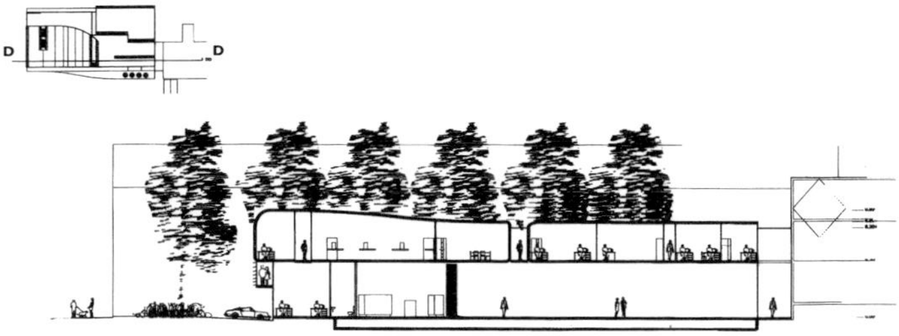

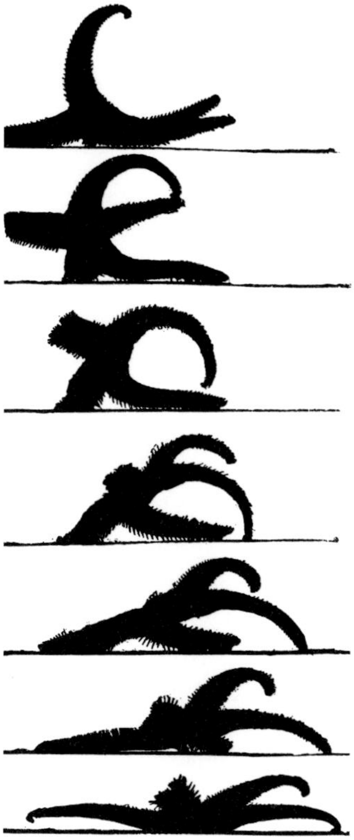

16 Arnhem Central Master Plan

ARCHITECTS Ben van Berkel with Tobias Wallisser, Sibo de Man DESIGN UN Studio in collaboration with Cecil Balmond (Ove Arup & Partners) LOCATION Arnhem Central, The Netherlands PROJECT 1996 – 2007 MASTERPLAN STUDY Freek Loos, Peter Trummer, Henk Bultstra MASTERPLAN Edgar Bosman, Astrid Piber, Oliver Bormann, Yuko Tokunaga, Ulrike Bahr, Ivan Hernandez, Cees Gajentaan, John Rebel, Andreas Krause TRANSFER HALL Nuno Almeida, Matthew Johnston, Antony Calcott, Ton van den Berg, Norbert Palz BUS DECK Jacco van Wengerden, Paul Vriend, Nuno Almeida, Phillip Koelher, Marco Hemmerling PARKING Jacques van Wijk, Ton van den Berg, Paul Vriend, Jacco van Wengerden, Mark Westerhuis, Eli Aschkenasy, Remko van Heumen TUNNEL Ger Gijzen, John Rebel OVE ARUP Joop Paul, David Johnston, Chris Rooney, Martin Walton, Patrick Teuffel, Charles Walker, Philip Jordan, Francis Archer.

This high-density project concentrates 160,000 m² of mixed programme on a 40,000 m² site. Six different transport systems converge on the station area and every weekday 55,000 travellers move through the location as they transfer from one system to another. Programme: transfer hall, underground car park, tunnel, shops, offices.
Deep planning: The Arnhem Transfer Zone focuses on the finding of overlapping areas of shared parameters and common values. Movement studies are the cornerstone of the proposal: the analysis of the types of movement on location includes the directions of the various trajectories, their prominence in relation to other forms of transportation on the site, duration, links to different programmes and interconnections.
The "Klein bottle" diagram served as a reference for the spatial transformation of a surface into a whole. A deformation of the diagram is applied to the transfer hall to realise the spatial integration of the area into a one-terminal concept.
The V-shaped shafts of the car park integrate functional, constructional and technical aspects. The shafts provide constructive stability, enable vertical public accessibility and regulate the natural air and light supply in the car park.

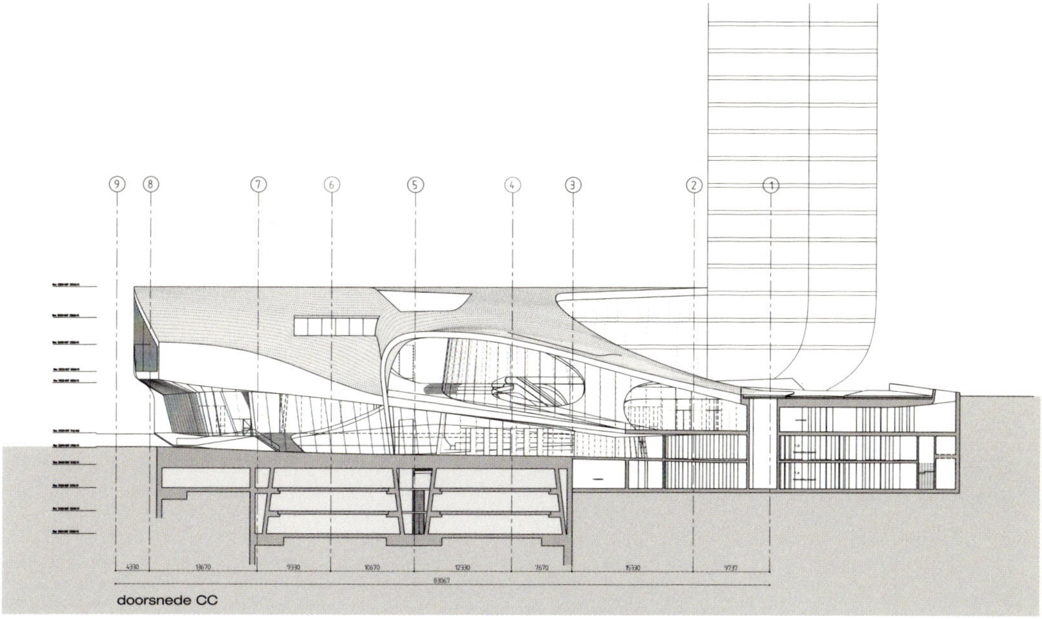
doorsnede CC

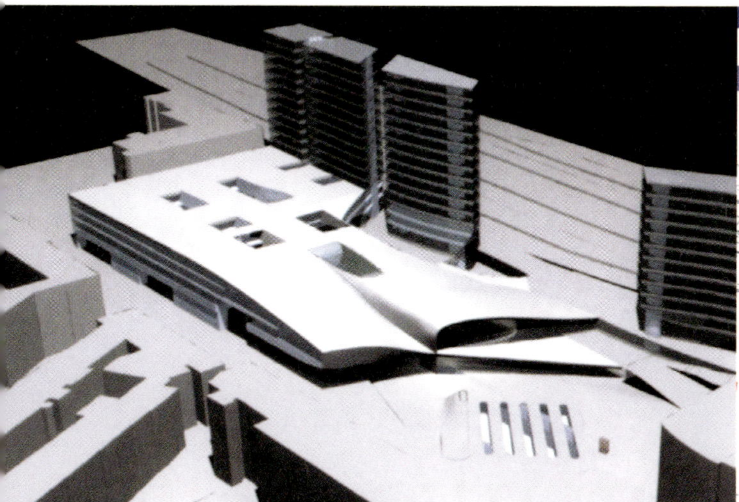

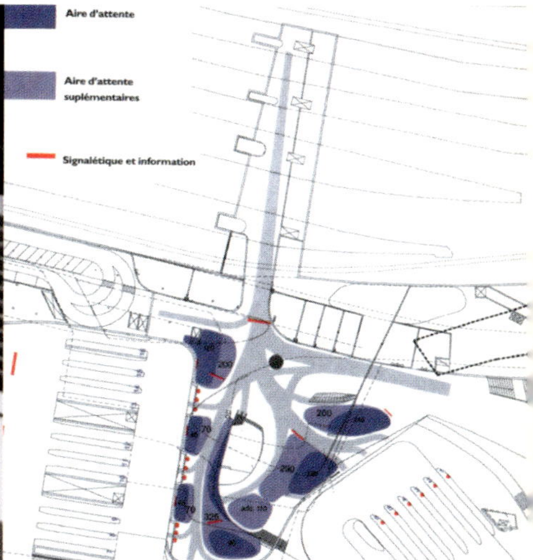
Aire d'attente
Aire d'attente suplémentaires
Signalétique et information

UN STUDIO

17 Penn Station

ARCHITECTS Ben van Berkel, Caroline Bos, Tobias Wallisser, Olaf Gipser PROJECT 1999, IFCCA Competition LOCATION New York PROJECT TEAM Hans Sterck, Jasper Jaegers, Philip Koehler, Stephanie Kulmann, Bas Kwaaitaal, Alexander Jung with Ludo Grooteman, Remco Bruggink, Andreas Bogenschütz Urban Filter.com (Vienna): Armin Hess. Susanne Boyer ADVISORS Ove Arup (London): Cecil Balmond, David Johnston, Paul Whitehouse, Juan Alavo Office 21 Fraunhofer IAO (Stuttgart): Alexander Rieck, Stephan Zinser

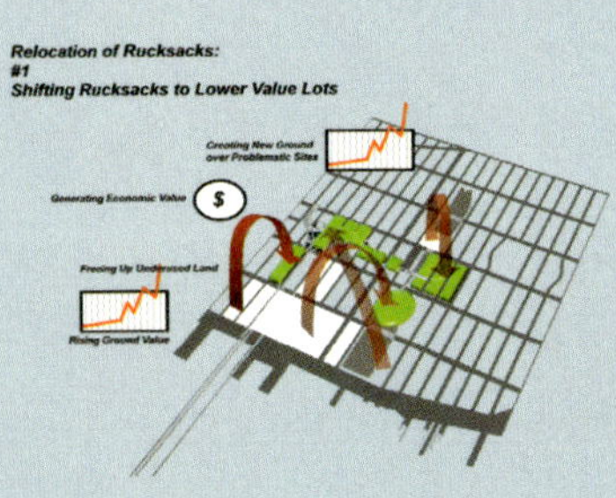

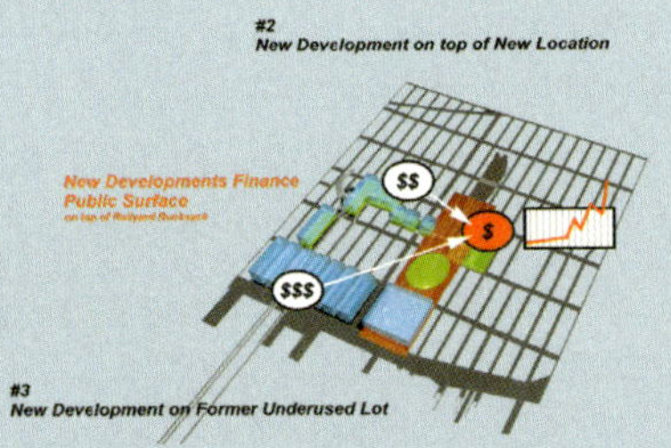

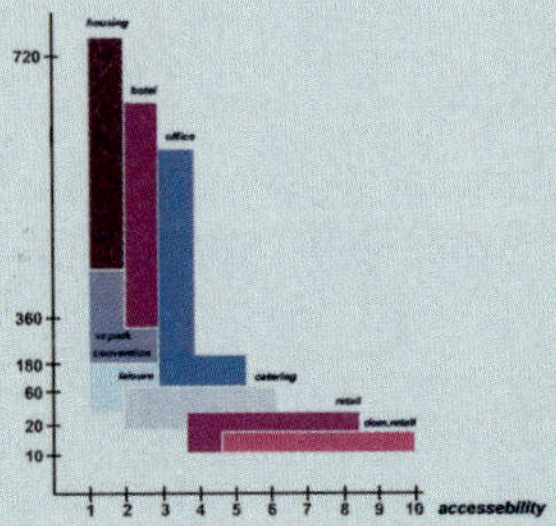

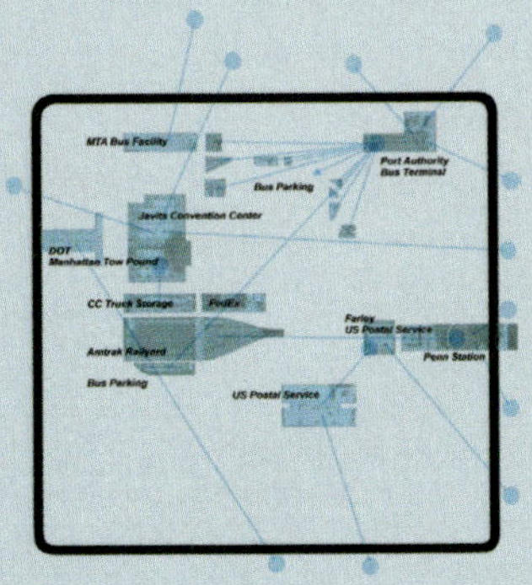

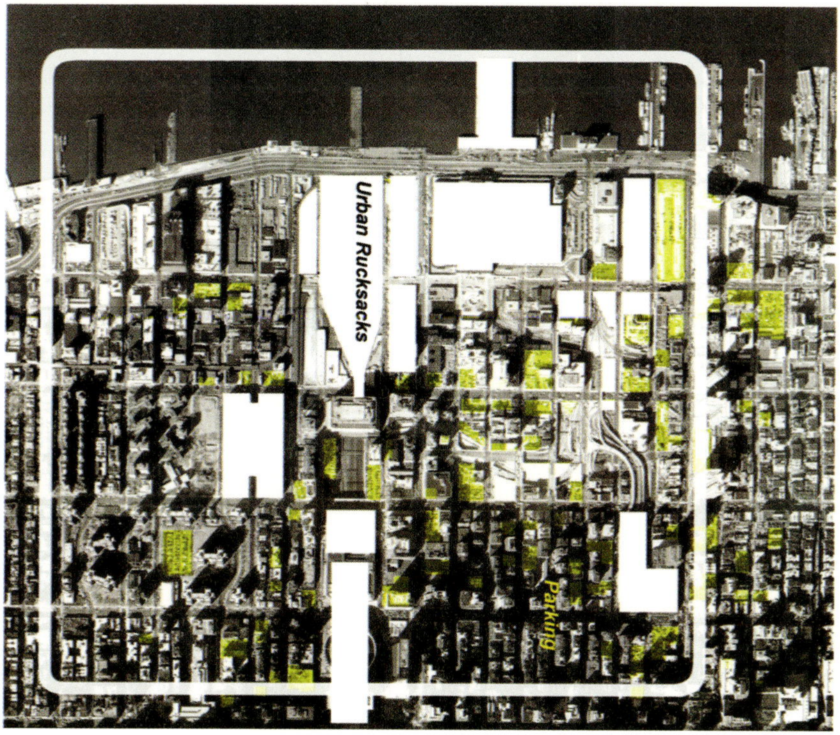

This proposal studies the Competition Site in relation to its historical development, to the greater metropolitan area of New York City and especially to its immediate surroundings. The subject of this study is the area between 42nd and 23rd Street. This area contains a number of service facilities that form obstacles in two respects: they constitute physical barriers that block fluent connections between the locations and they prevent the further development and full land use of several districts.
There are some ten facilities that are vital to the smooth running of Manhattan as a whole, but that have a negative effect on their immediate surroundings and thus block the further development of West Side, Chelsea, Clinton and the Garment District. We propose to concentrate as many of these facilities as possible.
Using funds and land generated by the rucksack negotiation strategy, the superblock between Pennsylvania Station and the waterfront is built over by a public surface incorporating routes, different types of landscape and urban spaces and three mixed-use clusters (living, working and service functions).
The new program we propose implies a considerable increase in housing, as well as functions that generate secondary local programs, such as restaurants, retail outlets and suchlike services.

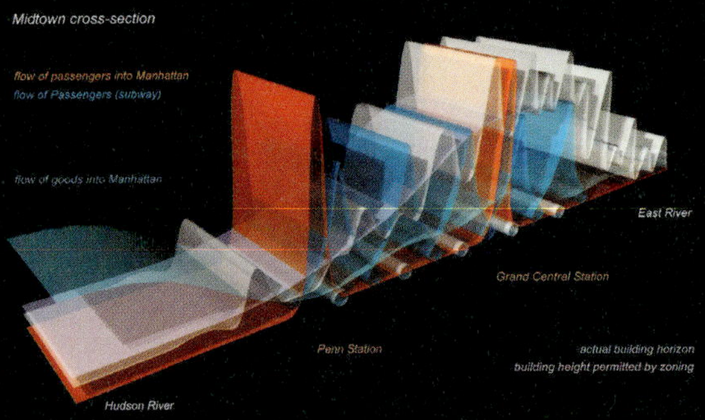
Midtown cross-section
flow of passengers into Manhattan
flow of Passengers (subway)
flow of goods into Manhattan
East River
Grand Central Station
Penn Station
actual building horizon
building height permitted by zoning
Hudson River

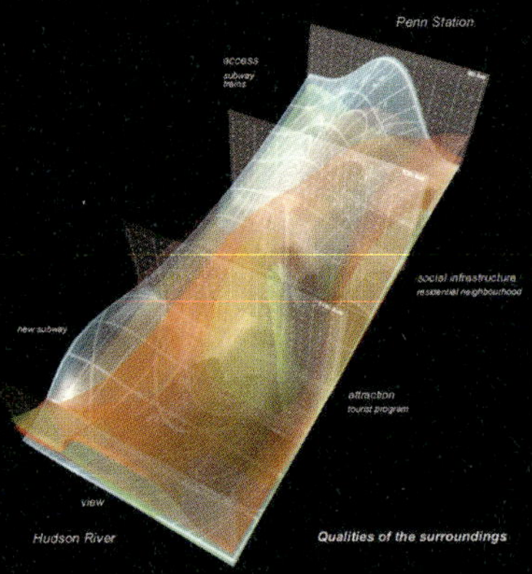
Penn Station
access
subway
trains
social infrastructure
residential neighbourhood
new subway
attraction
tourist program
view
Hudson River
Qualities of the surroundings

time [h]
living
residents
commuter
city user
metropolitan businessmen
consuming
consuming
producing
publicness
producing
producing
5 minutes
living
consuming
consuming
3 minutes
access

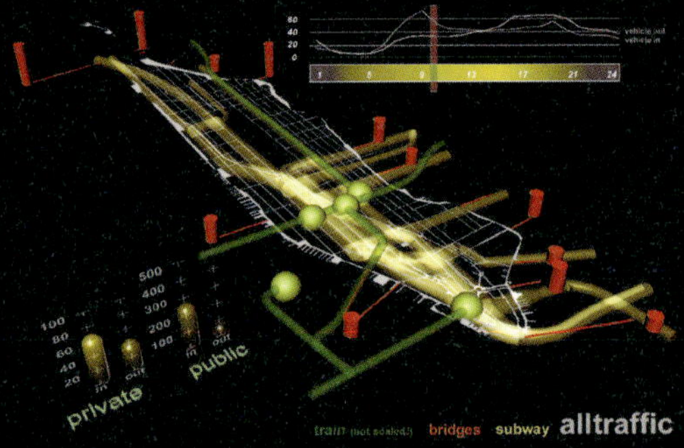
private
public
train
bridges
subway
alltraffic

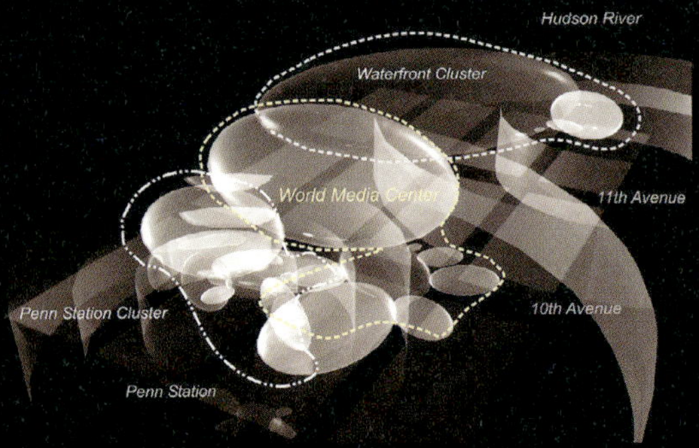
Hudson River
Waterfront Cluster
World Media Center
11th Avenue
10th Avenue
Penn Station Cluster
Penn Station

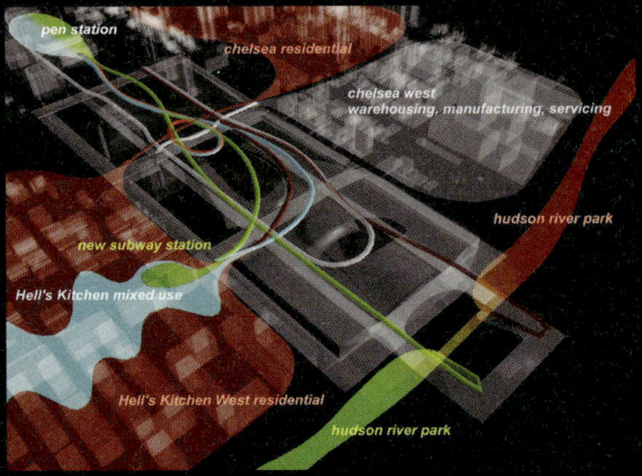
pen station
chelsea residential
chelsea west
warehousing, manufacturing, servicing
hudson river park
new subway station
Hell's Kitchen mixed use
Hell's Kitchen West residential
hudson river park

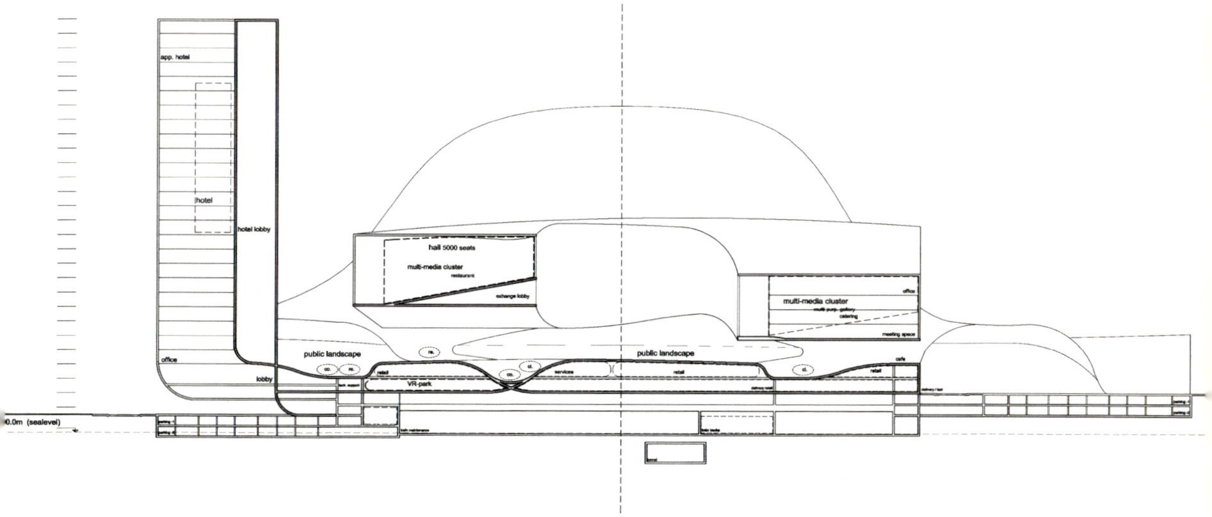

app. hotel
hotel
hotel lobby
office
lobby
hall 5000 seats
multi-media cluster
restaurant
exchange lobby
multi-media cluster
office
catering
meeting space
public landscape
public landscape
VR-park
services
retail
retail
cafe
0.0m (sealevel)

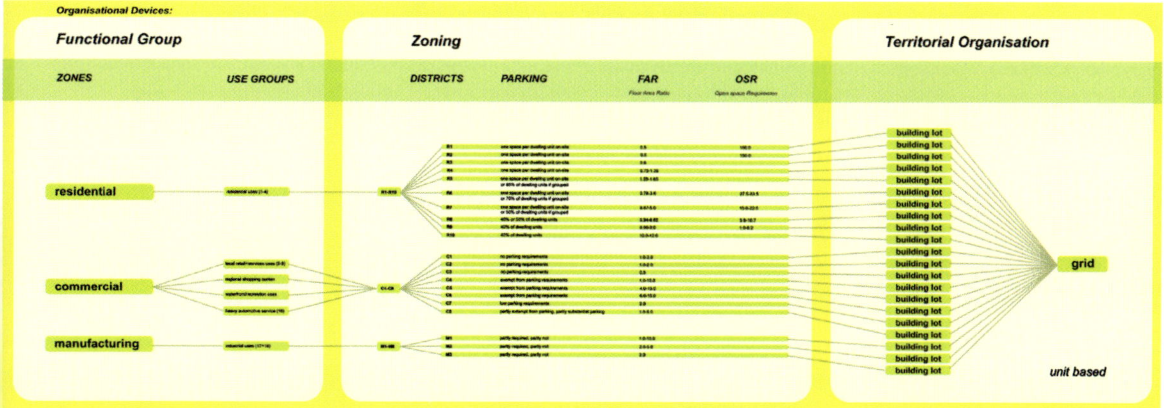

Organisational Devices:
Functional Group
ZONES
USE GROUPS
residential
commercial
manufacturing
Zoning
DISTRICTS
PARKING
FAR
OSR
Territorial Organisation
building lot
grid
unit based

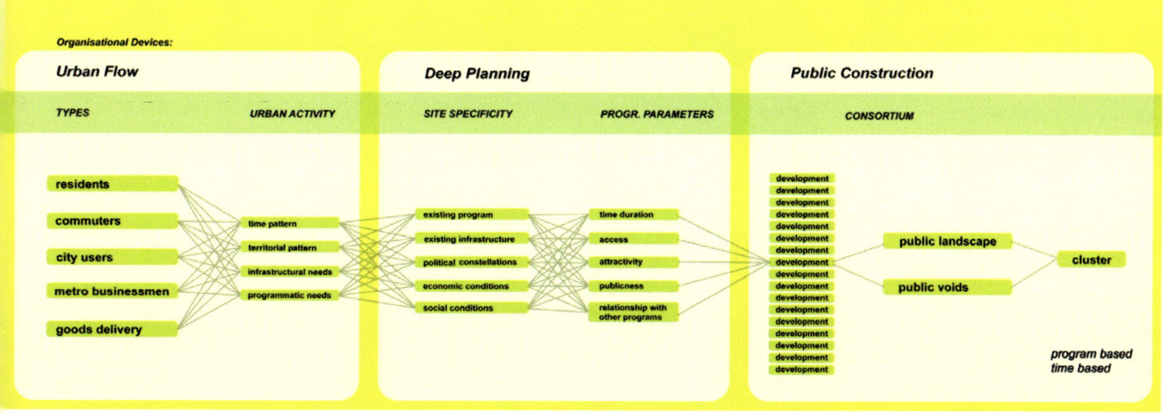

Organisational Devices:
Urban Flow
TYPES
URBAN ACTIVITY
residents
commuters
city users
metro businessmen
goods delivery
time pattern
territorial pattern
infrastructural needs
programmatic needs
Deep Planning
SITE SPECIFICITY
PROGR. PARAMETERS
existing program
existing infrastructure
political constellations
economic conditions
social conditions
time duration
access
attractivity
publicness
relationship with other programs
Public Construction
CONSORTIUM
development
public landscape
public voids
cluster
program based
time based

NOX 17

Oblique WTC
Paris BRAIN
Soft Office

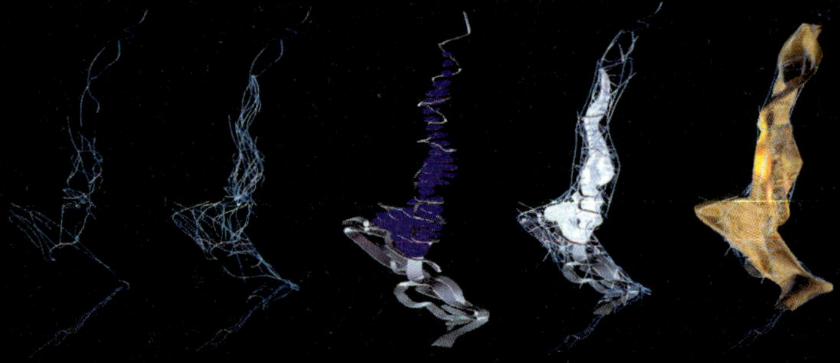

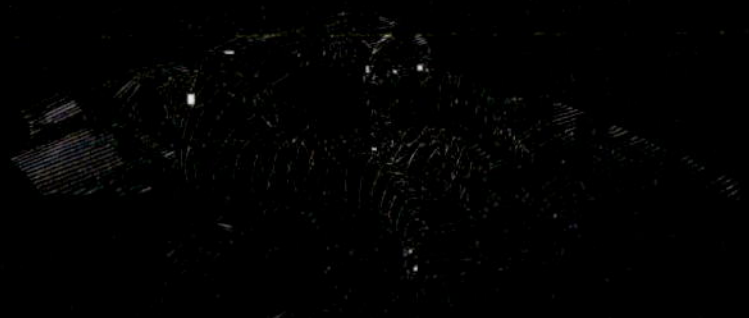

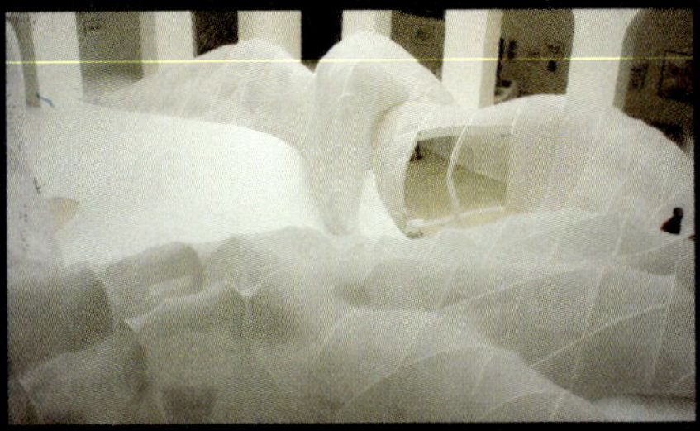

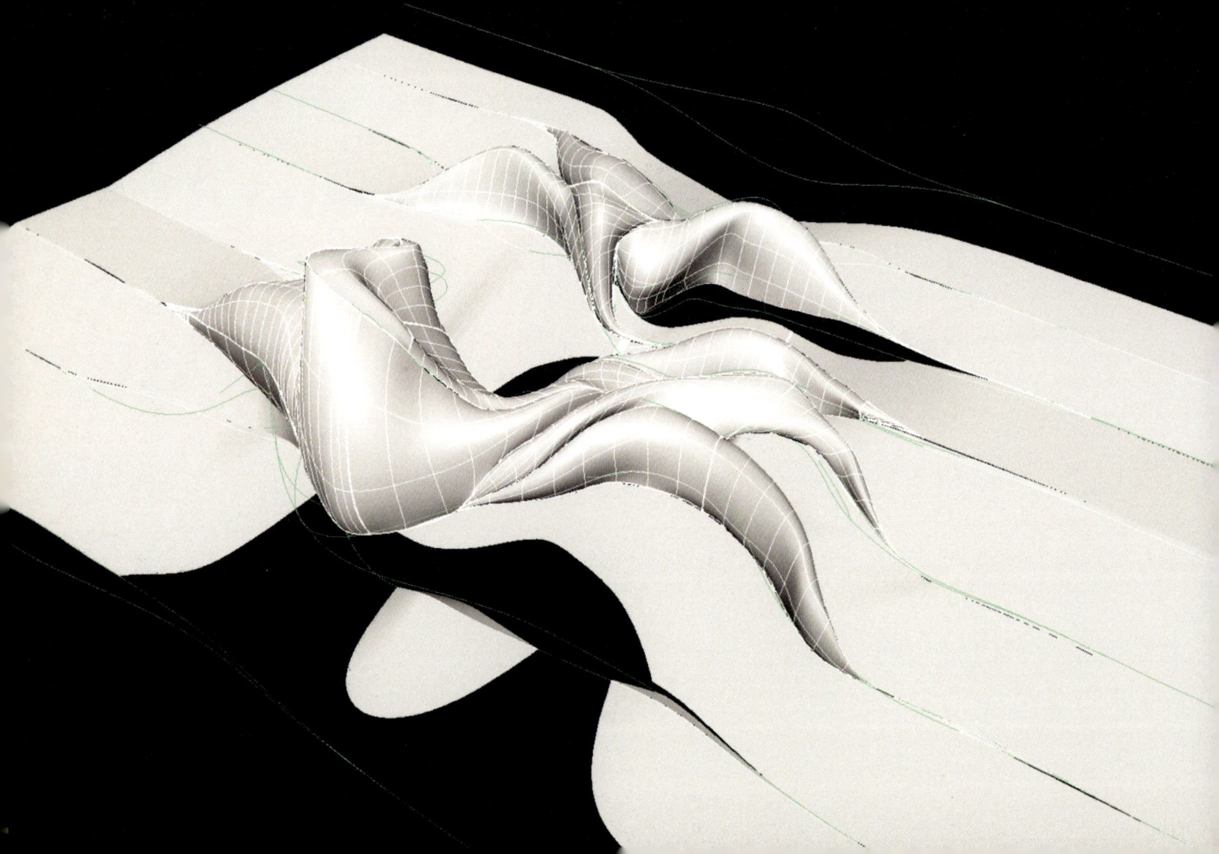

Wet Grid vs. Dry Grid

The dry grid is a system that separates movement from structure; the structure is of a solid, while the movement is of a liquid. The wet grid, Frei Otto's grid, is one in which movement is structurally absorbed by the system; it is a combination of intensive and extensive movement, of flexibility and motion. The organisation is wet, while the structure is dry. It implies that extensive, Cartesian, bodily locomotion is only possible when it is intensive first, both in the body and in the system. There is a direct relationship between the system of motion and the internal mapping of movements in the body. In the dry grid the body is acting as in an archive, it is constantly picking movements of the shelf, every act is a re-enaction – the body itself is a dry grid. The wet grid views the body as a complex landscape of tendencies and chreodes that form grooves (lines) in less defined areas that are surfaces. The dry grid is not very different in its ambitions than, say, the box or the hall in architecture: finding a structure, a tectonics that can absorb life, chance and change, while the structure itself must last and persist over time, to span the unforeseen with the foreseeable. The strategy of the grid and the box have always been to average out all possible events, to be general enough for anything. Our whole question here becomes a study of the relationship between flexibility and movement. In opposition to the cubist position, which states that movement is a deconstruction of form, we state here that nothing is as constructivist, as structuralist, as movement. But then movement must be viewed as information, as pure difference that can be absorbed by a system, which subsequently must be a (analogue) computing system.

NOX

17 *Oblique WTC*

ARCHITECTS NOX (Lars Spuybroek with Chris Seung-woo Yoo and Kris Mun) for the Max Protetch Gallery PROJECT 2001

1

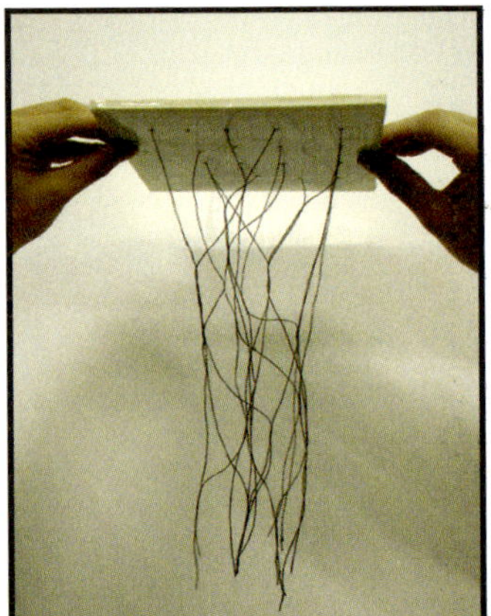

We should try to find *urban strategies* to deal with the Huge. In rethinking the mega, the Huge (which is slightly related to the High), we should be more concerned with the structure of the Huge than its size. In this project we reused the old wool thread modeling technique invented by Frei Otto and his Institute for Lightweight Structures in the 1970's. In our case we used one wool thread for each core of the destroyed or damaged buildings on the former WTC site. As an inverted model the wool threads hang straight down under the sole influence of gravity forces.
When dipped into water and taken out again all threads reorganize themselves into a complex network (with the cohesive lateral forces of the water now added to the gravitational system), comparable to bone structure. The structure is not formed anymore by a simple extrusion of a plan, but self-organizes into a networked megastructure where the whole is larger than the sum of its parts.
We thicken each of the wool threads into a lean tower that merges and splits up as it moves upwards. This enables the structure to comply with the New York zoning law that only allows high buildings to occupy 25% of the total site surface area. In this case however the 25% is always positioned somewhere else, making it both into one single Megabuilding with many (structural) holes in it or many thin towers that cooperate into one large structure. The towers sometimes act as a bridge, sometimes as a counterstructure for another one, and sometimes free themselves to become a smaller subtower. Most of the loads are transported through a honeycomb steel structure of the surface which is helped by an interior column grid, which follows the diagonals of the towers. Also the elevators form a highly complex structure of diagonals where at some platforms more than five or six different cores come together to form larger public areas. It is this network of elevators which makes the building not just a new type of tower but more like a new type of urbanism.

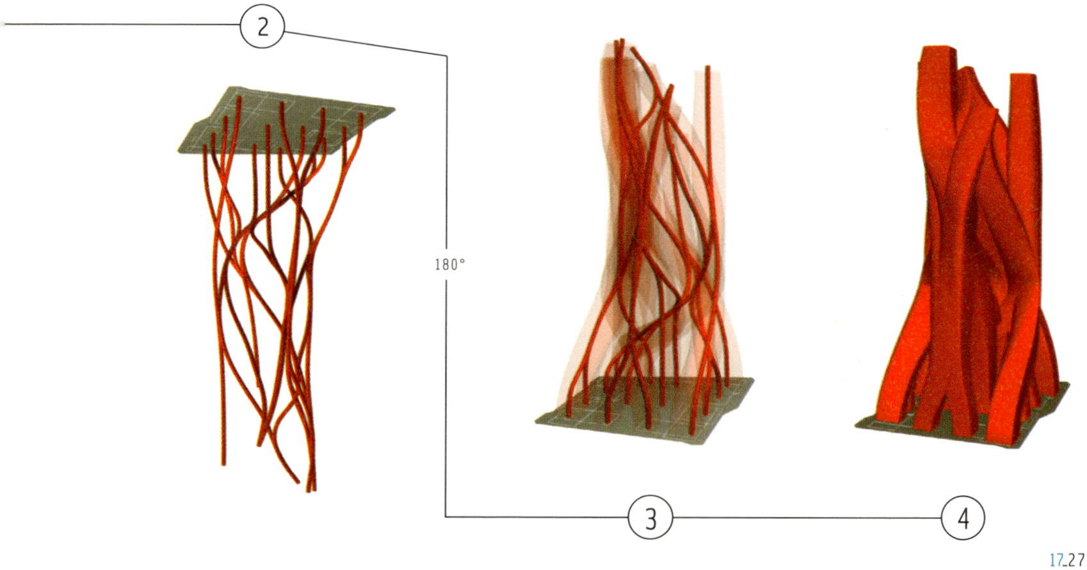

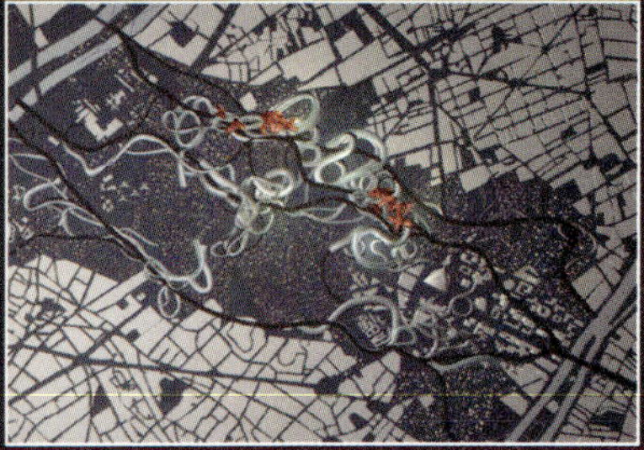

NOX

17 **Paris BRAIN**

A transurban scheme for the area west of La Défense, Paris ARCHITECTS NOX (Lars Spuybroek with Kris Mun, Ludovica Tramontin, Florent Rougemont and Chris Seung-woo Yoo) PROJECT 2001, installation for the *Expériences d'Urbanisme* exhibition at the Institut Neérlandais in Paris – for Els Hoek)

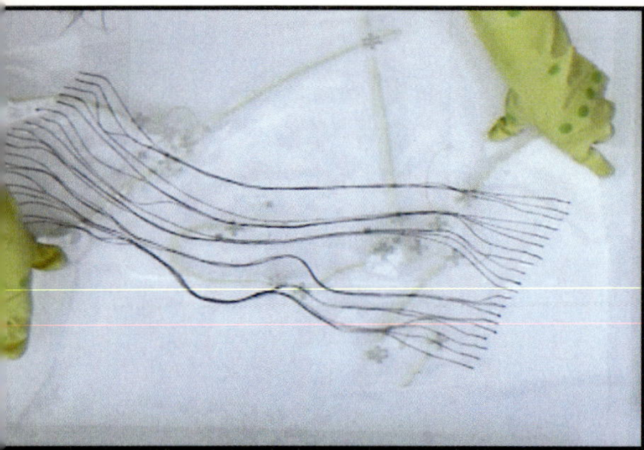

20 wool threads with 8 % overlength in the direction of the Grande Axe

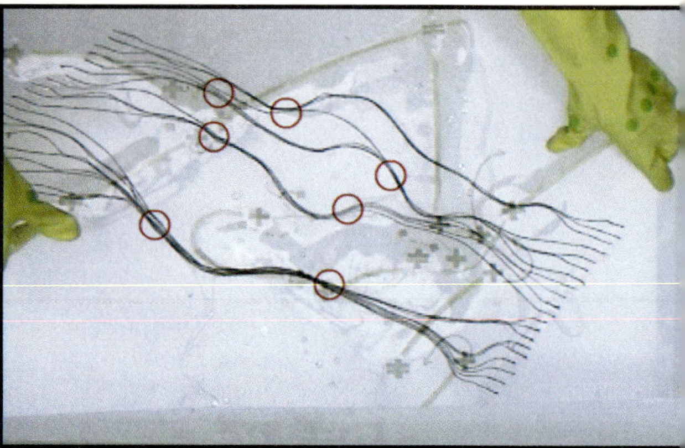

First insertion of loose ends at merged points

For the 2001 exhibition *Expériences d'urbanisme: Visions des Pays-Bas* at the Institut Néerlandais in Paris, we set up an installation that used intensive techniques in an experimental way. The exhibition included works like Constant's *New Babylon*, Aldo van Eyck's *Orphanage*, Piet Blom's *Kasbah*, Theo van Doesburg's *Aubette* and OMA/Rem Koolhaas' Yokohama project. We intentionally investigated these historical options and their relation to both early Situationism and contemporary experience design in the project ParisBRAIN.

a. Speakscape. Instead of making a horizontal wool-thread model with an open ring, we chose here to let the moving and merging lines interact with a smooth supporting surface, a sheet of transparent Perspex. The shape of the surface greatly influences the merging and bifurcating tendencies of the wool threads. We vertically deformed the shape of the surface into a landscape that would influence how fast the water ran off as the system was taken out of the tank after dipping. Its geography was a mapping of collective movements of the people in the area west of La Défense in Paris.

Speak Forces

Movement

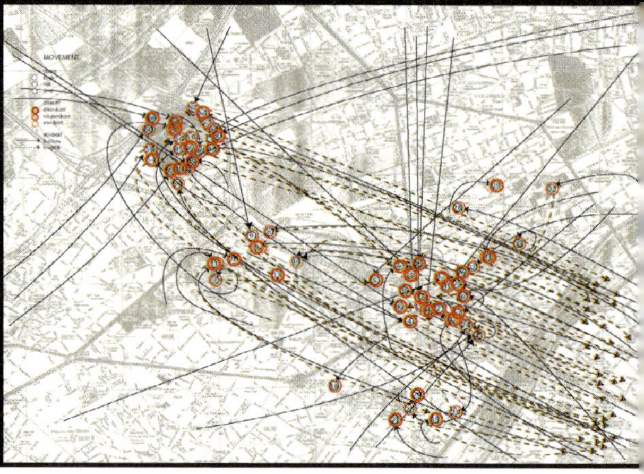

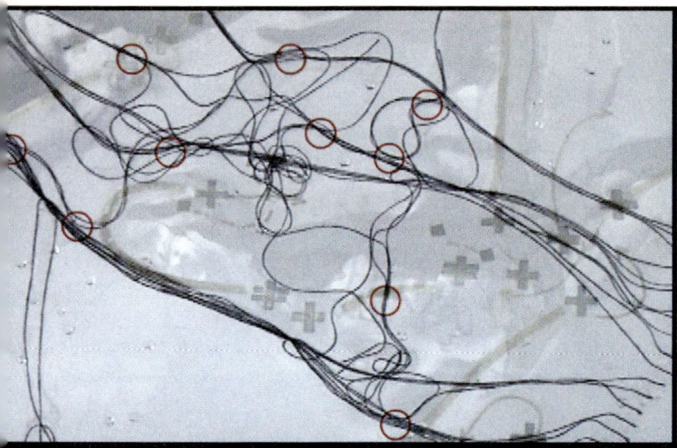

Second insertion of loose ends at merged points

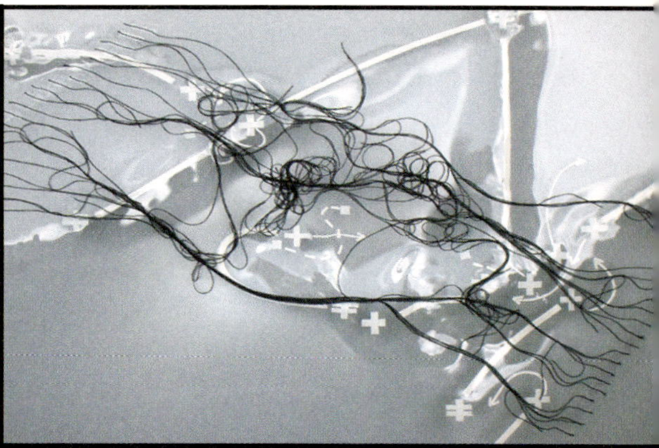

Dry structure of entanglements and merging

b. Entangled space (mega-architecture). We placed a set of parallel wool threads in the direction of the Grande Axe and attached them at the two sides of the Perspex with an overlength of 12%. The aim was to create a big shopping and leisure centre of airport proportions in the middle of an historic city. The five-by-two-kilometre area would connect to the La Défense area on the east side, and to several highways and a bridge on the west side. We shook the system under water and took it out slowly. Whenever we found merging groups among the wool threads, we tied them up with loose ends of decreasing length. We did this in four steps, organising the structure mainly through entanglements, spatial knots inserted to structure the "drifting" experience of strolling and shopping.

c. Dotted space (micro-urbanism). The system of tubular commercial buildings connected to global money flows would have an enormous effect on local land prices. The area between this shopping structure and the edge of surrounding nineteenth-century Paris should, we decided, be a conglomerate of *tax-free zones*, where local initiatives could develop freely, a *terrain vague* that would not be filled up immediately by buildings, but by an urbanism that would develop over a certain time span.

New Structure

Speak

NOX

17 **Soft Office**

ARCHITECTS NOX (Lars Spuybroek with Chris Seung-Woo Yoo, Kris Mun, Florent Rougemont and Ludovica Tramontin) PROJECT 2000-2005 - shop, interactive playground and headquarter office for an anonymous client, United Kingdom.

Soft Office is a building where work and play are deeply interwoven. It is a building where both children play and adults work. One half of the building is reserved for very young children to play with interactive environments (that are also present on the web), the other half for adults to work in a so-called *flexi-office* where no one has his or her own workplace, and where the environment is made for both functional, formal conduct as well as for more informal creative conduct like writing, discussions and presentations.

Soft Office is a project where intensive movement and extensive movement are closely related. We all know, being humans, that our emotions, moods and feelings influence the way we move in space, that our intensive movement is related to our extensive movement. Though modern management theory recognizes there is a necessary rigidity organizing tasks around set goals, a certain relaxation of their implementation has become vital. While short- and long term goals are a crucial, because they form the hinges of planning strategies, they shouldn't become so fixed they start becoming unproductive and oppose innovation and creativity What becomes evident here is that the architecture of group behavior with all its dynamics is directly related to the architecture of the building. A behavior of continuous grouping and regrouping, of solidifying into a certain configurations, then suddenly melting and regrouping in other fixed states. A behavioral vagueness paralleled by an architectural vagueness.

Analysis/Prediction Flexibility

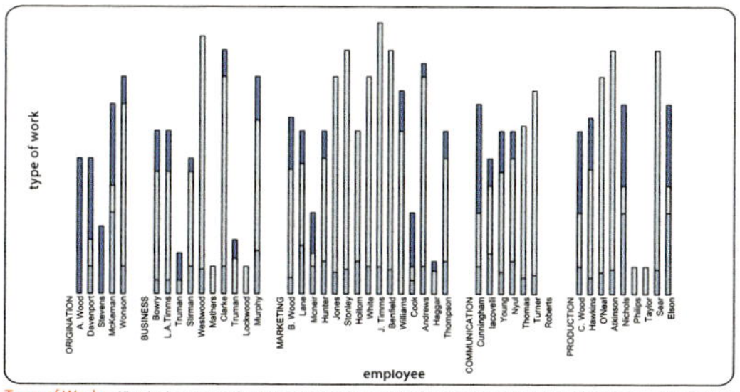

Type of Work ▫CELL: high autonomy-low interaction ▫ DEN: low autonomy-high interaction ▫ CLUB: high autonomy-high interaction

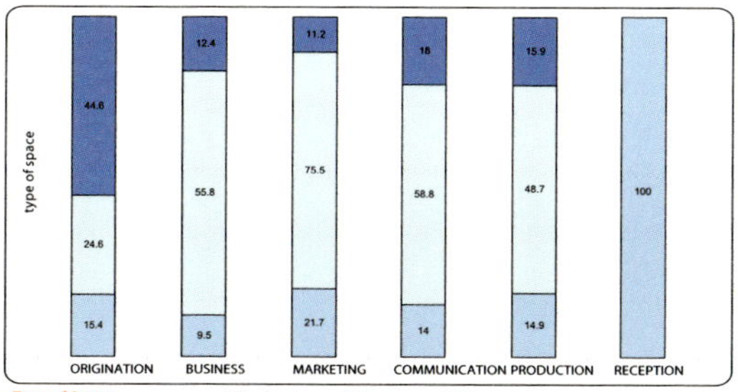

Type of Space ▫ CELL - closed ▫ DEN - open ▫ CLUB - semi-open

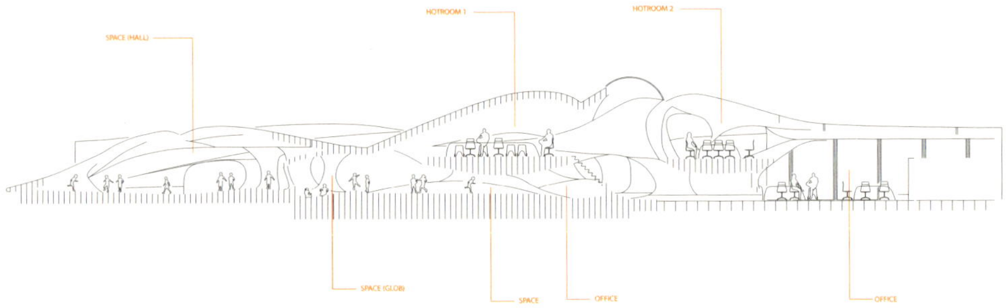

SPACE (HALL)
HOTROOM 1
HOTROOM 2
SPACE (GLOB)
SPACE
OFFICE
OFFICE

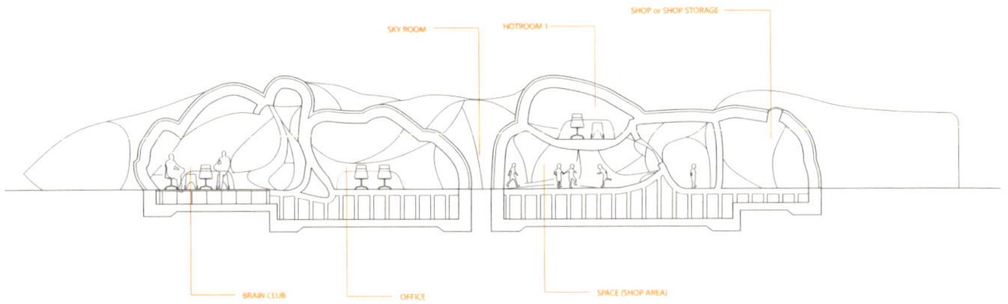

SKY ROOM
HOTROOM 1
SHOP or SHOP STORAGE
BRAIN CLUB
OFFICE
SPACE (SHOP AREA)

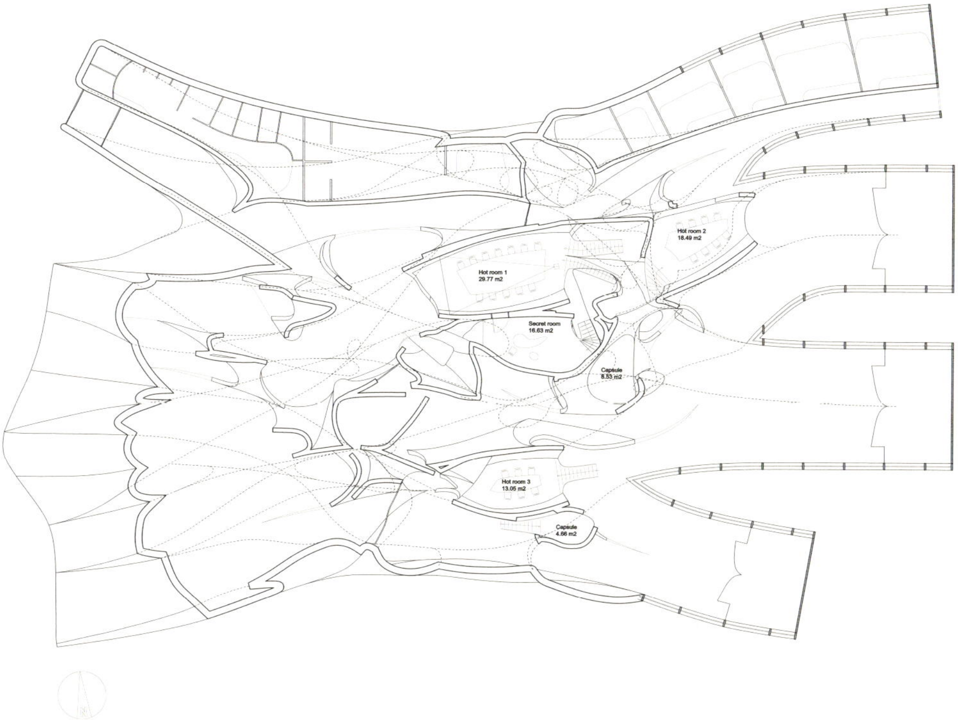
Hot room 1
29.77 m2
Hot room 2
18.49 m2
Secret room
16.63 m2
Capsule
8.53 m2
Hot room 3
13.05 m2
Capsule
4.66 m2

UCC

FOA

18

WTC

Yokohama International Port Terminal

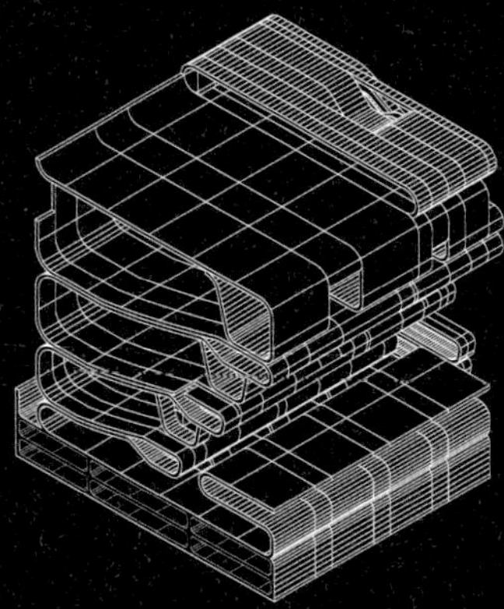
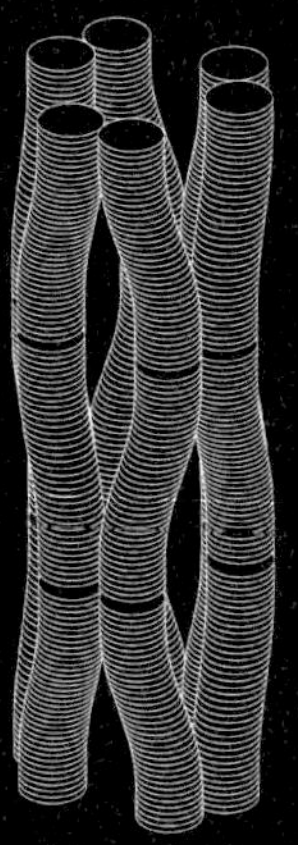
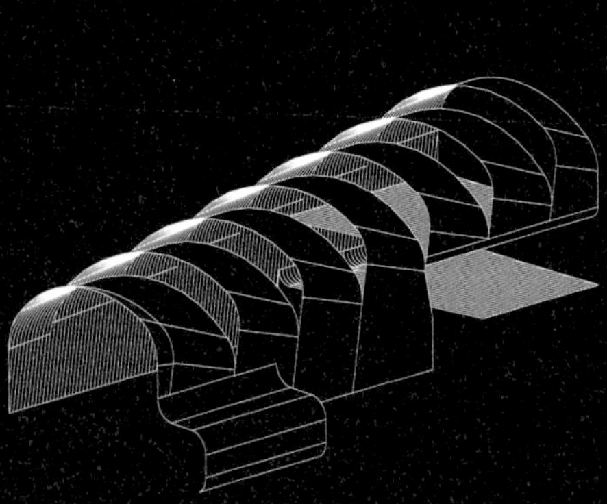
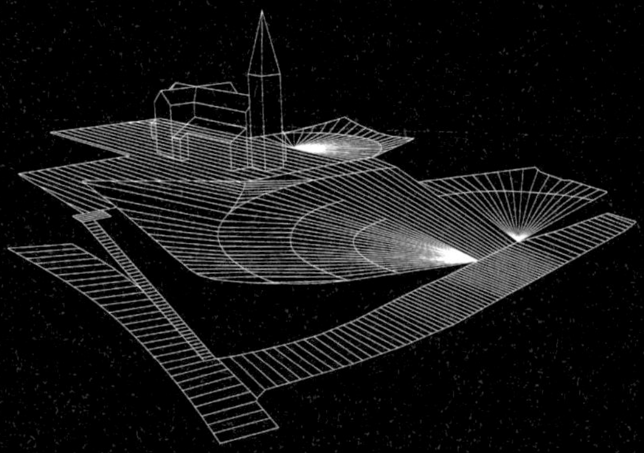
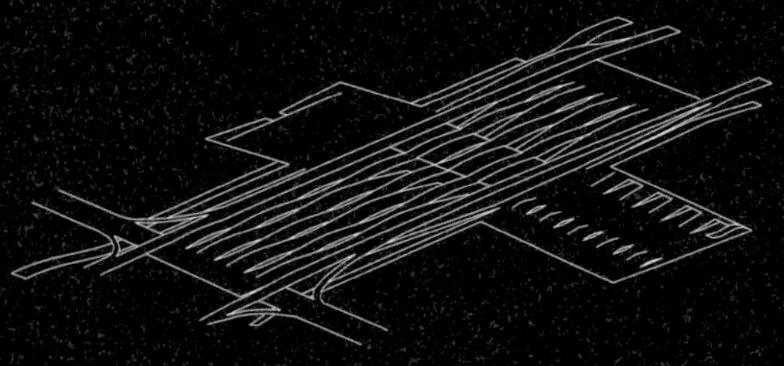
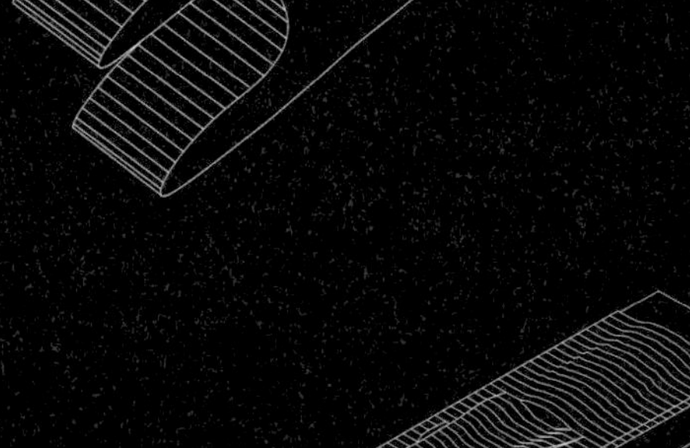
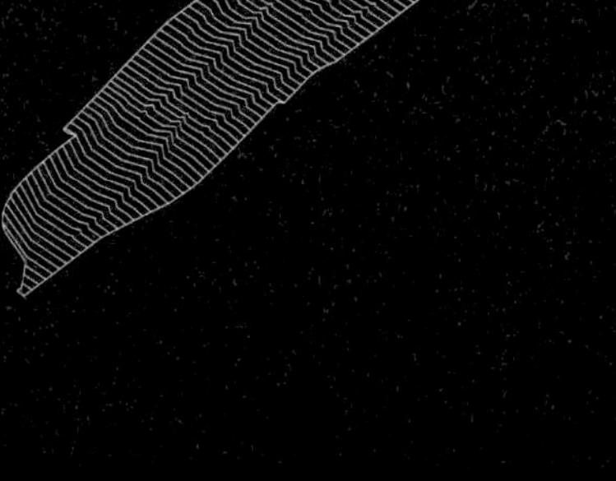
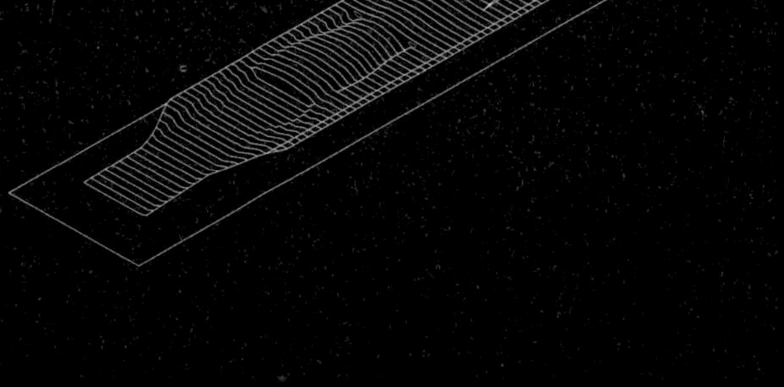

On Material Life

Architecture is not a plastic art, but the engineering of material life. We hope that this distinguishes our work from other complex architecture to which we have been associated on the basis of formal output. What fundamentally distinguishes the work we do is the process. Our main priority is to produce consistency in the process of construction and material organization rather than in plastic effects. In fact, we are not interested in having preconceived effects, but rather in exploring the materials –and here material, should be understood in the broadest possible sense– as a source of ideas and effects.

Processes are far more interesting than ideas. Ideas are linked to existing codes, operating critically or in alignment with pre-existing systems of ideas. Rather than making a project, the implementation of an idea, or the scaffolding of an image, we are interested in constructing engineering processes on different levels. A process is the generation of a micro-history for a project, a kind of specific narrative. The entity of the project is formed in a sequence where additional complexity is constructed to integrate incoming information. If geological, biological or human history, for instance, have something to teach us, it is that these processes of temporal formation produce organizations of far greater complexity and sophistication than instantaneous ideas. This is perhaps the most important development brought by information technology to our practice: we can design, synthesize and proliferate specific histories and scripts for a project; introduce a sequential development rather than deploying a form or an image. It proliferates, and waits for the emergence of the project. We are no longer trapped in the traditional compulsion to reproduce historical models, or to invent them from scratch. We do not have to produce a project as a reproduction, derivation or as the invention of a historical model. We do not need to produce complexity by making collages. We can synthesize the processes of generation as a kind of accelerated motion, integrally adding information to the construction. This sequential, integrative addition produces more ambiguous effects capable of resonating at different levels, rather than straightforward ideological statements, metaphors, allegories or reproductions.

FOA

18 **_Yokohama International Port Terminal_**

COMPETITION DESIGN TEAM Farshid Moussavi, Alejandro Zaera-Polo, Iván Ascanio, Yoon King Chong, Michael Cosmas, Jung-Hyun Hwang, Guy Westbrook ENGINEERING ADVISORS Ove Arup & Partners BASIC DESIGN STAGE 1 Farshid Moussavi, Alejandro Zaera-Polo, Felix Bendito, Jordi Mansilla, Kenichi Matsuzawa, Santiago Triginer BASIC DESIGN STAGE 2 Farshid Moussavi, Alejandro Zaera-Polo, Victoria Castillejos, Dafne Gil, Kenichi Matsuzawa, Oriol Montfort, Xavier Ortiz, Lluís Viu, José Saenz, Julián Varas, Thomasine Wolfensberger DETAIL DESIGN AND SUPERVISION Farshid Moussavi, Alejandro Zaera-Polo, Kensuke Kishikawa, Yasuhisa Kikuchi, Izumi Kobayashi, Kenichi Matsuzawa, Tomofomi Nagayama, Xavier Ortiz, Lluís Viu, Keisuke Tamura COMPETITION 1995 COMPLETION DATE june 2002 LOCAL ARCHITECTS GKK Architects STRUCTURAL ENGINEERS Structural Design Group (SDG) MECHANICAL AND ELECTRICAL ENGINEERS P.T. Morimura CLIENT The City of Yokohama COST ¥ 23.5 billiones BUILDING AREA 43.843 m² PHOTOGRAPHS Satoru Mishima, Ramon Prat

A passenger cruise terminal and a multifunctional civic zone.

- 48.000m² of construction to handle 53000 passengers.
- 17.000 m² of Domestic and International Cruise Terminal facilities including check-in, luggage handling, custom and immigration and related administration.
- 13.000 m² of Citizens amenities including conference space, shops, restaurants and multipurpose hall.
- 18.000 m² of Traffic facilities including public parking, pick-up and drop-off traffic plaza and coaches parking.

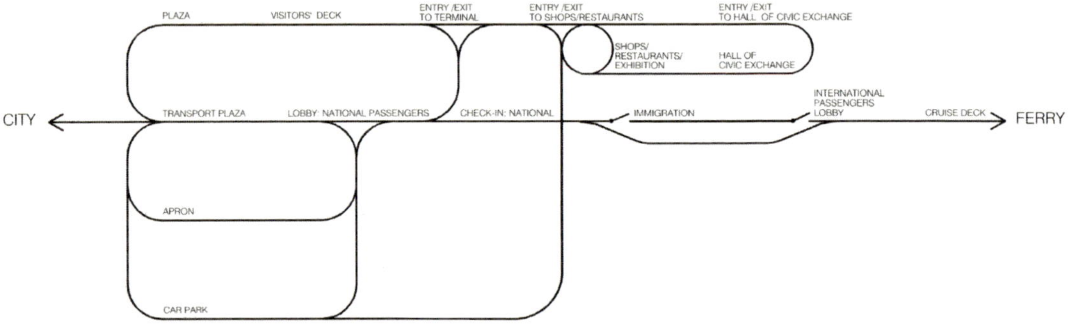

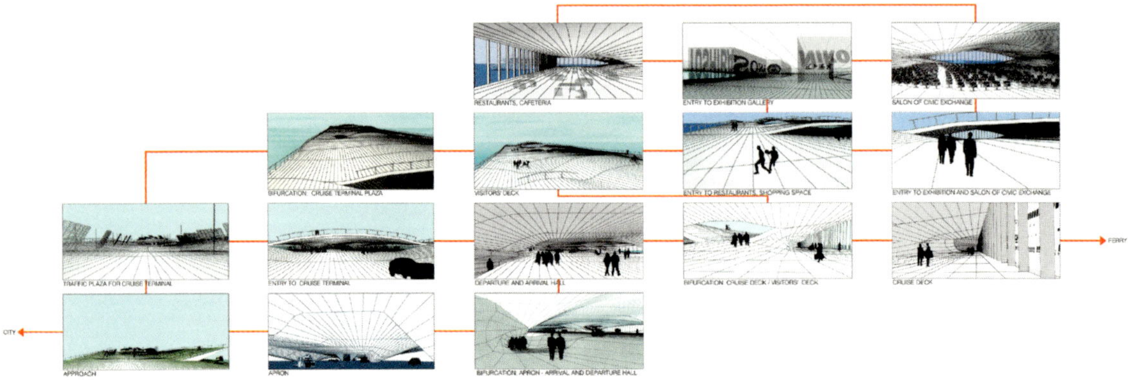

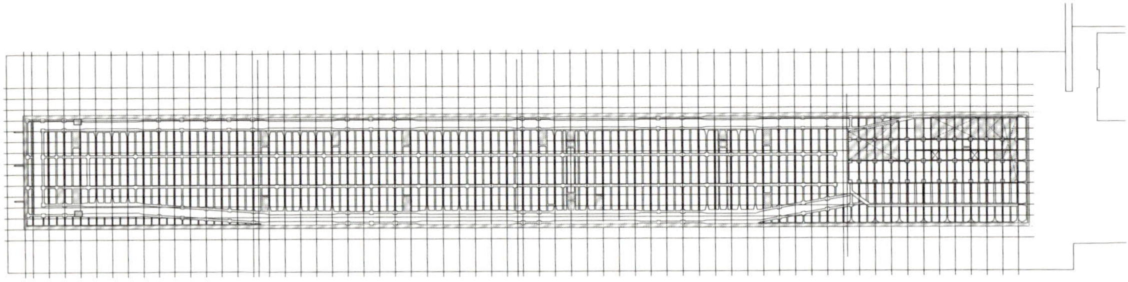

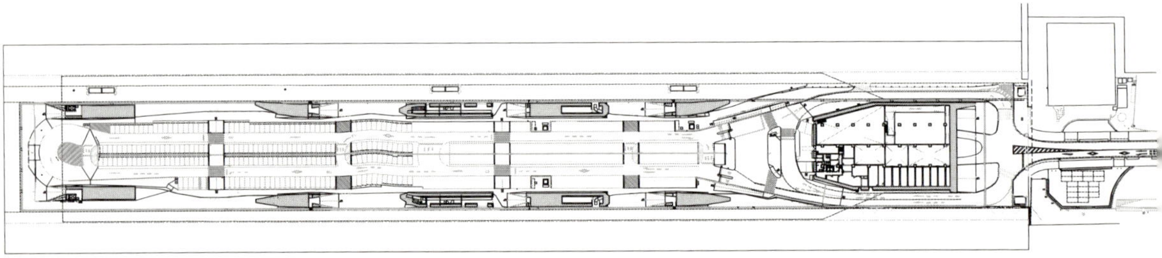

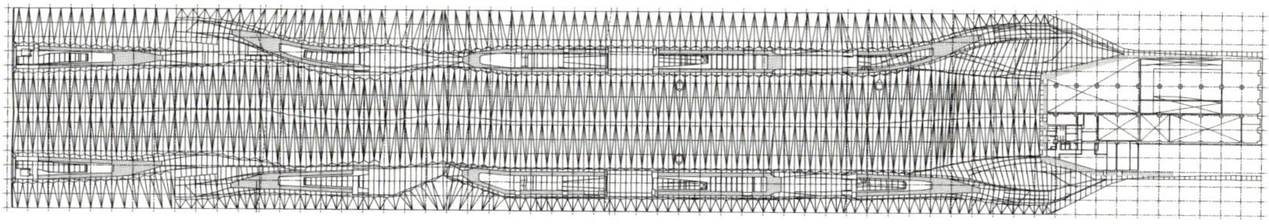

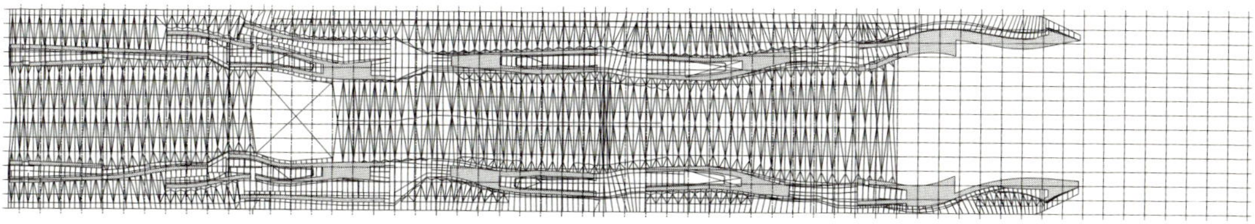

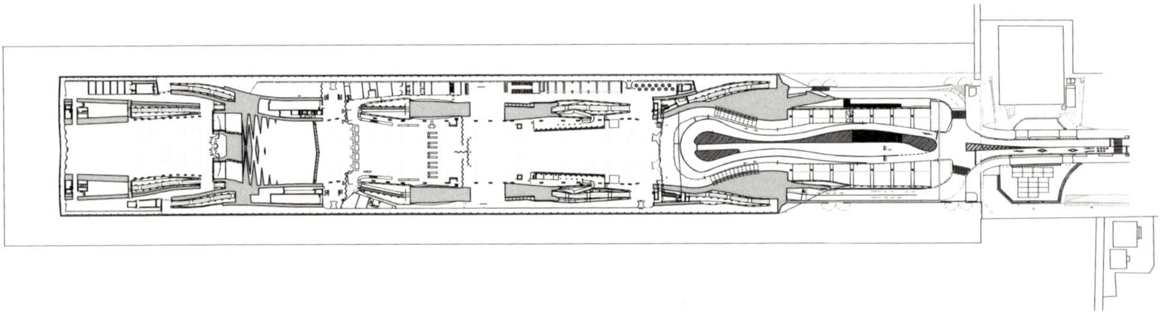

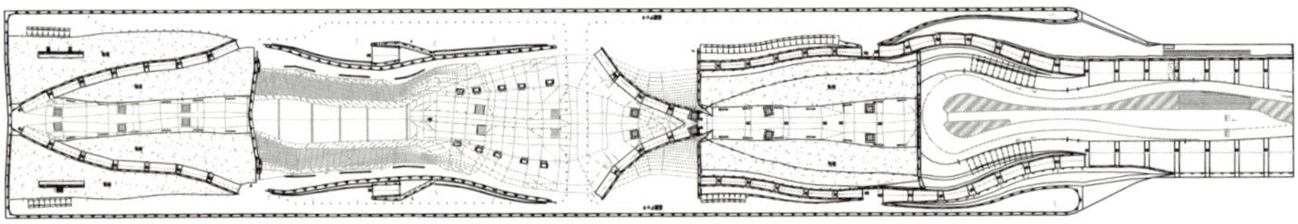

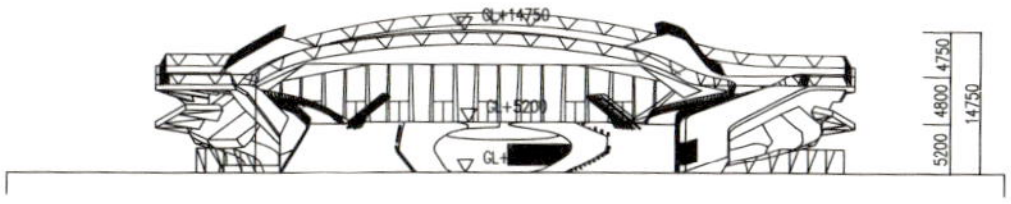
GL+14750
GL+5200
4750
4800
14750
5200

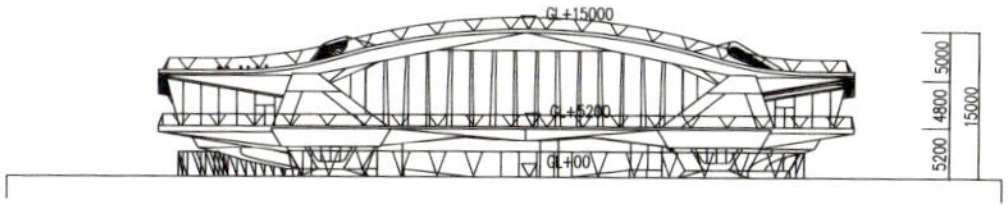
GL+15000
GL+5200
GL+00
5000
4800
15000
5200

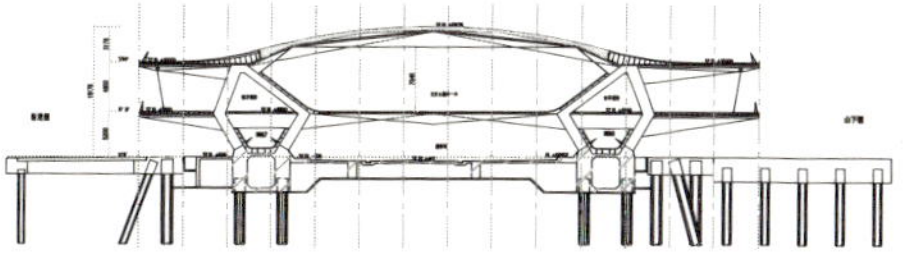

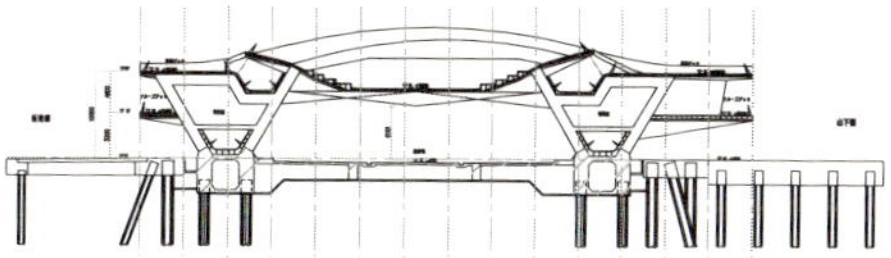

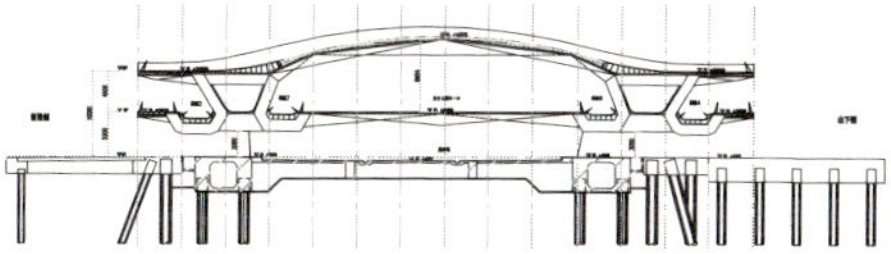

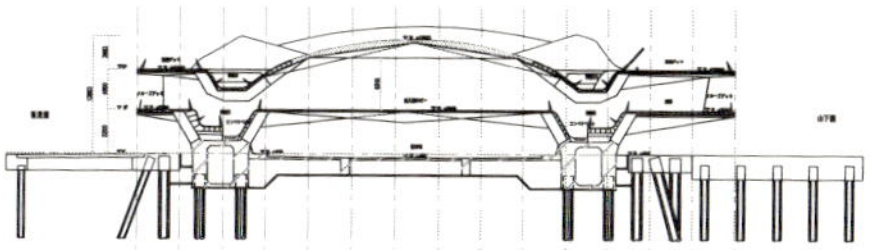

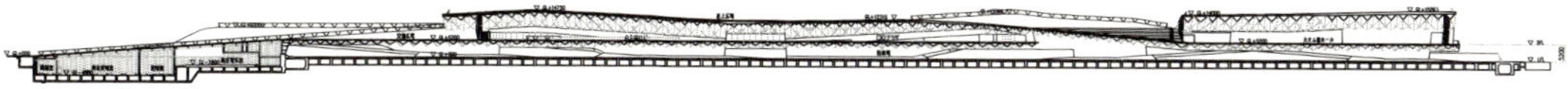

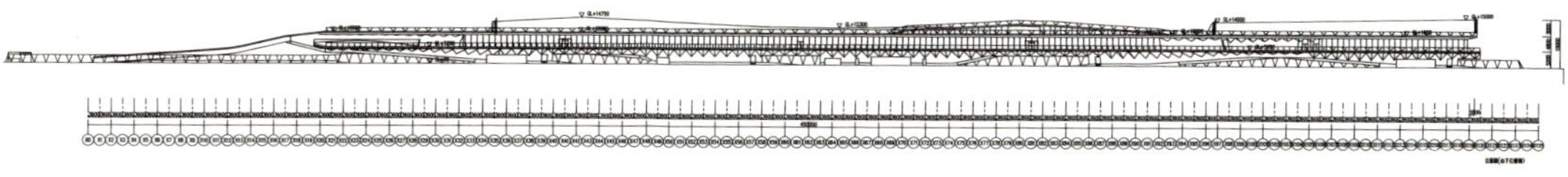

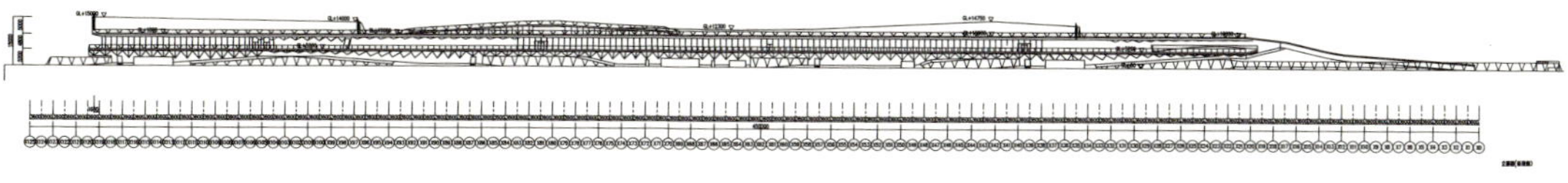

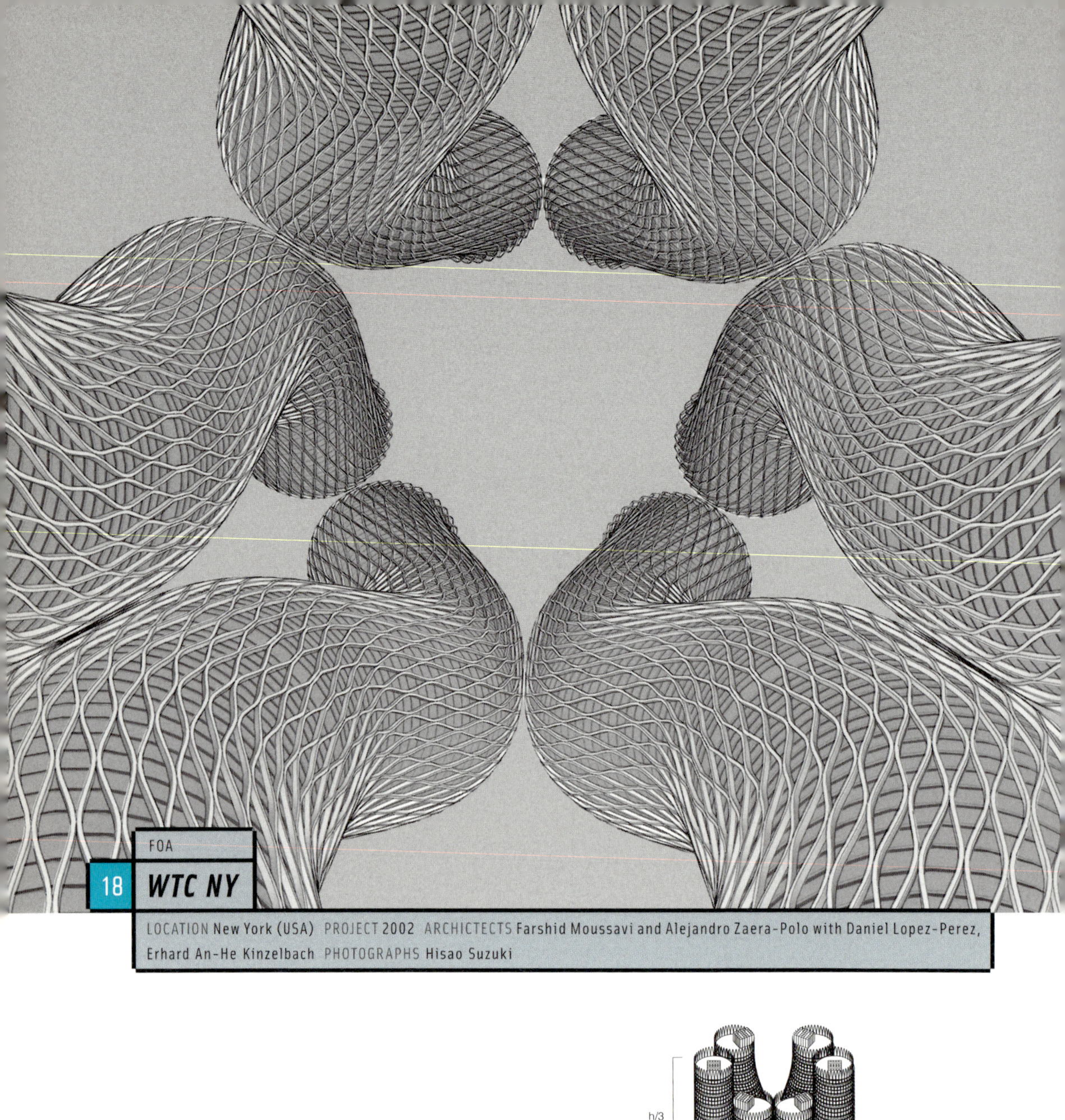

FOA

18 **WTC NY**

LOCATION New York (USA) PROJECT 2002 ARCHICTECTS Farshid Moussavi and Alejandro Zaera-Polo with Daniel Lopez-Perez, Erhard An-He Kinzelbach PHOTOGRAPHS Hisao Suzuki

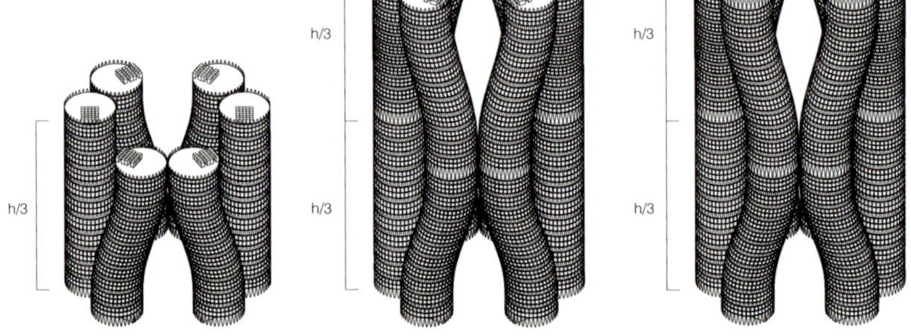

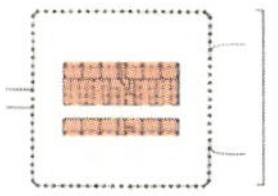

Original WTC

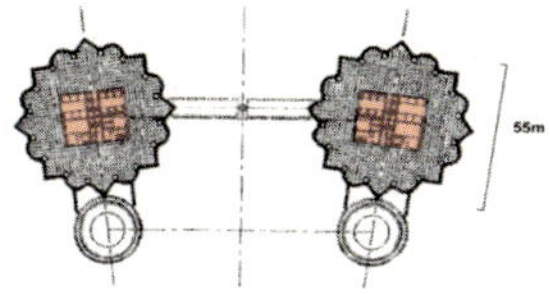

Kuala Lumpur Petronas towers

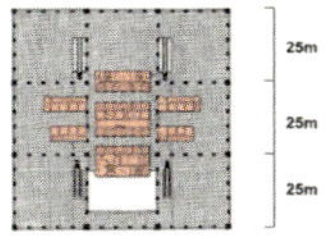

Chicago Sears tower

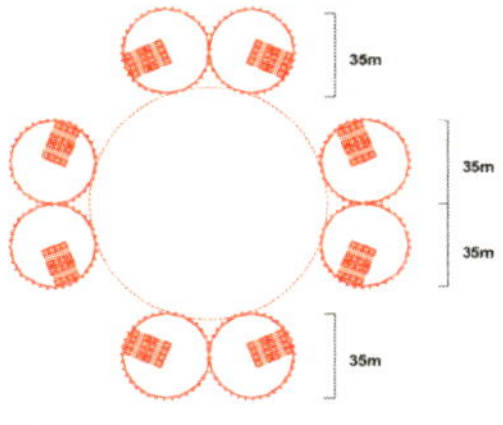

Bunch tower

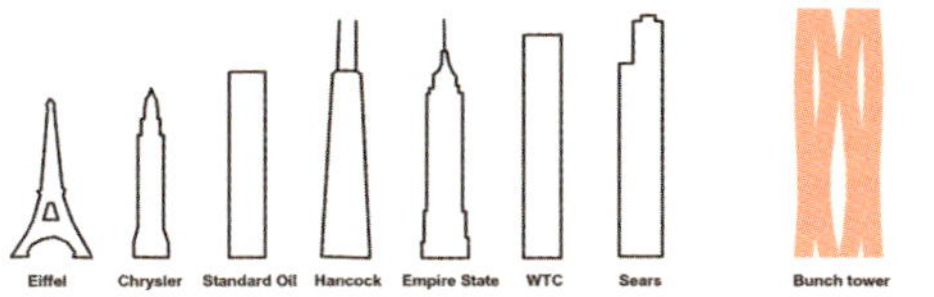

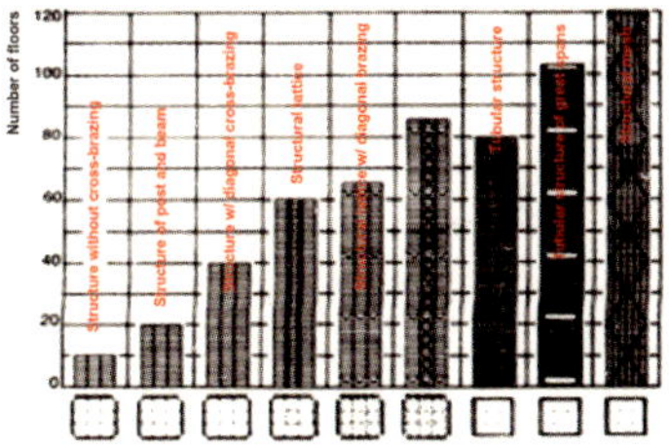

The world's tallest building back in New York
Let's not even consider remembering... What for?
We have a great site in a great city and the opportunity to have the world's tallest building back in New York. Ground Zero used to host 1.3M m2 of workspace, and that is a good size to attempt to return to NY what it deserves.
Our proposal is to form the complex as a bunch of interconnected towers that provide a flexible floor size and that buttress each other structurally, being able to increase the moment of inertia of the structure without necessarily increasing the floor depth and the total area. The average workspace floor size in New York City is 1000m2, and we have taken that as our quantum of space, or bunch scale in the new WTC NY: the size of the bunch towers will be approximately that size. As our target is to reach approximately 500m height, we are aiming at approximately 110 floors with a conventional floor to floor height of 4.5m. If we take the size of the former complex as a measure of total floor size, we have:
884,000 m2/110 floors = 8036m2/floor, which equals approximately to 8 towers of 1000m2 per floor.
In order to maximise the ratio between floor area and perimeter, and to improve the structural performance of the building, we have opted for a tubular structure with a circular profile with an 18m diameter, where the structure is concentrated in a structural lattice on the fasade of each tower. The tubes, organised in a circle, bend vertically to buttress each other approximately every third of the total height of the building, cutting the bending length of the towers to approximately 165m.
In order to maximise the resistance of the structural lattice of the tubes, the geometry of the columns will also bend, balancing the transmission of weight and the resistance to buckling and lateral stresses. The lattice of the tower structure and the geometry of the bunch tower are self-similar structures.

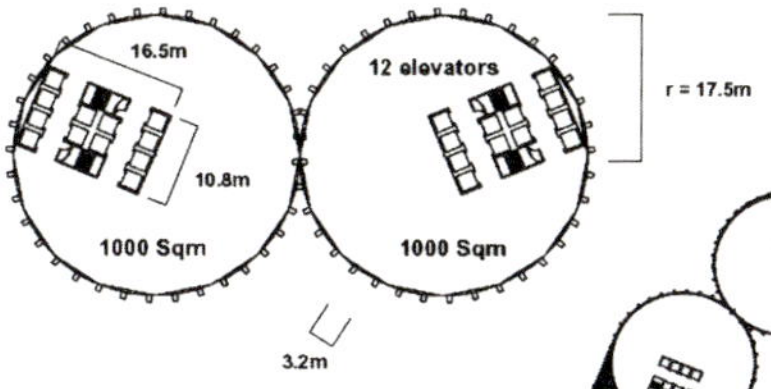

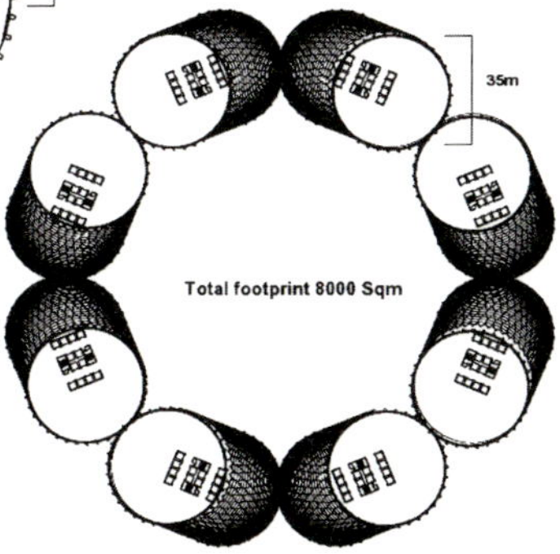

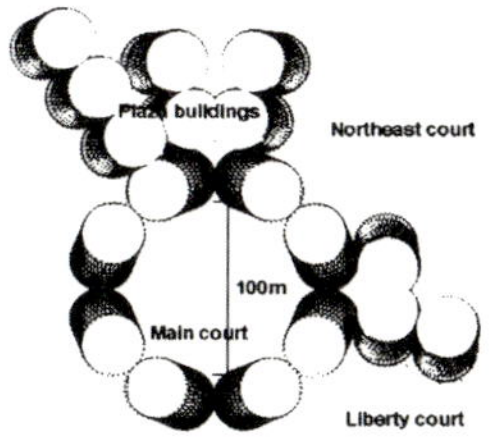

Total Area 1.3M Sqm

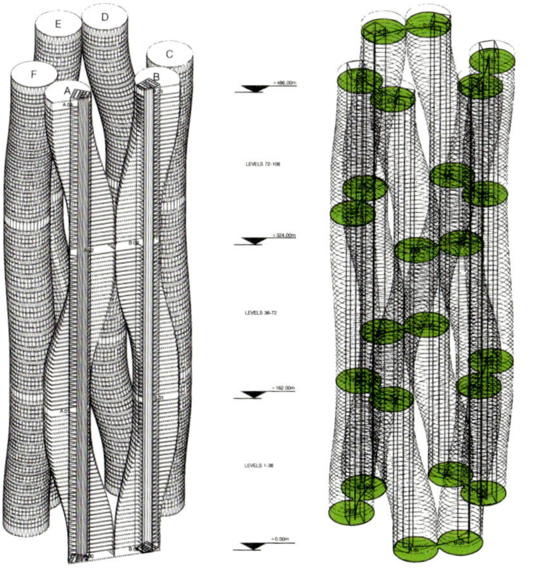

SECTION

SKY-LOBBY TRANSFER DIAGRAM

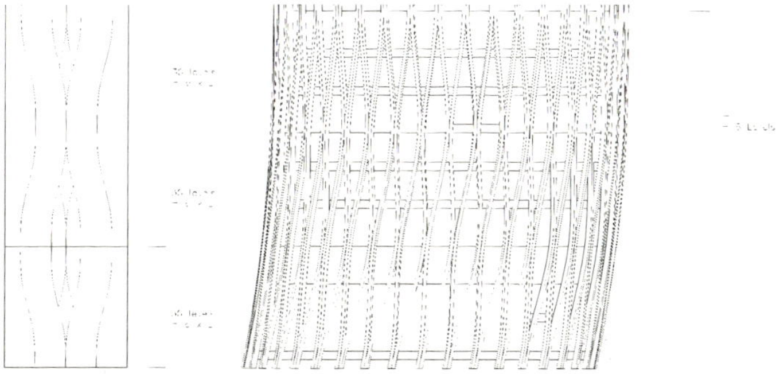

PUBLISHED BY
Actar

FOREWORD AND INITIAL CONCEPT
Manuel Gausa

GENERAL COORDINATION AND EDITING
Susanna Cros

COLLABORATION
Anna Tetas

GRAPHIC DESIGN
Ramon Prat
Reinhard Steger

TRANSLATION AND CORRECTION
Paul Hammond
Graham Thomson (Manuel Gausa's text)

PRINTING
Ingoprint SA

DISTRIBUTION
ACTAR-D
Roca i Batlle 2
08023 Barcelona
office@actar-d.com
Tel: 93 417 49 93
Fax: 93 418 67 07

DL B-24622-05
ISBN 84-95951-60-6

Printed and bound in the European Union
Barcelona, 2005